My Childhood Years

My Childhood Years

A Memoir by Peretz Hirshbein

Translated from the Yiddish by Leonard Wolf

My Childhood Years: A Memoir by Peretz Hirshbein
Translated by Leonard Wolf

Copyright for the translation is held by Jessica Hirshbein

White Goat Press, the Yiddish Book Center's imprint
Yiddish Book Center
Amherst, MA 01002
whitegoatpress.org

Paperback ISBN 979-8-9909980-2-5
Hardcover ISBN 979-8-9909980-3-2
Ebook ISBN 979-8-9909980-4-9

Library of Congress Control Number: 2024943594

Book design by Michael Grinley
Cover illustration by David Brinley
Yiddish copyediting by Yankl Salant

This book has been made possible
with the generous support
of Jane E. Gordon and Dennis Levitt

I dedicate my writing to my parents,
who made a home for my youth by pure water
between trees and meadows.

—Peretz Hirshbein
New York, *Teves 5676*

Introduction

At first glance, playwright Peretz Hirshbein's memoirs seem to resemble those of countless other Eastern European Jewish writers.
He treats his readers to closely observed anecdotes about home
life and the Jewish community in which he came of age, and he
chronicles his intellectual and spiritual journey from the world of
Jewish tradition and Torah study to his engagement with modern,
secular ideas and literature.

But despite its common themes, *My Childhood Years* stands
apart. Hirshbein had a distinctive literary voice, and his unique
outlook and way of viewing the world shine through in the stories
he tells from his childhood. One factor setting Hirshbein apart
from other memoirists is his birth and upbringing. Unlike most
other Eastern European Jews who became professional writers, whether in Yiddish, Hebrew, or other languages, Hirshbein
grew up in a rural environment rather than in a shtetl or major
city. Much of the book's activity literally and figuratively revolves
around his father's water mill, and Hirshbein writes about his family's surroundings with affection, though by no means uncritically.

As Hirshbein relates, the nearest shtetl to his home was about
three kilometers away. But as he recalls, "We didn't speak much
about the shtetl or the stuck-up shtetl folk at home. It was a foreign world to us." Hirshbein's folk are country folk, living lives at

one with nature and with the seasons. During the summer work is plentiful and the outdoors beckon. In winter the river freezes, the mill goes quiet, and money is often scarce. Like so many other writers familiar with hardship and hunger, Hirshbein retained a keen sense of how financially precarious life can be and a deep empathy with the dramatic characters whom he often placed in similarly poverty-stricken circumstances.

Though Hirshbein's path to becoming a pioneering Yiddish playwright was unique, its contours are familiar. The latter chapters of his memoir take us on a vivid journey from the mill to the shtetl to the city, and from the world of Jewish tradition to an environment where young men and women encounter secular ideas that lead them to rethink their purpose in life. Peretz Hirshbein would make the most of that journey. Readers will be the richer for accompanying him on it.

—Joel Berkowitz
Professor of English, UW–Milwaukee

First Steps

My memory carries me back over forty-nine good—as well as bad—years to a time when I could walk under a table by simply bending my head a bit. To a time when, though I was just beginning to form words, I was able to speak to my gentle mother with my eyes. I can still see my taciturn and truly good father snatching his yarmulke from his head to take a swipe at me for having committed some petty crime whose nature I could not understand. I remember how sweet my tears were when I was punished and how my mother gathered me into her arms and quieted me with kisses.

I remember how such unwitting acts of mine roused looks of fear in my mother, my father, and the other members of the household because it was the time in my life when I was too young to know that I should stand back from the bank of the river that turned the wheel of our mill lest, God forbid, an evil spirit pull me in. I remember too the anxious looks that followed me to the millpond's edge and the terrible attraction it had for me. We all drank from the pond—my father out of a pitcher, my mother out of a pot or pan.

The mill went *rattle rattle rattle, rattle rattle rattle*. What was it that made those noises to which I listened, amazed? Large wheels and small in motion; the shaking and banging of pouches and sieves.

My father and my brothers—and occasionally my mother and

sisters too—were dusted with flour. So I felt compelled to take flour from a sack or from a corner of the mill and turn myself white like everyone else. And that was one more provocation to my father to take a swipe at me with his yarmulke, producing more cries and tears. How delicious it was to wipe them from a face smeared with flour, to sob until I was overcome by sleep. Then my mother would put me into a wooden cradle she rocked with her foot as she sang "so your father went to deal in raisins and almonds . . ."

Again I see the expanses of boggy green meadow that every year produced much uneasiness in my heart. It was then that the adults took off their winter boots, rolled their trousers above their knees, and went rambling barefoot across the marshy springtime fields while I, longing to join in, gazed after them. I had no idea that the time would come when I too would join them in search of a horse or a cow that had somehow disappeared or that I would be sent to gather dry oak branches for the kitchen stove or sorrel for my mother who needed it to cook the tasty borscht she had promised us.

I remember when I thought of the trees that grew in the vicinity of the mill as no different from my brothers and sisters, my father and mother. I regarded the tall, straight alder trees, with their dark trunks, as fathers and older brothers and the wide-spreading willows, mirrored and washing their branches in the tranquil pond, as tree mothers with older sisters by their side.

I wanted to peer like them into the water. Only later would I be tempted to climb about in their parental branches. By then I understood which trees welcomed climbing children—the ones that bent low and spread their branches and had branches that did not scratch.

But that was later, when I was no longer supervised so carefully, when I was able to talk and had learned to carry water from the river for my mother, who did not protest even in winter if I slipped out barefoot to slide on the frozen pond beside the house.

I remember too the red rooster with his armored feet who, in the days when I went about wearing only a hand-me-down shirt, often pecked me in the stomach. I was afraid of that rooster. He would stretch his neck out, flap his wings, and utter his *cock-a-doo-dle-do* right in the house, where the barnyard fowl were welcome. The duck scared me too with his *quack, quack* as he chased after me, snapping at my feet.

I can remember the time when there was happiness at home because the peasants were coming to our house. They were different from us and spoke a language I could not understand. They came in horse-drawn wagons loaded with sacks of wheat they put on their shoulders and carried into the mill. At such times my silent father beamed and my mother turned cheerful. She kissed us children and sang, wanting us to sing along with her.

The mill was always in motion, and there was flour dust and the noise of turning wheels and hissing water everywhere. The dust covered us and covered the long garments of the peasants who brought their wheat to us in their wagons. Why was I unable to understand their language while everyone else in the family could?

I remember that those festive visits of the peasants took place when it was no longer cold and we could see out of our unfrosted windowpanes. I would climb up on the bench on which I slept and, looking out the window, discovered that what had been winter snow was now black with soot. Outdoors there were rivulets murmuring everywhere and fresh breezes whistling through the trees.

I still remember those spring days when my long nursery shirt seemed oppressively warm, when I yearned to run out barefoot to dance in the puddles outside the window and watch the peasants who had brought the wheat that set the mill wheel turning, who got my parents, brothers, and sisters singing and talking cheerfully and being kind to one another. Those strangers liked the youngest boy with the flaxen hair. Yes, they loved to grab and toss me upward—high, high—till it seemed that any second my head would strike the ceiling. I was scared and could not understand what was so funny, though I remember that my father and mother laughed even as some huge fellow with a hairy, prickly face tossed me up and down. Eventually I cried and put my hands out toward my mother, who took me in her arms and tickled me till I laughed, to the delight of everyone.

I remember those days when the mill was quiet, the wheels stopped, the water still. My father and mother were sad—my sisters and brothers spoke little. I myself crawled under the bed, somewhere behind the oven, or even in with the chickens under the oven. I started crying without even knowing why.

My memory brings me back to my earliest awareness: blood running from my finger, my tears suppressed, afraid to come out of my eyes.

Here's what happened: My father and brothers waded into the water fully clothed, where they caught the fish my mother had many times pointed out to me in the pond. They came out of the water soaking wet and brought the fish into the house, where they shook them out of a sack onto the floor. There was one long fish lying among smaller ones that kept opening and closing its mouth. I managed to put my finger into that mouth just as it closed. I shrieked and tried to pull my finger out, but I succeeded only in dragging the fish about. At my outcry, my mother appeared and pried my bloody finger from the fish's mouth. From then on I was terrified at the sight of blood.

I remember being conscious of the smells of spring as the trees around the mill turned green and bloomed. My older brother and sister came back from the woods bearing blossoming branches. They put the blossoms to my nose and I inhaled. Ah, the sensation!

I recall envying older people who knew everything and were permitted to do everything—who could pick up an ax and cut a tree down with it or who could use a knife to cut into a huge loaf of bread from which I was given a morsel. I envied the trees their height and strength. I wanted to put my arms around a tree to shake it, but it was so hard to get my arms all the way around.

I slowly became aware of nature and became a part of it. I learned to talk and to call things by their names. For some time I had words just at the tip of my tongue, but now I could say them as needed. I also understood the mill better. I even started to understand the people at home: my father, mother, sister, brothers.

Then there was my grandfather, my father's father, who was to become my friend, almost a playmate.

When I grew bigger, I was sent by my mother to fetch water from the pond, but she held me by my shirt so I wouldn't—God forbid!—fall in. The time soon came when my father would say a few words to me as if to someone who understood. He would ask me to bring a piece of wood for my mother to fuel the kitchen stove.

I felt closer to the river, as if it were becoming a part of me. The trees too became closer and more understandable. I recognized the birds that flew away somewhere and came back again flying and singing among our trees.

Spring, summer, fall, and winter—everything became part of me. The mill where I was born and grew up was my home until my twentieth year.

Where was this mill? In what country? In what city or shtetl? Next to what river? Near what body of water?

My father and mother, sister and brothers, grandfathers and grandmothers, uncles and aunts, peasant men and women, ducks and chickens, horses and cows, land that was marshy and green during the summer and got marshy and cold in the fall and was hidden under the snow for a string of winter days—

Where was all this and where did it all take place?

How much I remember; how hard it is now to tell it all—and how pleasant.

Lippe's Mill

In a part of Poland that was formerly Russia, the low-lying shtetl of Kleshtshel hugged the earth between Bialystok and Brisk and between the smaller cities Bielsk and Visoke-Litovsk. At the town's center there was a circular marketplace occupied by Jewish-owned shops. Narrow streets lined by small Jewish homes radiated out from the marketplace. Farther out, the streets led to streets on which Gentiles lived in thatched-roof houses and beyond them to open country. The Jews had one synagogue in town.

My father's mill was three kilometers from the shtetl. In summer the young villagers used to stroll out to the mill. Their route led from the marketplace, through the rabbi's street, and past the Gentiles' houses. Farther out the road passed market gardens and then boggy fields. The road going upward was intersected by train tracks running southwest, and from there it went on through alder and willow trees. To the left there was a pond; to the right, marshy fields with dense undergrowth. Not far from there you caught your first glimpse through the trees of the shingled roof of Lippe's mill, where the road ended. Near the mill there was a bridge that led to distant meadows on the other side of the river.

My father, Lippe, a gnarled man of middle height with a thick, copper-colored beard, was a taciturn fellow who had a genial look in his blue eyes. Though he was already past fifty when I was a child, he always looked young to me because of the contrast with my grandfather Yehoshua, who was then close to a hundred years old. My grandfather was a lively man with a small blond beard. He was much more talkative than my father and always went about with a song on his lips.

My father and grandfather seemed to me to be a couple of huge trees. My mother, Sheyne—or Sheyndl, as my father called her—was like a supple sprig. She had a narrow face and gentle dark eyes and hair. I used to wonder how a woman who was by no means strong could cook, wash, and carry heavy things about all day. Some good impulse prompted me to help her whenever I could by carrying a bucket of water or pieces of wood for the fire.

Our house was an integral part of the mill, through which one passed to get to the family quarters. To accommodate the mill wheel, the house was built on stilts over the water. It consisted of two rooms that were separated from each other by a bank of ovens. One of these was a wall oven that heated the house in winter and the other was a baking oven that was heated twice on Fridays. There was a window on one side of the house that looked out onto the river and a window opposite that faced the meadows. When the mill was working, the pond water was led through an open sluiceway from which it fell onto the paddlewheels, making them turn. Then the walls trembled and we could hear the sibilant murmur of running water under the house.

Of the older children in the family, the first was my tall, blond-bearded brother, Binyomin Khayem, who lived in town with his wife and small children. Then there were my slow-moving and very pious blond brother Kalmen and my spirited, lively sister Bebl. And finally there was my brother Moyshe, who cared more for the mill than he did for school, which is why my father often cast irritable glances his way.

Our mill, with its two large waterwheels, really came to life only in spring when the snow melted and water was plentiful. That was the season when the peasants brought their wheat and rye to be turned into sifted flour for the coming holidays. Those peasants were the source of our income—though occasionally flour merchants from town would give my father a bit of wheat to sift. We didn't speak much about the shtetl or the stuck-up shtetl folk at home. It was a foreign world to us.

In the fall when the rains began there was never a lack of water in the river. As soon as summer came the river hid its stream between its banks. The pond was dense with water lilies, and the mill ran only a couple of hours each day.

In winter, when our district was frozen over with ice and snow, life was hard. An anxious silence reigned in the house. I have then two quite different memories of childhood. One is of a home that in summer was bright and cheerful and the other is of winter, which was hushed and cold.

At the beginning of summer not only horses, cows, chickens, and ducks came alive in the nearby meadows, water, and woods. My family too turned spritely. My grandfather, who spent the winter on his warm place on top of the oven, no sooner felt the coming of summer than he revived and turned into a boon companion of the outdoors.

The crowdedness indoors expanded outside. In summer every one of us gravitated to his or her tree, beneath which we slept, or to the fragrant hayloft, and my mother found excuses to leave the hearth and go outdoors. It was the season when we drank directly from the river, when the cow gave milk, the hens laid eggs, and birds arrived from distant lands to sing their songs in the trees. In summer we chewed the blades of sorrel that grew among the riverside grasses, and we gathered currants and mulberries.

It was the time of year when the stork came and searched among the alder trees over the pond for his nest of last year. The patter of his bill against the trees always announced his coming. We were eager to see the stork because our luck for the coming year depended on whether we first saw him standing, walking, or in flight. It was very bad to see him standing on one leg because then our luck would be bad.

When I recall my earliest childhood years my memory most often takes me back to those summer days. By their rhythm I grew in harmony with the trees and with the full flowing of the river. The warm outdoors drew me, and there were endless inconsequential things to think about. It was a good time to mimic the grown-ups. If they went barefoot, so did I. If they were talkative, I prattled along with them.

All I remember about winter is that it was cold. I slept in my mother's bed, and I remember that even under the covers it was so cold that I cuddled against my mother for warmth. Winter encased us in silence and in the sorts of troubles winter brings, like childhood illnesses. But I was then too young to understand those winter problems. Only later would I learn there was no money to buy Shabbos candles and that even a miller may need to buy flour to bake his challah because the mill wheel, without flowing water to turn it, was at a standstill.

We could see winter through our windows. There was the frozen millpond and the pile of snow outside that had to be cleared away each morning before we could leave the house. Everyone was overworked. Ice had to be chopped away from the waterwheels and a round hole chopped in the pond's ice, through which we could draw our drinking water. In the morning everyone went to wash their hands and face in the hole in the ice and then hurried back into the house all wet. I remember asking my sister Bebl to lower me to the ice so I could scoop up water to drink. More often I would end up running out barefoot into the snow.

I remember, from my very earliest days, how vibrant the family became on Friday nights. All day long my mother busied herself with household duties. I remember particularly the fires she made in the stove and the glow on her face as she fed it with wood the older children had managed to find somewhere. (Later I would learn where that supply of wood came from.) I remember getting ready on those Friday evenings to take our places at the table, on which a white tablecloth was spread. And I remember my mother bending over the candles as she blessed them, the men reciting their prayers, the array of Shabbos foods and the songs that were sung mid-meal and later. And there was grandfather Yehoshua, waving one hand as he sang while my father and the older children sang along with him. Grandpa pointed at me with his finger, encouraging me to sing as well, while I, sitting on my mother's lap, wanted to sing but couldn't.

Some years later, when I was able to carry a tune, I sat on my grandfather's knee and stroked his blond beard as he taught me his melodies. It was about that time that I began to think of my grandfather as being like the cherry tree that grew behind the stable. Later my reasoning matured enough to distinguish my grandfather from my father, to understand my older siblings and eventually the world in which I was growing.

From that early period in my life I remember the death of my little brother Hirsh-Yudele. I remember sitting on the oven not feeling well, my head aching and my throat constricted. The body of my brother lay on the floor with his face covered and lighted candles at his head, while my mother and sister wept without restraint.

From that time on I was watched over especially carefully. If I reported that my head no longer ached or that my throat no longer hurt, my father would take me up in his arms and dandle me while my mother, looking on, beamed. Then my father looked to my mother with much kindness.

Out of our window we could see the train passing a quarter kilometer away as it left the forest bordering our district. Its whistle and noise of rattling steel terrified me. If I happened to be outdoors when the train went by I fled for home.

I was quite young when I mastered the use of a wooden spoon to feed myself. About that time I acquired a taste for rye bread because my mother used to pop a morsel of it wrapped in a rag that had been sprinkled with sugar into my mouth. Later one of my great pleasures would be to gnaw at the heel of a loaf with my own teeth.

It was about that time that I first heard the word *heder*—"religious school." I knew it was somewhere in town; that summer and winter, my older brother Moyshe left the house every morning and came back at dusk, too unhappy to eat. When my mother unbuttoned his trousers and looked at his bottom, she called my father and showed him the black and blue marks. And I remember my father's anger. Later I learned there was a schoolmaster in the heder, that his name was Mattes, and that it was he who had beaten my brother.

Pointing at me, my mother said, "I won't let that thug get his hands on my Peretz." My brother Moyshe was four years older than me. I was probably about three years old at that time, and I already began to grasp that I too would be taken to the shtetl, and there my bottom would also be made black and blue.

My brother Kalmen was perpetually covered with flour. He carried heavy sacks of grain on his shoulders. I remember how he looked in winter, all wrapped up, wearing his heavy leather coat. Ice sprayed over him as he hacked at the ice that interfered with the mill wheels.

With much kindness Kalmen would carry me into the loft, where he showed me how the grains of wheat ran down from the hopper and were ground between the millstones. I remember how he put my hand to the vibrating paddle that guided the grains into the hopper, from which they fell between the grinding stones.

My older sister Bebl used to take me out into the fields, where she taught me to recognize ripe currants. It was she who rolled up her skirts and carried me deep into the millstream so I could get close to the waterfall under the paddle wheels. She put my feet into the water, but when I got frightened she hoisted me onto her shoulders.

What else did I know in those days? That my father was called Lippe the miller; that my home was Lippe's mill, where I was growing up, a sapling among trees. Like the willows in front of the house, I could see myself reflected in the water.

Blood Relatives

Slowly I began to distinguish the various grown-ups in the family and to recognize each one's character.

My father was quick to anger at almost any provocation. But his anger lasted only a little while. I could tell whether his mood was good or bad by the way he would search for his snuff box, the way he grasped the snuff between his thumb and forefinger, and how he snuffed the snuff up his nostrils.

In a bad mood he would hastily stuff two pinches of snuff into the same nostril. In a good mood he did it at a more comfortable pace. He would grub about with his fingers deep in the snuff box and apply his pinches of snuff slowly, first to one nostril and then to the other, keeping his eyes half closed as he appreciated the to-bacco's fragrance.

Another of his habits was to find fault with other people's work, though I understood early on that my brothers and sisters knew the work of the mill as well as he did and sometimes even better.

He was stockily built and could carry heavy sacks of grain from the wagons into the mill and from the bottom floor up the stairs to the hopper. But his young sons could do the same thing. They had no trouble carrying heavy loads. Even my grandfather could put a not-inconsiderable weight on his shoulders and carry it up to the loft.

My mother loved the outdoors, where she was alert to the

smallest changes in her surroundings. To her children she would say, pointing, "Do you see, children, how the clouds are poised over the water? Look—can you tell that this year the leaves on the trees are denser than they were last year? Do you see how that branch on the willow tree has begun to grow crooked?"

Spring made my mother younger. Her every movement was more youthful. Coming in from outdoors, she would drive the children out, crying, "It smells so good out there; it's absolutely wonderful. Look, children. The birds have come. Go on out. The cherry tree is blossoming. Go on outside. There are blossoms out there. Go pick some of those yellow marsh marigolds; they'll make the house smell nice."

My oldest brother in the house, Kalmen, was extremely pious and would take a long time reciting his prayers—a very long time. My mother would urge him to hurry so he would have more time to eat.

It was about that time that I learned my hardworking brother was both my brother and not my brother. He was not my mother's son, though she was as good to him as she was to the other children.

My sister Bebl, eight years older than I was, loved to carry me about slung across her shoulders like a little lamb and would take me out into the bogs in search of currants. On one such occasion I fell from her shoulders into a dense clump of nettles. I was so badly stung my whole body was blistered and she was afraid to take me home.

About this time I became aware that my brother Moyshe did not want to go to heder anymore because the teacher Mattes beat him and pinched him and pulled his ears so hard he drew blood.

On the other hand, young though Moyshe was, he really understood and loved the work of the mill. With his ax he could hew a wedge out of the hardest wood. My father was pleased with him. He often sent him into the mill to check on the hopper or outside to bring in a bucket of water. Or to the meadow to catch the horse and bring it home.

Slowly I learned to understand my grandfather Yehoshua. Old man though he was, his beard was shorter than my father's and his posture straighter. He had grandfatherly ways. He would take me up in his lap and say, "I hope you live to be my age."

When my grandfather went out to split wood beside the barn it would sometimes happen that he would have trouble with a log. Though he spat on his hands and raised his ax high and cried out "Split!" the log was stubborn and refused to split. Then my father would come and take the ax from him. Without raising the ax very high, he would deliver a single sharp blow, and the log split obediently in two.

Then one day a second grandfather appeared among us—my mother's father. He was a strange grandfather, and I was a bit frightened of him. He stood straight as an arrow and had white, white hair and a long forked beard with sharply pointed tips. And what long, ringleted side-curls he had.

He did not wear boots the way everyone else in my family did, including my grandfather Yehoshua. He wore white stockings and shallow slippers.

His wife, my grandmother, came with him. She was even smaller than my mother— so small! She kissed all the children; me she kissed on both cheeks. Because it was summer she brought pears and apples. The whole house smelled of fresh fruit.

My white-haired grandfather lifted me into his lap. He lifted me high up until our faces were level and he looked with his keen eyes deeply into mine. "Can you find an aleph in the prayer book yet?" he asked, his voice at once stern and kind.

I didn't know what to say. I looked down at the floor and started to crawl down out of his lap.

My mother was happy to have these guests. She said that, God willing, if we could manage it, we would go one day to Meleytshitsh, to my grandfather's house.

My mother, her eyes brimming with tears, asked my grandmother whether people still strolled in the forest near the town.

That's how I first became acquainted with my white-haired grandfather, who was called Reb Yossl Itzl. And that was the first time I saw Peshe Reyzl, my tiny grandmother.

There was an uncle who arrived driving a wagon. I gathered

that he came from some distant town called Orleh. That was my uncle Moyshe Linever, whose wife, my aunt Blume Rokhl, came with him. My uncle had a long, fair beard. His eyebrows were so thick they entirely shaded his eyes so that he peered out from under them. He spoke very little.

He was always at his prayers, always washing his hands. My aunt Blume Rokhl brought all sorts of cheeses with her. Dry cheeses. Moist cheeses. Everyone in the house got to taste bits of cheese. No one spoke much to my uncle.

Aunt Blume Rokhl was one of my father's sisters. Tears came to my father's eyes when he saw her. She, gazing at him, wept silently. After that a few words were exchanged with my uncle.

"Yes, yes, they do get to see each other from time to time."

"Well, well. Thank God everyone is well. That's what counts, thank God."

"We're getting along. Getting along. We take each day as it comes."

"This summer was better than the last one."

A shadow of sorts fell on the household with the coming of Uncle Moyshe Linever. I was pleased he was leaving us that very same day. When he was at the table everyone seemed discouraged and looked down at the ground while he sat in silence.

Before he drove away he turned to me and said, "Well, Peretz, you're big enough now to be going to heder."

My father said, "Of course. Yes. Certainly it's time for him to begin heder. But"—indicating my mother—"she insists on keeping him at home."

My mother said, "He's nothing but skin and bones, poor thing. The sickness took its toll on him. Next year, God willing, when he's a full five years old, he'll be sent to the teacher, Moyshe Mordkhe."

I sat, head bowed, because I knew they were all looking at me. Then suddenly my uncle handed me a kopeck and pinched both of my cheeks as he said to the assembled company, "Be well." My mother wiped the tears from her eyes. We all went outside to watch my uncle and aunt drive away.

Yet another uncle came to visit us. An uncle with a black

beard—Uncle Avrom Tumener. Aunt Soreh came with him. I could tell that Aunt Soreh was my mother's sister. They embraced each other and shed tears of joy.

Uncle Avrom took me up in his lap and tickled me to make me laugh. "Hey, youngster, when are you going to visit us?" he asked, handing me a kopeck.

My mother put a pot of water on the fire to make tea. My uncle Avrom loved tea. He ate very little, but he did drink tea. Slowly, drinking one cup after another, he emptied the entire pot. Having emptied it he became very jolly. The conversation turned to cows and how much milk they gave. There was also talk about children. He knew everyone by name. He had children the same ages as those in our family. Among them was a daughter named Sheyndl, who was my age. "God willing," he said, "when I come again I'll bring Sheyndl with me."

My mother's name was Sheyndl—and he had a Sheyndl too!

"What makes him so pale, your Peretz?" my aunt Soreh asked.

"He won't eat," my mother replied.

"If you don't eat you won't have the strength to study Torah," my uncle scolded me.

My aunt Soreh picked me up and, feeling my bones, said, "Let him eat plenty of butter and sour cream."

"You'd do better to take him home with us, Soreh," said my uncle.

I was sorry to see my uncle and aunt preparing to go.

The uncles and the aunts came to visit us in summer. They brought green cucumbers and blackberries. Wild pears and new potatoes. The house was filled with relatives. All the people we ever talked about showed up. They came from what to my childish mind seemed distant places and stirred thoughts in me of unknown, far-away worlds. Their presence was felt in our house even after they were gone.

From our mill, if one looked far, far off into the distance across bogs and meadows, past stands of alders, we could make out a hill on which there stood two windmills. When there was no wind they stood with their sails outspread, like wings. When the wind was blowing the sails went round and round, cutting circles out of the sky.

One of my mother's brothers, Uncle Avrom Moyshe, lived in the higher of the two mills with his wife, Aunt Rivke, along with a number of children of all sizes. Often we looked in his direction, while they often looked toward us. In summer, on a Shabbos afternoon, we rolled up our trousers and, walking barefoot, started across the fields and bogs to Uncle Avrom Moyshe's house.

My uncle Avrom Moyshe was a scholarly Jew in whose home there were shelves with many books. He too pinched my cheeks and demanded to know why I was not yet attending a heder. My aunt Rivke agreed with my mother that I was all skin and bones and that such a child ought not to be sent to heder. That heder began to loom large before me. Everywhere I turned there was someone raising the heder question.

Then one day, just after Pesach, my father wrapped me in a tallis, and—though I was quite capable of getting into town on my own two feet—he carried me all the way. My mother walked beside him. It was the beginning of spring, and the road was still very muddy. The alder trees were still leafless. The weeping willows bowed their green heads and looked down into the pond. My father carried me silently along. My mother, beside him, was silent too.

The alders followed our progress. The weeping willows lifted their heads to watch Lippe the miller carrying his Peretz, wrapped in a prayer shawl, to Moyshe Mordkhe's heder.

My Grandfather's Melodies

I did not learn much Torah from Moyshe Mordkhe, the teacher of the youngest students. My father brought me into his heder wrapped in a tallis. My mother was at our side. In the crowded heder, the pupils were droning.

The teacher Moyshe Mordkhe had a red beard and was nearsighted; he couldn't see anything beyond his beard. He sat me down at the table, placed in front of me an alphabet glued to a tablet, and with a wide pointer showed me the aleph. An "angel" threw a kopeck down to me from heaven. I saw that it was my father who did it: he was standing behind me and he tossed the kopeck so it would land on the *alef-beys*.

When my father and mother left I cried. There were strange children around me; I didn't like the teacher. He lay his whole head on the *alef-beys* and was hiding the letters with his beard. He wasn't a bad man, but if you didn't get what he wanted right away he would give you a jab in the side with his pointer. Immediately I began to yearn for home.

Someone always brought me to heder. They were afraid to let me go by myself. In the evening someone came again from home and led me back by the hand. Whenever my mother came for me she would pick me up and carry me over a mud puddle if the road was muddy.

Whatever I learned I didn't understand. I learned the *alef-beys* and to recite prayers from the prayer book. I was soon able to recite the order of daily prayers, and I knew the Shema by heart, but my mind was not on my work. It was back at the mill.

I was frequently ill. Moyshe the physician, with his smooth, dark beard, would come to look at my throat and tell my parents I was to stay home. As a result I did not actually go to the heder every day.

In winter I really did get sick with scarlet fever and, after that, measles. Moyshe Mordkhe, the heder teacher, came to find out how I was. A good fellow, Moyshe Mordkhe. Just the same, I didn't like him. And it was all the fault of my home because I hated leaving it every morning to go to the strange shtetl. It seemed to me that the very trees looked on unhappily as they watched me on my way. That, no doubt, is why they greeted me as a relative at night when they saw me on my way home. Then everything I passed seemed familiar to me.

As soon as I crossed the high railroad embankment I was greeted again by the world I knew. Here was the pond whose sparkling surface I glimpsed through the trees. And there were the two tall alder trees growing like twins beside each other. When the wind stirred in their branches both of them groaned. And I recognized each stone my family had placed on the dam to serve as stepping-stones after a rainstorm when the path grew difficult. And there was the one and only cherry tree behind the stable, and beside it the little plum tree with several green plums on its branches.

I could already hear the *plop plop* of the mill wheels turning and the sound of rushing water below them. The ducks greeted me with their quacking; the rooster with his evening *cock-a-doodle-doo!*

Now that I was attending heder I was treated with greater respect by the grown-ups. Sometimes my mother would ask me to help her carry out on a pole the feeding tub for our cow. But she would give me just the pole so it wouldn't be too hard for me. I proved useful too when the millstones needed trimming—when the heavy upper mill wheel had to be lifted from the lower one, then turned upside-down so it could be trimmed and shaped. Of course the grown-ups could perform the task of removing and up-ending it, but they needed me to slip a piece of timber between the two stones.

I understood why I had to recite the Shema before I went to bed at night. It would keep evil spirits from doing me harm.

Even the grown-ups were terribly frightened of uncanny creatures. Everyone was afraid to leave the house at night to answer nature's call.

During the day, however, every tree was familiar, every rivulet and the sounds it made. During the day, especially in the summer, it was a delight to creep about everywhere searching for wonders. There was nothing to be feared either from the bogs or from the distant woods.

At night, when darkness surrounded the mill—especially on moonless nights at the end of the month—we were frightened even of our own shadows. Then we regarded every speck of darkness outlining a tree or a stump with suspicion. Here and there, around the pond, there were upended trees with dark holes where the roots had been. Who could tell what might be sitting among the roots of such a tree?

When the mill wheels turned, life was lively at home. Even at night the noise of their turning kept fear away. But when the wheels stood still the unimpeded water rustled its way under the house. When a breeze played among the trees we all listened anxiously because there was no one in the house who had not encountered an evil spirit. My grandfather, and my father too, told stories of encounters with evil spirits. One night my brother Kalmen came home pale and frightened because, driving back from town, he had seen something or someone supernatural sitting at the side of a ditch waving at him.

In winter, if it was the end of the month and someone had to go outdoors, we would find some excuse to get someone to come with us.

My grandfather could not admit he was afraid to go outside, so he would say to my father, "Let's go out together so we can check the force and direction of the wind. Maybe there's a thaw coming."

If my father had to go out he would call my brother. "Come. Let's go see if the stable is properly closed and if the horse has been well fed."

My mother would ask my sister Bebl to go with her. "Come, daughter. Let's see if all the ducks have returned to their pen. I have a feeling the gate was left open."

Bebl, for her part, if she had to go out, would call me or Moyshe. "Come on. Let's go see how cold it is outside. Come on, Peretz, let's go see if there are stars in the sky."

One frosty night, when the wind was howling and frost had entirely obscured the windows, the family was sitting around in the mill. Suddenly our dog started barking right under the window. He raced to the barn and was back at the window, still barking.

"Thieves. Thieves, that's what it is. They want to break into the barn and steal the horse." There was consternation in the house. We all looked at each other.

"Who'll go out with me?" my father asked. "Let's all go," said my grandfather.

We searched the mill for sticks, for iron bars. Everyone armed himself with something. My grandfather seized a poker. Slowly we opened the mill door and went out, single file. It was dark. And the dog, who was waiting for us at the mill door, ran, straight as an arrow, to the stable, where he began snapping at what looked like the coattails of someone dressed in black.

We approached the stable but the person in black did not budge. When we came closer it turned out that what had frightened us was an old cloth coat hanging on a pole near the barn. It was a wet, swollen coat that had frozen stiff and was waving back and forth in the wind, a fact that irritated our dog. And though each of us reassured himself by touching the coat, it was some time before we were able to get back to sleep.

My brother Moyshe, who often brought me home from heder, would tell me stories of evil spirits. While passing the church that stood in the middle of the shtetl marketplace, Moyshe ordered me to take off and run.

My grandfather, in those days, was very pleased with my prog-

ress in heder. When I found his place for him in the prayer book—
which he could not do without his glasses—he would reward me
by setting me in his lap and teaching me some of his melodies. Ah,
those melodies.

"Come, Peretz, and we'll sing the red melody together." Or
"Come, grandson, and we'll sing the blue melody." My grandfather
Yehoshua also had a yellow and a green melody. And a speckled
melody. Little by little he taught them all to me. I loved his speckled melody best of all and have remembered it all these years.

He used to say, "Remember, Peretz, if the western sky at sunset is red with yellow stripes, that's a good sign for the windmills
because it means the wind will blow in the high places. If the sun
is obscured by a cloud and doesn't appear again until sunset, that's
a sign of rain. When the hens flutter their tail feathers, there's certain to be a storm, and when the cat scratches at the legs of a chair,
that too is a sign of wind coming. The north wind is a wicked fellow.
When he blows he brings the cold and the frost, but when that good
fellow, the south wind, blows he brings warmth. When he nods toward the west, that's a sure sign of rain."

The adults would walk about out of doors, sniffing the wind,
checking, by its smell, what the weather would be. I too sniffed at
the wind. In summer I could understand from the songs the birds
sang that within three days' time it would rain. And I knew which
birdsong predicted the end of rain within a day.

Because Moyshe Mordkhe, the teacher, had taught me how to
say my prayers, my father required me to say them every day. He
made me stand beside him as he recited the *Shemoneh Esreh*, the
Eighteen Benedictions. He would point to his place in the prayer
book and make me recite after him. I would recite and recite without understanding a word, though it's true that standing beside my
father I felt myself getting sensibly older, especially when he said
that very soon he would turn me over to the teacher, Mattes, because it was time for me to be someone.

My mother would not abide it. She refused to hand her Peretz
over to the hangman who had pinched and bruised my brother
Moyshe's body black and blue. But my father said that any child

who was not sent to Mattes would never properly amount to anything.

The winter passed, and then, in the days between the beginning and end of Pesach, the teacher Mattes came to our house to talk about my coming to his school at the beginning of the next term. Mattes was a stocky man with a flushed face and a long, copper-colored beard. He was a good head taller than my father, and he had huge, soft, hairy hands.

Mattes pinched my cheeks. My mother, tears in her eyes, said softly, "God forbid, Reb Mattes, you mustn't beat him."

My father said angrily, "Reb Mattes will teach him so he can be somebody."

My brother Moyshe, who no longer studied with Reb Mattes and was, therefore, no longer afraid of him, gave him a dirty look. Mattes was offered a glass of Pesach wine, and it was agreed that he would be paid eight rubles a term for my tuition.

And so I began to attend Mattes's heder, alone. I followed the path alongside the dam, going my own way. Alone.

My Teacher, Mattes

At the time when my brother Moyshe was attending Mattes's heder, the teacher had a three-thonged whip whose middle thong was tipped with iron. It was the whip with which he beat the naked bottoms of his pupils. That was why, each evening when Moyshe came home from school, my mother had reason to grieve over the black and blue marks on his body.

A few years later, when I went to his heder, Mattes had grown more restrained. The townsfolk had complained that his behavior was excessive after he had beaten his own son to a pulp. "Beating them is fine, but within reason and with justice . . ."

His heder was on a side street, in the house of the widow Gedalyekhe. In that low, narrow room, Mattes seemed much bigger than he appeared when I saw him at our home. In his domain his pupils looked even smaller than they were.

Gedalyekhe, the widow, was a large, bony old woman with a red face. Among the peasants in the district she had a reputation as a blood-letter who used cupping glasses and leeches. She was a healer who received her patients near the door, beside the fireplace, which usually meant that, while we children were studying Torah or Gemara at the table deep in the room near the window, there was always some peasant—man or woman—sitting near the door on a footstool while Gedalyekhe busied herself over the peasant's naked shoulders.

There were some ten pupils under Mattes's care, ranging in age from seven to ten years old. I was one of the youngest and certainly the smallest. The first week, when I was a little slow to repeat the translation of a Torah passage he read to me, he pinched me affectionately on the cheek. For the rest of the day I felt as if ants were crawling about under the skin where his fingers had touched.

Some of the children had studied with him before, but from the first day of class they were not spared his blows. Mattes had a nickname for each of his pupils. Mordkhe Zalmen, the smith's son, a plump boy, was called "Bondeh." Elye, whose father came from Zalishin, was called "Mozsheh." One of the boys was called "Shmegdeh" and another "Glovatskeh." I inherited my brother Moyshe's nickname: I was Shtshenyuk (a whelp). When it pleased Mattes to beat one of his pupils, he would add the word "crook" to the nickname, as in, "Bondeh, you crook!" and "Mozsheh, you crook!"

Mattes enjoyed grabbing a pupil's ear and, using it as a handle, banging the boy's head against the wall. His soft hands distributed forehand or backhand slaps generously, but his greatest pleasure was to whip a pupil. These whippings he accomplished with great ease. He usually stood behind his pupils as they were reciting. When a recitation displeased him, he seized the offending boy by the shoulders and flipped him around and over. Putting the boy's head firmly between his plump, soft knees, he reached a hand up to the rafter where his whip was concealed, then lashed the boy's bare bottom.

During my first days in his heder I had plenty of opportunities to see how Mattes turned boys into men. My narrow shoulders grew even narrower. My pale, thin features grew paler and thinner. In those first days a change occurred in my childhood. I suddenly became a sensible person. Forty-three years have already gone by since I started going to Mattes's heder.

I remember that time when I encountered the world with eager curiosity. I felt the soft earth with my bare feet. I reveled in the mill and its surroundings and the path I walked from it to heder. And I felt how my soul was being strengthened by powers in me that, until then, I had been unaware of. It was exciting to be thrust out into the world, to learn to cope with it on my own.

At the beginning someone from home brought me to heder. Often someone came to pick me up at dusk. A little later that summer I walked to heder on my own. And since the children were let out on time in the summer I mostly found my way home by myself.

I didn't walk home. I ran the entire three-kilometer distance from the shtetl to the mill. I was a fast runner, the fastest in my heder. I ran so quickly my coattails flapped behind me. Just the same, I had time to pause occasionally to look about me, to take in whatever was new on my way. I had time to lie beside the pond and look into its clear waters at the swimming fish. I knew all the nests in the trees on both sides of my path. I had a gypsy knife in my pocket, and I knew how to whittle a whistle out of a willow twig. On my way to heder I sometimes whittled several to give to my friends. I had time too to check each tree stump between whose roots currants grew and to note which of the berries would be ripening soon.

That was the part of the path stretching from the mill to the first Gentile barns and houses, the part that had water and marshes on both sides. It was familiar territory to me. I would shout into a clump of trees, and from a distance there would come an answering shout. I piped to the birds, and they replied. I mimicked the cuckoo, and from wherever she was she replied, "Cuckoo, cuckoo, cuckoo." When I came to the railroad crossing, I never failed to put my ear to one of the rails to hear whether a train might be coming. There were needles on the rails where my sister Bebl and my brother Moyshe had put them to be flattened by the train. One of the needles was mine. It lay there embedded in the rail with its eye unbroken and gleaming.

That was my world, but when my path approached the fences of the town's landholders I entered hostile territory, a world where Gentile boys would call from behind a barn or a house, "Kike, kike, take a hike." Sometimes they might follow me, and I would find myself struck by a thrown stick or stone. I pretended I saw no one, but if I started to run, that was the signal for them to dart out from their hiding places to chase me, stick out their tongues, and throw sticks or stones. They threw more or less for form's sake rather than with any serious intent to hit me.

In those non-Jewish streets, geese and ganders were among the worst of my enemies. The ganders would chase me, hissing, and often enough would succeed in grabbing the hem of my kaftan in their bills.

There was one house at which a not especially large red dog waited for me with his head on his paws as if he did not have me on his mind at all. But the minute I came near he leaped toward me and gave chase. A couple of times he succeeded in tearing my coattails.

The first few times I had to pass through the Gentile district I crept over fences and made my way through back gardens to avoid my enemies, the Gentile boys, the geese, and the dog. Later I felt ashamed to be doing that. Instead I found a good supple stick and carried it with me under my kaftan. The children, sensing its presence, developed respect for me and instead of calling after me talked to me. I gave them a bit of the challah my mother had given me, and a peace was established.

Later that summer, when the gander tried to snap at my coattails, I grabbed him by the neck, lifted him high in the air, and flung him among the geese. "Quack, quack, quack," scolded the geese as they scattered across the courtyard.

The time came when I showed the red dog that he should be afraid of me even though I was only a little boy running past his owner's house on the way to heder.

What happened was this: As the dog was chasing me—when in fact he had both paws on my shoulders and was on the verge of biting me on the neck—I turned and grabbed his tail, yanked him off the ground, and swung him over the fence and into a nettle bush. He uttered a yelp and ran off wherever his legs would carry him while I, with my heart beating as if it meant to leap from my chest, set my legs in motion and ran off helter-skelter. From then on, whenever the red dog saw me coming, he put his tail between his legs and slunk quietly out of my way.

Mattes the teacher sent word to my father that I was a good pupil who should be kept in heder a long time and that, if I continued to apply myself, I might amount to something. That was told to me by my mother after my father told her. It was on a Friday afternoon when I came home early and my mother was, according to custom, washing my hair.

My grandfather Yehoshua quizzed me from time to time, making me translate passages from the Torah, totally buddy-buddy with me. With his spectacles tied to his head with a string, he would search our old copy of the *Humash*—Pentateuch—for the passages I had been studying in heder that week. On Friday, the two of us— he with all of his hundred years and I with my seven—went through the entire Torah portion of the week, squeakily intertwining our melodies.

Among the children in my heder there were some who, because their fathers were bigwigs, were treated with special respect. Those fathers had shops in the center of the marketplace and seats in the synagogue right next to the prestigious east wall. I, however, was only the son of Lippe the miller, who did not have a place beside the east wall. Indeed, he sat far from it.

When, on Shabbos, my father took me with him to the synagogue he would look at the men sitting at the east wall. There they were, those big shots. So far, far away. I saw my fellow pupils standing there next to their fathers. They looked toward me, and I understood they were not permitted to come talk with me. Nor would I leave my place to join them.

I felt isolated at heder. I did not always take part in the children's pranks and games but kept my eyes buried in my book so I would remember what Reb Mattes taught us. I made a silent contract with myself that Mattes could slap me or pull me about by an ear or pluck my hair. But one thing I would never let him do was beat me on the backside the way he did the others. My brother Moyshe couldn't believe it. He pulled down my trousers and was amazed to find no marks on my body.

I didn't like the shtetl. Once I was let out of heder I ran home. The heder didn't draw me away from me from the mill. The heder didn't distance me from my family.

Though my mother was proud of my Torah learning, that did not keep her from sending me up an alder tree to pull down a dead branch she could break across her knee when she wanted to kindle a fire in the kitchen stove.

My father, even though he was constantly interrogating Mattes to see if his Peretz was making progress, was delighted to see how Peretz was carving out his place.

Mattes had said that one day I would amount to something. I had been a pupil of his for an entire summer, and yet in all that time he had not beaten me once.

ᕈᓍ The Landlord

On the way to heder, on the first street that led to the circular marketplace, I passed two houses with thatched roofs. As I neared the first I always hurried and was afraid even to peep through the gate to catch a glimpse of the yard; on the other hand, as I neared the second house, which did not have a fence around it, I was often tempted to go in. And I did.

Shrinski, the wealthy peasant from whom my father rented the mill, and for whom everyone in my family slaved, lived in the first house. In the second there lived Arye the tailor and his wife, Rokhele the kasha maker.

Arye the tailor was a graying, nearsighted man who sat continually hunched over a broad, heavy table sewing cheap peasant clothing while his wife, Rokhele, a small shrunken woman, almost always stood at the door turning the handle of a small grinding mill. She made a living grinding buckwheat groats and oat grits for the entire town. She also baked round loaves of rye bread. A couple of times a week she baked small round buckwheat cakes, which she sold to Jews and Gentiles alike. Arye and Rokhele had two sons, the younger of whom was Alter, a boy my age.

I was drawn to their house by their mill and by the smells of groats, dried oats, and buckwheat that hovered in the air when Rokhele baked her bread. Rokhele's hand grinder appeared, in my eyes, to be a diminutive mill. There were many times Arye the tailor appeared at our mill carrying a sack of dried buckwheat on his shoulders to be ground into flour and then sifted. And we in turn always used our wagon to bring his grain to be milled into rye flour.

I used to run into their house on my way to school to say good morning. My mother would often ask me to stop by to get a half quart of groats for her. Arye never took his eyes off the rough cloth at which he was working as, in his slightly nasal way, he asked if the mill wheel at home was turning or how I was doing at heder or whether Mattes was beating me hard.

Rokhl ranged much further with her questions. But first she handed me a buckwheat cake, then she kissed my cheek maternally. She wanted to know whether my mother was suffering from headaches, and had she baked bread? And how had the Shabbos kugel turned out? My mother and Rokhl frequently visited each other. Neither of them liked the people who lived around the circular market very much. They were intimate friends who poured out their hearts to one another. But my mother never carried anything that was said to her in Rokhl's house beyond those walls. When Rokhl and my mother talked about how bitter life was, or about the joys and sorrows of children, Arye never lifted his head from the coarse cloth he was sewing.

I felt much differently about the first of the village houses I came to on my way to school. That was the home of Shrinski, our landlord. I was not the only one in my family who hesitated to come near it. We all shied away from the place because the landlord and his sons were for us a constant source of worry, of anxious days and my parents' sighs during the long winter nights.

Shrinski was old and bowed. His face was round and flushed and covered with spiky hair. When he was around people he kept his small, watery eyes on the ground. He had two sons. The older one, Yuzik, was dark and wore a mustache. The younger one, still unmarried, was called Yaske. Yuzik was the clever son of the Haggadah story, but he also had a mixture in him of the wicked son. Yaske was pale, flaxen haired, and was the simpleton of the Haggadah tale, but he too had some aspects of the wicked son in him.

Our landlord was entirely wicked. He never had a smile on his face or uttered a kind word. He was always muttering into his own belly. He owned our mill. He owned the meadows and the trees behind the mill and all the fields that bordered the stream. He controlled the access rights to fields that were not his and would charge a toll to the hay wagons that crossed his bridge over the river.

One of his habits was to come into our neighborhood and stand there examining his property. He did this especially in the summer. He checked to see whether his fields were being overgrazed and whether my father had by chance turned his cow or his horse loose into them. Though he had difficulty raising his head, he himself looked up to examine his trees. If he found a tree that had been chopped down or had a broken branch he was furious and slapped his sides in vexation.

Seeing him as he wandered about the fields or trudged along the dam muttering imprecations at an invisible enemy, it was easy to imagine we were seeing a man possessed by evil spirits.

His sons were rarely seen in our neighborhood except when they came to mow the hay or to pass on some evil tidings. My father ground all Shrinski's grain for free, and the landlord's sons had a way of showing up to have their wheat ground and to watch the grinding carefully "to keep the miller honest."

Shrinski sometimes did come to our house. He usually showed up early on a Friday evening to ask for his rent money. Then he would wander about looking over his property, and later, when my mother had finished blessing the Shabbos candles, he would come into the house and, without so much as a "Good evening," he would sit down, muttering. When the blessing of the wine was over, my mother usually gave him a piece of challah and a glass of brandy, which pleased him. Blood suffused his face, and he would talk about how sinful the world was and about his son Yaske, who could not find a bride. He always managed to tell us he had been offered more rent money for the mill, and therefore, after Pesach, Laybko—that is, my father—would have to pay a hundred and fifty rubles a year for the mill instead of the usual hundred and twenty.

And if he didn't, well, then Laybko had been given fair warning and would have to look for another mill.

Of his two sons, Yaske was the one who most liked to show up on a Friday evening. He would come in and seat himself on the sleeping bench near the window and watch us while we said our evening prayers or as we washed our hands and made the blessing over wine. He always thanked my mother for the piece of white bread and the glass of brandy she gave him. When Yaske had downed the brandy, he would smile foolishly and tell us his father would never rent the mill to anyone else because he respected Lippe the miller. But Lippe would have to pay more rent because, Yaske confided, "It's your Jews who are butting in. Your very own Jews are the ones who want to drive you from the mill because they think you've got a gold mine here."

To thank him for his news, my mother gave him another piece of challah and poured another glass of brandy, which made him laugh foolishly again as he said in Russian, "Jews know how to live!"

Then, pleased at how clever he was, he went off, having spoiled our Friday evening for us.

Yuzik, the older son, rarely came to our house. He had a better sense of how to behave; he gave polite thanks for his bit of challah, and he talked sensibly. He even ordered that dried branches among the trees be collected. When the brandy he drank had relaxed him, he would praise Lippe the miller. "My father will never put anyone else into the mill, but you'll have to pay more rent starting with the new year. It makes no difference to me. I'm not going to live in the town in any case. I'm going to leave. My wife says it's not good for her here. My wife ... yes ... if she should give birth to a boy, well ... yes."

At that point my mother gave him a second piece of the Shabbos challah, telling him to take it to his wife.

Just like that they appeared from time to time in the summer and winter. Even in the fall, at the time of the cheerless, autumnal mires, they did not fail to come. Sometimes it was the landlord himself, at other times one of his heirs. In the fall they fit right into the mood that reigned in our house.

The fall brought all sorts of troubles, all sorts of heartache.

With the coming of the rains the narrowing streambed meant that the water overflowed its banks. Because of the flooding, and because the roads had gotten so bad no one could make their way over them to the mill, there was no work for the miller. There was more than enough water to turn both mill wheels and both pairs of millstones day and night. Indeed, there was so much water in the mill race we could not control it, so we had to open the sluices and let the water flow where it would.

The sounds the destructive waters made flowing under the house seemed to tease us. The water flowed continually away, laughing at the miller who had sluices next to the bridge, in the trough next to the wheels. The wind whistled through the damp alder trees—and poverty whistled, cutting at our hearts. It was not a pressing sorrow but a gnawing pain. I too felt the anguish of the adults.

As the water flowed away unfettered, and there was no flour in the mill with which to bake challah, we greeted the Shabbos with mournful faces. Flour had to be bought in town. Though in truth the challahs made with store-bought flour were whiter than those made with our own, still the loaves seemed foreign, and the Shabbos table was a gloomy one.

It was at such times that old Shrinski, the landlord, came to us. He walked in, stamped his muddy boots at the doorway, and squinted at the light, which was unusually bright because in honor of Shabbos the glass in the cheap wall lamp had been cleaned and filled with oil. In addition to the lamp there were the four candles my mother had blessed burning in the brass Shabbos candelabra.

Shrinski enjoyed our white Shabbos bread though it had been made with flour bought on credit from a merchant in town. "A Yid can't do without challah," he muttered as he chewed. "Has to have challah for the Shabbos. Therefore," he began, raising our hopes, "since there is no work in the mill and," he continued, "since the water is flowing uselessly away, I'll bring you a wagonload of my wheat to be ground so I'll have enough flour for the winter."

Whether it was because my mother had given him a smaller slice of challah or because of the brandy he had drunk, he waited until he was already at the door before he said, "See that you don't let anyone cut wood from the trees. The goddamned thieves, may their bones rot . . ."

His appearance in our house was a premonition that we were in for a hard winter. In those dark days, when my mother buttered a couple of slices of bread for me to take to heder, she would say, "Remember, my son, to stop at Rokhele's house to see if she's baked any buckwheat rolls. Let her give you one. With God's help, we'll pay her for it."

And if my mother's heart was so oppressed by the rumor that someone was offering to take the mill away from us, she would slip over to pour her heart out to Rokhele in Arye the tailor's thatched-roof house, which faced our landlord Shrinski's home.

Torah and Wet Cupping

For Mattes, my teacher, there was a time for everything. A time to distribute harsh blows or mild ones. A time for whipping and a time for smiling, even a time for pinching a cheek affectionately.

His good days were usually at the beginning of the month. It was then that the pupils brought their tuition money. Sunday could also be a good day because that was when we began the study of a new Torah portion or a new problem in a tractate of the Gemara that the pupils were not yet required to know well.

Wednesday was always bad. Though the pupils studied in pairs, each member of the pair had to prove he knew the material. Thursdays were dreadful since each pupil had to recite on his own. It was not unusual that on a Thursday a pupil had his ear pulled so hard it bled. Mattes required us all to know the work by heart.

On Friday things eased up. Then we were in school only half a day, and we went over the weekly Torah portion and looked through the Shabbos prayers. We also worked a little on the haftorah selection from the Prophets that follows the reading of the Torah portion.

Shabbos afternoons, especially in summer, were good. It was then that we studied the *Ethics of the Fathers*. Mattes was sleepy from the effects of his Shabbos cholent and kugel, so even at the study table we could get away with catching an occasional fly.

Whether good or bad, Monday was a special day. What made it special had less to do with studying than with the school itself. It was special because Monday was market day in the village of Kleshtshel.

Though Mattes did not do any business himself, he felt the pull of the market. Who could tell whether he might not meet a peasant who would offer him a bargain of some sort? So on Mondays Mattes was always a bit distracted and occasionally left the school in "confusion," as he put it.

Because of the widow Gedalyekhe, on Mondays the school was transformed into a bizarre sort of butcher shop. It was then that the heder's landlady sat in the doorway near the fireplace and received the country peasants, men and women, who were her patients and on whose shoulders she applied dry or wet cupping.

Sometimes one of her patients showed up in the middle of the week, but Monday was the day when Gedalyekhe's business thrived. Peasants young and old flocked to her. They sat on stools near the fireplace beside the doorway and offered their blood without restraint.

This is how she did it.

She sat the patient down with his face to the door and his back to the room—that is, with his back to us, the children at the study table. She had a dozen or so tin cups standing in a bowlful of warm water. A small smoky lamp burned on the mantelpiece. When she had washed the patient's bare back with a damp cloth, she brought a wet cup close to the patient's back, then inserted the flame of the lamp into it for an instant, after which she pressed the cup to his skin, where it stuck.

The patient sat there in his bowed position for a quarter of an hour while Gedalyekhe dozed off. She woke just in time to pluck the cups from the patient's back. Each of the cups gave a little hiss as it was removed, and in the place where it had been a red circle now glowed. There could be as many as ten, twenty, or even thirty such circles stretched taut with blood.

If the patient wanted dry cupping, the process was now over and Gedalyekhe smeared grease over his back with her bare hand as she said in Russian, "To your health!" The patient paid the few groschen that were her fee and replied, "Thank you."

When the patient wanted "punctured," or wet, cupping, Geda-lyekhe further treated each red circle by thrusting into its center the sharp, corroded tip of a brass instrument that caused three blood spots to blossom there. That done on each, she placed a heat-ed cup again over the area she had just punctured. It was not long before the cups filled and then fell off the patient's back of their own accord, splattering blood. Blood ran down the patient's torn-up back as well, making him look as if he had been skinned.

Gedalyekhe wiped the blood off her patient's back with her hand, then smeared the raw red skin with stinking unguents as she said, "To your health." The patient groaned, barely able to straight-en his back, paid his fee, and replied, "Thank you."

There were young backs and old, fat and lean, broad and nar-row. There were those who accepted the cupping as if it were a blessing and there were some—especially the women—who shud-dered and recited prayers while Gedalyekhe drew their blood.

We pupils, sitting at the study table—we concentrated neither on Torah nor on Gemara. Our attention was focused on Gedaly-ekhe's basinful of cups. We silently counted the number she had applied to someone's naked back. Mattes, meanwhile, did not de-liver so much as a slap or even a punitive pinch on Mondays be-cause he was ashamed to punish the children in the presence of the peasants.

As a result, those of us who were especially daring on Mondays paid dearly for our behavior on Tuesday, when he reminded us of what we had done.

"Boyteh, you crook, yesterday you counted the cups on the peasant woman's back. Not a thought for your Torah studies. There. Let that pay you."

That year I started to study the Gemara tractate Bava Met-zia. But it was the stories in the Humash that agitated my mind. I particularly studied how God created heaven and earth and ev-erything under the heavens and upon the earth. "God created the world in six days, and on the seventh day He rested."

I began to think about the world as it was described in the Humash, in Genesis. The path I took from the mill to heder and from heder back to the mill seemed to me to resemble the world after its creation. I found myself thinking more and more frequently about God, especially since I had begun to study the Tanakh. I talked about how God had created the world with a fellow pupil of mine whom the teacher called Glovatski.

I never understood why Mattes called my friend Glovatski. There was a Gentile in the village named Glovatski who had all sorts of skills. He could pull a tooth with the help of a key. He could copy a key and he could shoot birds. It was said he was a magician. I had seen Glovatski in the vicinity of the mill studying the trees and then shooting at the birds in them.

Glovatski, my fellow pupil, became a close friend. We shared our thoughts on the vastness of the world, on the distance that separated heaven from earth. I confided secrets of the mill to him, explaining how grains of wheat were turned into flour.

Mattes had not yet beaten me. It may be that I had done nothing to deserve being beaten, or it may be that my mother had pleaded with him not to beat me.

But once in that first summer he struck me in the face with his fist so hard my face swelled up, after which I was left with a black and blue mark under my eye.

Just before it was time to go home, Mattes called me to him and, out of earshot of the children, said, "When you get home, tell them you tripped on a stone." I kept my word and never told anyone, not even years later, that Mattes had given me a black-and-blue mark with his fist. I felt that so far he had treated me differently from my fellow pupils, and so I wanted to keep his good will.

One Friday, following an exceptionally difficult Thursday, the pupils got together and decided to steal the teacher's whip and hide it somewhere. Each of the pupils offered a different suggestion. One said we ought to cut the whip into tiny pieces and scatter them somewhere. Someone else suggested we burn it. A final suggestion was that I take the whip home, fasten a stone to it, and drop it into the stream. I was scared, thinking Mattes might have supernatural powers and that he would know what I had done.

We finally decided we would hide the whip under a washtub filled with dirty laundry. Mattes of course suspected we had stolen his whip. He beat us unmercifully with twigs he broke from the broom or with a rope. Eventually Gedalyekhe, as she was preparing to do her laundry, lifted the tub and found the whip, now grown moldy, and returned it to Mattes.

Mattes demanded a confession from whomever it was who had stolen the whip. The pupils wept and denied absolutely that any of them had taken it. Then he whipped and flogged and flogged and whipped until he had worn the mold off the whip's thongs.

All week long my head was filled with Torah. My mother complained that my strength was being sapped by my studies. Every weekday morning I downed a dish of groats, after which my mother would give me a couple of slices of day-old white bread spread with butter, which I scraped off and threw away. After the day of studying I took off running from heder in a hurry. When I got home I was too worn out to eat the supper my mother had made.

It was only on Fridays that I relaxed. Then I came home at midday and had plenty of time to enjoy the life of the mill. My mother had already baked the challahs; the oven was glowing, ready to keep the cholent warm over Shabbos.

I was glad when my mother sent me on errands. "Peretz, darling, go see where the cow has run off to." "Run up to the attic, dear. I heard a hen clucking. She must have laid an egg." "Go on out, Peretz, and gather some pine branches so we can strew them about the house."

My grandfather, feeling congenial, pulled down a copy of the Humash from the bookshelf to test me on what I had learned that week. "Ah, my grandson, it's a good thing there's a God in this world. Now you know all that God has done. If you want to be a rabbi, you can be a rabbi. If Mattes says of a boy that he's going to be someone, then he'll be someone. So, then, let's sing the red melody."

My sister Bebl took me out to the river behind the mill, where she bathed me, washing me all over.

My brother Moyshe, now a grown-up, flour-dusted miller, was

much bigger than me and already very strong. It bothered him that Mattes had given me the nickname that he, Moyshe, used to have. He still remembered much of what he had learned in school. He would take the Humash down and show me what he knew, but I could see he felt troubled as he did it. I had some idea of what disturbed him. He felt my father had taken him out of heder too soon.

When my mother said, "Oh, I forgot to buy pepper. Run into town, would you? Here's a piece of *kikhl* cookie to nibble on your way," I ran. The ground under me seemed to fly away. When I reached the marketplace I grew shy, and to give the appearance of poise I slowed down. I went into Shimen-Velvl's grocery store and bought pepper. Then, when I had cut across the market square and was in the non-Jewish street, I was off and running again. Fleet as the wind, I was back at home with the pepper in my hand.

"Oh, dear. Too bad," my mother said. "I forgot to tell you to buy sugar. There won't be any for our tea." At that, my brother Moyshe gathered up his coattails and sped away. It would be hard to catch up with him.

My father returned from town flush from his visit to the mikveh, where he had gone to get himself cleaned up for Shabbos. There he had talked with Mattes, who told him that he, my father, had reason to be proud of me. My father came home feeling pleased and reported what he had heard to my mother, and she too was pleased.

My father turned to me, saying, "I talked to Mattes. We're going to get you a pair of boots this winter. I've already ordered them from the shoemaker."

And that was the way the first summer in Mattes's school ended. I had studied Humash, Rashi, and Gemara. The High Holy Days were around the corner. I was free, but I had the fear of God. I could now see God's presence everywhere in and around the mill. I could feel Him moving over the fields each evening when the sun went down in the west.

And as night fell, I was scared to go outside by myself. Lying in bed I listened to the sound of the water under the house. Sometimes it murmured, and it seemed to me I could make out the words it said, but no matter how hard I listened their meaning escaped me.

I still slept in the same bed as my mother, and sleeping next to her I was still a small, small child.

In my heart I was happy Mattes had not beaten me once during the entire term.

✍ "Love Thy Labor"

I overheard a conversation one evening between my father and mother, who were sitting on the ground outside the mill sorting the cucumbers my father had brought from town and which he and my mother were going to pickle. A nostalgia hovered over the fields. Leaves were turning yellow and falling from the trees.

My father said, "If we can't find a teacher for him in Kleshtshel we'll have to send him to some other town to study."

My mother said, "Don't even think of sending him away just yet. He's still a child. Think what can happen to him in some strange town."

My father examined a cucumber that had turned yellow and said, "No. It's on my mind. With God's help he'll be a rabbi."

My mother replied, "Why do we have to think of what he will be now? So long as he's healthy. I see no reason to make him work so hard." Turning to me she said, "Go on, Peretz, dear. Cut yourself a slice of bread. And here, have one of these tasty cucumbers."

So I understood my father wanted me to be a rabbi and that he was already thinking of sending me away to study.

I went into the mill. There was a back door that opened out toward the river with a view of the meadows. I looked out and watched the water that fell from the wheels flowing farther and farther away from our mill.

I knew that far, far in the distance, if one avoided the swampy fields and cut through a small wood, one would come to another mill on the same bank of the stream as our own—a mill that belonged to a Gentile named Lapinski. When his pond was at its fullest, Lapinski let its water turn his wheel, after which it flowed away. Upstream from us, in the shtetl, there was a mill that belonged to a man who was called "the only son." He had a rich father named Moyshe Podbilyer, a landholder who built a mill in town for his son. The water from "the only son's" mill flowed down to us. From us it flowed to Lapinski and from there . . .

When I thought about what my father had said and tried to imagine the route I would have to travel to become a rabbi, what came to my mind was our river and the way it wound between shaded green banks, between alders, willows, and bird-cherry trees. I had no idea how far the river went. I had no idea how far my route would be if I had to leave home to study, as my father said.

My father said he hoped, God willing, that Peretz would be a rabbi. As it was, the only rabbi I had known until then was the rabbi who lived on the street in Kleshtshel that led to our mill. He was blind, and people led him around by the hand. On Shabbos there was always a minyan praying at his house, including my father and grandfather. People came to him for answers to questions about ritual. He had a salt-and-pepper beard. He kept his eyes wide open. Dark, dark eyes. He was deeply learned and knew everything by heart.

My father took me to see him once, and I could tell the rabbi was blind. Totally blind. My father said, "Rabbi, this is my youngest son. He is already studying Gemara in Mattes's school."

The rabbi reached toward me with both hands and touched my head, my face. As he passed his soft fingers over my face he said, "Study. Study Torah, and all will be well."

I was frightened by his dark, wide-open eyes that saw nothing. In Mattes's school I had learned that in *Ethics of the Fathers* it is written "Ye shall love work and despise the rabbinate." Rabbi Mattes never made clear to us why one must love work and hate the rabbinate. Still, because the teacher had taught the phrase to us, I thought about my family.

I thought about my father, my brothers, and about my oldest brother, Binyomin Khayem, who already had a wife and children and who lived in town, where he worked as a dyer, dyeing wool and thread for the peasant women in the neighboring villages. When something broke down in our mill, Binyomin Khayem was the only one who could fix it. He was a tall, straight man with a blond beard and light blue eyes. When he came in, he threw off his kaftan and went into the mill, where he took the machinery apart. I envied him—the way he held an ax in his hands and the way the ax was obedient to him. Dry, coarse logs, hard as steel. He hacked so precisely the chips flew under the blade. When he was shaping a piece of wood, the shavings fell away from it smoothly.

When he trimmed the millstones one could hear the rhythmic sound of his hammer. He chipped at the large stone with his pointed hammer. Bits of stone flew in all directions, landed in his beard, and struck him in the face, but he continued to wield his hammer cheerfully.

Why had my father not let him become a rabbi?

When I thought of work one could love, it never occurred to me to think of any other work than that of a miller. I knew my father worked hard. All of the older children worked hard. But any work that did not leave one covered with flour had no appeal for me. I was already studying Gemara but, though my father talked of my becoming a rabbi, I loved our mill. When Binyomin Khayem came to us and started fixing the mill, I ran about at his feet, following him step by step. When he was sawing something, I studied the way he held the saw, and I could see why his cuts always came out straight.

Skillful as he was, it was clear to me Binyomin Khayem did not like doing miller's work. He hated having his kaftan and hat dusted with flour. Before he left us he brushed off every last speck. Still, I envied him because he could do so much.

My uncle Avrom Moyshe, my mother's brother, had a windmill on a hill beyond the fields, beyond the woods and marshes. We often visited him. In summer we went barefoot across the boggy fields to his mill; in winter, across the frozen fields. My uncle had a small brown beard and intelligent eyes. Though he was always dusted with flour, he was also something of a scholar. Along one wall he had shelf upon shelf of large, thick books. On Shabbos, if we came to visit him, we would find him studying Gemara without having shaken off the workaday flour from his clothes. He gave to his Gemara reading a melody that pervaded the whole house.

"If he would have had drive enough in his youth, he could have become a rabbi," my mother told me of Uncle Avrom Moyshe.

If we came to visit him after dinner on a Shabbos afternoon, his wife, Aunt Rivke, offered us kikhl and tea. Then I dashed off into the family's windmill, where his children explained what made windmills move—how the force of the wind drove the sails, which then turned the millstones, and how the entire mill could be shifted so its sails faced the wind.

But across from the mill, not far at all, was the town's Jewish cemetery. I was a bit scared of the mill too because it was so close to the cemetery. When I went back into the house I saw that my uncle was sitting before an open book as he listened to my aunt and my mother talking about me. I was embarrassed.

My uncle said, "So, Peretz. You don't want to be a miller?"

I was too shy to say anything. My mother said, "Lippe wants to turn him into a rabbi."

My uncle said, "A town will have to be built for him."

I felt the blood rush to my face. I felt my uncle was right. I watched him from a corner of the room. There he sat with his broad forehead beside his Gemara. He could have been a rabbi and had chosen not to be one. I saw that under his bookshelves there was a workbench with planes, chisels, augurs, and an assortment of saws hanging above it. I thought again of the passage in *Ethics of the Fathers* where it is written "Love thy labor, despise the rabbinate."

And I understood now how my father and mother were unlike Isaac and Rebecca in the Bible. Isaac admired his hunter son, Esau, while Rebecca had wanted her son Jacob to study only Torah. Not everything was clearcut in my mother's life. Though it was she who daily stood face to face with the outside world, she was not quite certain what path her child should take.

I remember it was during that summer that my mother and I started off one morning to go to town. The sky was overcast by dense clouds. As we passed the railroad crossing a flash of lightning dazzled us. Almost at once there was a thunderclap that felt as if it was directly over our heads.

My mother fell to the ground, stunned, and sat there beside the path. When I too sat down, I saw she had turned pale as chalk, with enflamed red circles on her cheeks. The thunder had truly frightened her. She sat there for a while without getting up, gazing silently at me and caressing my face with a cold, trembling hand as she said, "That's what scares me. I don't understand it. There are many things I don't understand. But when a thunderclap like that one goes off above my head, my heart stops. Maybe you'll understand such things so your life will be easier."

A while later her face brightened. "Look. See the rainbow off there in the east? How beautiful it is with all those colors. It's worth a scare." We got to our feet and admired the rainbow arcing now above the green fields.

Later, in the days before the High Holy Days, my father woke us at dawn so we could go into the town to say the penitential slichos prayers. Kalmen was easy to wake, but my father had to literally drag Moyshe out of bed. When it came my turn, my mother rescued me. "What do you want of the child?" she said. "Let him sleep. He'll have time enough for slichos services all the rest of his life. If he doesn't get his sleep now, when will he?"

I heard her drawing him away from my bed. Though I was awake, I kept my eyes closed. I was not myself sure whose side I was on, because it was soon going to be Rosh Hashanah. Everyone in the family, including my grandfather, went to the synagogue for slichos. I heard my grandfather's footsteps in the house. And my mother wouldn't let my father wake me up.

My mother prevailed, and my father went away, saying irritably, "Maybe at least one of my children will grow up to be somebody. You're spoiling him. When you come to the synagogue, you'll see how many children get up for slichos."

That left me feeling sad. They all went away, leaving me and my sister Bebl in the house. I wasn't sleeping. She didn't have to go to slichos. I thought, "Why does mother want me to sleep? And why does father want me to get up before dawn to go to the synagogue? Which of them is right?" It seemed to me that my father was. I wasn't sleeping anyway.

Later in the morning I got up from bed. I looked up at the bookshelf above the window. It seemed that the books were scolding me. "Sleepyhead! Everyone's gone off to slichos services, and you stayed in bed. You and Bebl. But Bebl is a girl. She doesn't have to study Torah. And you—your father wants you to be a rabbi."

Bebl asked, "Why are you up so early, Peretz? Climb up here beside me. Crawl under the quilt and go to sleep."

I obeyed my sister. She slept, but I stayed awake because of the emptiness and gloom the departure of the rest of the household had left behind. And I thought, "It must be that mother knows what is written in *Ethics of the Fathers*: 'Love thy labor, despise the rabbinate.'"

⤜ The Days of Awe

It was about to be Rosh Hashanah. My grandfather had been going into town to pray the whole summer. As usual, he came back a bit tired and hungry. Once he had a bite to eat, he'd be happy and start looking for work to do to pass the time. Now, ever since the slichos days had begun, he came back from synagogue sad.

He took a new calendar from his pocket and showed me, "Peretz, my grandson, this is a new calendar for the year 5648. You see, the calendar says that from the month of Heshvan on the winter will start in earnest. In Kislev there will be smaller frosts and bigger frosts. In Tevet there will be severe freezing weather. A cold winter, my grandson. The shammes, poor man, has not been able to blow the shofar lately. It's stopped up . . ."

While setting the table my mother said, "Very soon even the fish in the water will start trembling."

"Yes, my daughter," said my grandfather, "he couldn't blow the shofar. The devil snuck into the shofar beforehand."

I could see my grandfather was a bit frightened. Even my father wasn't himself. My brother Kalmen kept quiet and listened to my grandfather describe how the shammes was unable to blow the shofar. I knew my brother Kalmen definitely did not sin. He did not sleep without a head covering, never drank a drop of water before saying a blessing, never put a bite of food into his mouth before washing his hands.

My brother Moyshe and even I myself had more sins than him. On my way home from heder, I'd sneak into someone's garden and fill up my pockets with kidney bean pods; I would pick the broad, flat beans that I loved my mother to cook; I would pick cucumbers, pull up carrots and beets . . . Yes, I sinned more than Kalmen. And he was the one afraid. He fasted practically every other day. He recited the Psalms with such a sad melody.

The Days of Awe were really about to arrive. My grandfather brought them to us with the new calendar and the bad news that the devil had snuck into the shammes's shofar. My father was also agitated. Next to the house he found a knife stuck in the ground—it was my mother who stuck it there because it was a meat knife and she had cut cheese with it. The knife became kosher if it was stuck in the ground for a few days. My father did not like it. He said the knife had to be polished and koshered. The entire summer it didn't bother him when my mother stuck the knife in the ground; this time he pulled the knife out of the ground and threw it away like a loathsome object.

After breakfast my grandfather went outside, looked around at the trees, contemplated the yellowed leaves. He sat there under a willow next to the pond and gazed far off toward the meadows that lay spread out to the west. Mowed meadows, here and there with dark spots where haystacks still stood, not yet carted away and turned black because of the still-falling rains.

It had already been a week that I hadn't been going to heder, and being with my grandfather was beginning to make me feel sad. Instead of singing his speckled melody or his red melody, he began to hum the melodies sung during the Days of Awe.

"Yes, grandson, a man does not crumble . . . the summer went too fast."

Grandfather did not like to be asked how old he was. He reckoned his age in *shoks*, sixty-year units. When a peasant asked him, "Shayke, how old are you?" he replied, "A *shok* and a half plus a couple of years." Yes, my grandfather who counted his years in *shoks* was now sad before Rosh Hashanah.

My mother sensed his sorrow. She could not stand having people turn gloomy and fearful just because Rosh Hashanah was coming. She said, "I haven't sinned. I haven't harmed anyone. I have no reason to be afraid." That was how she talked to my grandfather when he started listing the sins a person can commit in a year.

Listening to my grandfather, it occurred to me that ever since he had come home from the synagogue in a dark mood even the trees bowed their heads. Traces of summer still lingered in the fields; one could still find an occasional late raspberry or a withered yet sweet black currant. And then grandfather had to come along to tell us the shofar had refused to obey the shammes in the synagogue.

It was not long before our roosters and hens sensed the coming of the Days of Awe. Until now they had gone into the hutch to spend the night. They knew their places there. The ducks too spent the night in the hutch. But now, as night came on, the roosters craned their necks toward the trees—*cluck, cluck, cluck*—checking them for the branches easiest to reach when it came time to roost. Eventually they took to flying into the trees to spend the night and were soon followed by the hens. They flew upward from branch to branch until, when it was finally dark, they reached the uppermost branches, where they settled for the night.

The ducks sought resting places in tree stumps by the pond or in the high reeds. Both the chickens and the ducks sensed that the Days of Awe were coming. Soon Yom Kippur would be here. Very soon, one by one, they would be caught and bound and, in the *kapores* ritual that precedes Yom Kippur, they would be waved above someone's head, then sent to the *shohet* to be killed.

My father said, "It used to be that children your age got up early in the morning to go to services. Next year, God willing, you'll get up too. You're a big boy now. You're already studying Gemara."

About the time my father was talking about slichos a heavy, cold dew settled over the fields. If you got up at dawn and went outside barefoot, your feet could freeze. At dawn there was already white rime on the fields. The dew was so heavy and cold on the trees it turned the leaves yellow, so that soon afterward even a little breeze would make them fall.

The water from the river had already gotten colder. You didn't have to go looking for a cold drink in some wellspring among the tree stumps, water that was reddish and smelled of mud—now it was already refreshing to plunge one's whole face into the river and drink, drink.

My father told us he had rented an entire pew in the synagogue for the Days of Awe so his sons could stand near him while he recited his prayers. It was pew five east—that is, the fifth bench from the east wall. Taking some holiday prayer books down from the shelf, he called me over. He chose one and tapped it so the dust flew, after which he riffled its pages until he found the Rosh Hashanah prayers. "Do you know the meaning of these prayers?" he wanted to know. I pleased my father and surprised myself when I showed how well I understood them.

It was a poignant time around our mill. The setting sun itself seemed nostalgic. I watched it going down much more to the left, to the south, as its crimson glow lingered over the distant fields and alder trees. Summer would soon be over. Each evening our stream stayed on fire a little longer between its dark banks.

The day before the New Year, my mother seemed anxious. All day long she baked challahs decorated with birds instead of braided ornaments. My father brought three watermelons and a cluster of green, tart grapes over which to make the special blessing of gratitude.

On Rosh Hashanah people hurried to the synagogue. Though we started off very early, it was considered sinful to walk slowly. My father, striding, led the way, followed by my grandfather and my mother and then by Kalmen, Moyshe, and myself. Bebl, who was not required to go to the synagogue, stayed home.

Once in synagogue, when the recitation of prayers from the holiday prayer book began, it seemed to me we would never get through them all. It was a long service. Halfway through there was an interval during which the men of the congregation were sold the privilege of reading publicly a portion of the Torah. One by one the Torah portions were auctioned off as the men bid against each other. Once they were read, it was back to praying from the holiday prayer book.

I got increasingly tired. Finally my father noticed that he was expecting too much of me. He signaled for me to go outside for a while. It was understood that I would return later.

When I came back I recited the prayers at the top of my squeaky voice, feeling that small though I was, I was a Jew among Jews. I even knew that the Jewish year was 5648.

When it was time to blow the shofar it refused to make a sound. The shammes blew and blew. Though he was entirely enclosed in his prayer shawl, still the shofar refused to obey him. It gobbled like a turkey. Everyone in the congregation trembled and looked with amazement at the shofar blower. Upstairs in the women's section, the women began to weep. I too felt my heart tremble. Any moment now some disaster would strike.

Finally the shammes blew so hard he expelled Satan from the shofar, after which he blew it easily enough. The congregants lifted their heads, relief showing on all their faces.

When the service was over we left the synagogue. My mother came down from the women's section with Rokhele the kasha maker. Her husband, Arye the tailor, walked with the men. Nobody hurried. We walked deliberately, step by step, through the marketplace. Everyone wished everyone else a happy new year.

Though we were very hungry we walked with a measured tread toward home, enveloped in holiday calm. Coming out at the dam we paused to see what had happened to the trees over the summer. My grandfather saw signs that this year winter would come early and would be severe. The pond was still. A duck swam by, its wake dividing the stillness of the pond in two. There was some conversation about the man who had led the prayers and whose voice, on this first day of Rosh Hashanah, had turned hoarse.

Grandfather told me that before Rosh Hashanah one is supposed to forgive people; that one ought not harbor anger or vexation. But I harbored anger against my teacher Mattes because a couple of weeks ago he had suddenly—provoked by something less than trivial I had done—twisted my head down between his knees and tried to unbutton my trousers so he could beat me. I had bitten him on the leg. Blazing with fury, he had grabbed me by the head and flung me onto the table on top of the Gemaras and tried to unbutton my pants there. But I had flailed out wildly with my legs, yowled at the top of my voice, and would not let him expose my naked bottom. Hearing my yells, old Nakhum the glazer, who was carrying a box of glass panes on his shoulder, looked in the window and cried, "Ruffian, why do you torment little children?" Mattes turned me loose, and I leaped down from the table. Later he did slap me, but he did not try to whip me again.

All through Rosh Hashanah I tried unsuccessfully to drive the anger against Mattes from my heart. He had acted tyrannically. There had been no reason to whip me. But looking around at the people in my home, all so good and so pious, I was saddened by my enmity against Mattes. I had thought that before Yom Kippur came around I would go to Mattes and tell him I forgave him.

But on the night before Yom Kippur, I had a new sorrow. We had to perform the ceremony of kapores, loading our sins onto a barnyard fowl. So the chickens were chased down from the trees. A duck was caught and bound, and everyone in the family took turns performing the ceremony. Then the fowl were put in a basket, and my sister Bebl and I carried them into town to the shohet to have them killed. It was the first time I had ever seen the shohet, how he held the knife in his mouth. There were a great many fowl waiting for him. He took his time. Working slowly, he took a bound hen or a rooster and twisted its head to one side, then plucked a few feathers from the place on its throat that he would later stroke with his knife. When he had slit its throat, he squeezed a bit of blood from the wound and then threw the bound body of the "sacrifice" aside. The bird continued to flap its wings, beslobbering itself in its own blood.

He killed our "sacrifices" too. There was a duck among the fowl—he killed it. We put the slaughtered fowl back into our basket and went home. There it turned out that the shohet had both killed the duck and *not* killed it.

"The duck's alive!" Suddenly there was a tumult in the house.

The bird was untied. The duck, its throat cut, started to walk away. Someone offered it water, which it drank. The water poured from the gash in its throat. Ah, what anguish, what sorrow, and oh how much fear did that unkilled duck generate in the house. All through Sukkos time, that duck wandered about. One would have thought it was possessed by a spirit. Questions were put to the rabbi, but he did not know what to say. I watched my mother weeping silently every time the unkilled duck came into the house. My grandfather shook his head and said, "Never seen anything like it in all my days. Never heard the like."

The duck survived Sukkos. At the end of the holiday it dropped dead in front of the house and was buried behind the stable. For some little while, I was afraid to go near the place.

And my grandfather turned out to be right in his prediction that an early and hard winter would come upon us.

⁓ Winter

Overnight, a white winter was upon us, turning the black ferment of autumn rigid, then covering it with frosty white. The first snow that fell was so thick it covered all the neighboring fields, the dam, and the trees, and it lowered the sky so far it seemed to be touching the snowy tips of the branches.

The snow was followed soon after by severe frosts; winds drifted through the evenly dispersed snow, making hillocks behind every fence and around every tree stump. The wind piled a small mountain of snow up before our house and hid the causeway that led to town. Distances contracted before our eyes, and the sun, which usually went down in the far, far distances where the fields seemed to border the sky, now seemed to set in the branches of the nearby alder trees, which had shed their leaves long ago. The setting sun illuminated the two windmills on the hill, in one of which my uncle Avrom Moyshe lived.

When the wind had covered our world and the surrounding countryside with snow, the little white horse, when I caught sight of him through our window, was not nearly as white as he had looked when my father turned him out of his stall. Not only that, but he appeared to have grown smaller. As he looked up at me at the window he seemed to be wanting someone to take him into the house where it was warm. The chickens and ducks stood beside the door and waited to be allowed into the house. And indeed, we cleaned out a space under the oven to accommodate them.

With the coming of winter, everyone in the house became aware of the oven. My grandfather continually tapped its sides to check whether it was frozen. Winter came and froze the pond in front of our house. When the water approached from the river, it flowed over the ice. The ice shattered with a dull crack. Then the water oozed out through the cracked ice and darkened the white covering of snow. Behind the house, in the place where the water flowed under the wheels, the waterfall prevented ice from forming, and it was in that clear water that the ducks lived by day, flapping their wings and quacking cheerfully in the face of winter.

Eventually the mill wheels, blade by blade, were encased in ice. The rigid wheels grew heavy and jammed the sluiceway. The boards and timbers gleamed. One had to be an adept walker to keep from slipping near the wheels. To free the wheels and the sluice-way we hacked at them from time to time with sharp axes that sent a spray of ice into our faces and hair.

Because the house overhung the water and was not sheltered from the wind it was hard to keep it warm in winter. Our windows iced over, and it was not long before we began to see frost flowers on the panes; then frost trees appeared . . . whole forests of trees. Later those forests appeared to be covered with snow. If we wanted to see what the winter was doing outside, we had to clear a circle in the middle of a windowpane with our warm breath.

Everybody in the family donned warm clothing: sheepskin coats and quilted jackets, woolen gloves for our hands, heavy leggings for our feet, and to keep our feet warm and dry we put straw in our boots.

With the coming of winter the trees, our stream, the nearby woods, and the sky seemed smaller and nearer. The winter diminished everyone, just as it made the days shorter. The horse, the cow, the chickens, and the ducks looked shrunken. My grandfather looked especially small, particularly when I saw him out of doors wearing his sheepskin jacket, his head wrapped in a shawl. My father too looked smaller, as did the children. The winter blended everything together, just as it wound the day and shortened it.

Despite the gloves the men wore, their hands were so severely chapped they sometimes bled because they had to handle wet things in the bitter cold. On the night before Shabbos, we would steam wheat bran in boiling water, and the men would dip their chapped hands into it, softening them as they steamed the hard week away.

In winter Shabbos too seemed bent over and anxious. The whole family somehow managed to find places to sit on the clay oven, although the Shabbos teapot, covered with sheep pelts and pillows, occupied the place of honor.

After dinner on Friday night, my grandfather was the first member of the family to climb, groaning with pleasure, onto the warm oven. After him followed the younger members of the family. There, before bedtime, we enjoyed rubbing our bare shoulders against the oven's warm sides. My mother or my brother Kalmen would hold me against it so my young shoulders too could get warm.

At the end of Shabbos, as my mother recited the God of Abraham prayer, we heard the cow mooing in the stable, begging to be fed and milked. The men recited their prayers. Then the tallow Havdalah candle was lighted, and my father performed the ceremony ushering out the Shabbos. "May we have a good week."

Through the breath-warmed circles on the frosted windowpanes, the winter work week once again peeked in.

On those mornings, the younger members of the family had trouble getting out of bed because winter had crept into the house overnight, and it was hard to get rid of. None of the younger ones had much enthusiasm for the idea of crawling out from under their quilts. Still, you had to get up. The bran for the cow had to be steamed. Wood had to be brought in so my mother could heat the oven. Our mill, far from any settlement, stood amid a world of alder trees, and yet there was no firewood in the miller's house. To buy firewood at the market seemed a crying shame. To drive to some distant forest to buy it at a lower price seemed equally dismaying considering that we lived surrounded by trees. But we could not touch those trees because they belonged to the mean landlord, Shrinski.

The solution was to cut young trees or to break off branches secretly so Shrinski would not notice. Sometimes we would swipe wood from around the tree stumps for heating.

When my father tried to rouse us in the morning, we all pretended not to hear him and feigned sleep. So he told my mother to wake us. She pleaded with us so pitifully, so tearfully, that we had to get up. Meanwhile my father had turned the cow out of her barn, and she came to stand under our window, where she mooed sadly.

Kalmen, Moyshe, and Bebl were the first to jump out of bed from under their quilts. Nor was I, just because I was studying Torah, allowed to linger in bed. So we ran outdoors to wash our hands and faces. The ice hole had frozen during the night. We had to break it open with our feet. The water was blue and so cold a vapor rose from it. After wetting our hands and faces, we ran back into the house. The skin of our moist hands stuck to the frozen iron of the door latch. We dried ourselves with a rough towel, rubbing the skin hard to warm ourselves. After that we hurried into our sheepskin jackets and wrapped warm scarves around our ears, leaving only our noses to stick out. With one of us carrying an ax under a coat, we were off into the stumps through the deep white downy snow.

The branches of the trees were covered with frost and ice. We cut a sapling far below the snow line so no one would notice its absence, then we gathered up the wood chips so there would be no sign of our work and went home, carrying our felled tree with its cold, frozen branches. Meanwhile, the house was getting colder and colder. At home we cut the tree up with an ax, broke its branches across our knees, and shoved the wood into the stove. My mother arranged the wood, lit the fire, and blew on the kindling. The wet green branches sputtered and spluttered and began slowly to burn. My mother grabbed up handfuls of straw from our bedding and stuffed them into the stove until, as if she had given the fire a good idea, it burst into flame. Immediately she put large kettles of water on the stove, in which she would later steep the grain for the cow.

Soon after that, the male members of the family started reciting the morning prayers. My father and my grandfather each wore their tallis and tefillin. Kalmen and Moyshe wound the leather straps around their bare left arms. Their constricted left hands turned blue. The prayers were recited loudly, hurriedly, as the men strode back and forth. The floor seemed to groan under their pacing. Occasionally, sparks flew from the stove. I too recited the prayers in my squeaky voice.

The next thing we did was to scald the tub in which food for the animals would be mixed. The rising steam warmed the house and made it smell of chaff and scalded bran. The scent of that food, intended for the animals, made us feel terribly hungry. But the horse and the cow had first call on it, then the ducks and the chickens.

My mother had already cooked a barley soup. We were all going to eat. We brought a frozen loaf of rye bread in from the cupboard in the mill. To cut a loaf like that required real strength, but Kalmen, Moyshe, and Bebl were able to do it. My mother ladled out a large bowl of barley soup for each of us. We ate with wooden spoons and could feel the warmth of the soup spreading into all our limbs. Wiping the sweat from our faces, we recited a prayer of benediction.

The older ones went to their work. As for me, my mother put me into my sheepskin coat, wound a shawl around my head, and sent me off at a run to school and to Mattes.

I was studying Gemara, which was supposed to train the mind. The classroom was still in Gedalyekhe's house, and in winter it seemed even more cramped than usual, the children even smaller and Mattes even larger. In winter Mattes beat the children more frequently. Along with more beatings, he stuffed more Torah into their heads. There went a whole day. There went a whole week.

I continued to run to school alone, taking pleasure in the crunch of the snow under my feet. I scooted into Arye the tailor's house, where his wife, Rokhele, gave me a warm rye bun. Around seven or eight in the evening someone would come to fetch me. Sometimes I would stay in town at my brother Binyomin Khayem's house. When my brother Moyshe came for me, we would wait until we reached the outskirts of town, where we recited the Shema and made a "fig" in our pockets with our fingers to ward off evil spirits.

When I reached home I found the mill, the house, and the people sunk in silence. Probably during the day the mill was running a bit. During the day it was certainly lively inside and around the house, just as we started the day in a lively way. Before the day began the house was warmed up. Now as I came in, a blast of heat struck me. My grandfather lay on a bench near the oven half dozing, half awake. My father sat at the table near the window, his chin in his hands. Who knew what he was thinking? My mother, not far from the oven, was plucking feathers. The younger members of the family lay near the oven too, winter thoughts in their heads.

When I came in, my mother rose and got me out of my winter clothes complaining that children were kept so late at school. "Made a tasty dinner, and now it's grown cold."

She filled a bowl with thick farfel and potatoes, getting it from the bottom of a large cast-iron pot from which the other members of the family had eaten long ago. "Would the Torah be offended if they let the boy come home a little earlier?" my mother murmured as she got the beds ready for the night.

One by one each of us drifted toward bed. My grandfather on his bench beside the window. My father in a bed in the other room. My mother and I in the other bed. Moyshe and Kalmen together beside the oven. My sister Bebl on a sofa. Someone turned off the tin lamp, and suddenly it was pitch dark. We could hear the night speaking on the other side of the window and the water talking under the mill.

None of us was a heavy sleeper. We lay there in the dark in an uneasy silence and listened to the quiet speech of the world. Everyone in their beds in the dark house: my grandfather with his small blond beard who would soon be a hundred years old; my anxious father; my profoundly sensitive mother; the blossoming Bebl; the pious Kalmen; the tough young Moyshe; and me, the Gemara student. All of us listened to the trees and birds, the water and mill wheels, the roosters and hens and ducks and ravens. The speech of wind among the frozen trees. And from time to time the sound of the train rushing by on the rails under the deeply drifted snow. All of it dream and reality.

In the course of the night one could hear my father's long, drawn-out "Oy, oy" as he sighed into the night. My mother replied with a gentle, incomplete sigh.

A nighttime world, a secret world, peered into the house through the frozen windowpanes and whispered something to those in their beds.

"Mama, why are the windows so white?"

"Sleep, my child. Morning is still a long way off. Sleep. It's the frost crossing the frozen river or maybe the wind blowing over the ground, driving the snow against the house." The fowl in the hen coop under the oven were awake. Suddenly they made a disturbance, as if startled by an intruder. "Sleep, my child. It's probably a water rat frightening the hens."

The cat prowled the mill. The black cat moving about all night in the flour-whitened mill, its steps barely perceptible.

"Sleep, my child."

The night proved more powerful than my mother. It would not sleep and would not let her child sleep. It woke my grandfather. "Huh? Children! Can't you hear the horse beating its head against the stable door?"

"Huh? Who will go out to check the stable?"

"Huh? What?" someone in one of the other beds asked.

Cock-a-doodle-doo! It was the rooster under the oven letting us know it was midnight.

Making the Mill Kosher

When a warm wind began to blow from the southwest and rain fell instead of snow, when the ice on the pond began to break and the piles of snow heaped against the windows shrank and grew dark, we all felt the loosening of winter's grip over the mill. Around Purim time, the sun seemed to shine more brightly, melting the ice on the mill wheels. We sensed the welling of the water under the ice and understood the meaning of every new sound we heard coming from the river at night. Spring was near.

About that time, several Jews from town came to discuss with Lippe the miller the koshering of the mill for Pesach. They brought all sorts of wheat samples to display. The men, looking very serious, sat around the table. Carefully they unwrapped their canvas sacks and shawls, from which they brought out samples of Pesach wheat. My father put his glasses on and wrinkled his forehead. One by one the children drew nearer and nearer to the table. And the simple kernels of wheat, which looked just like every other grain of wheat grown at any other time during the past year, seemed now to have their own special look. Jewish kernels of wheat. Thoughtful kernels.

My mother brought a thimble to the table with which the men measured thimblefuls of grain. The grains were then spilled onto the table, where each kernel was examined separately. Any kernel with rootlets at its tip or any other sign it had sprouted was put aside. Such kernels triggered a suspicion of chometz: the grain had probably been under the rain; the rain soaked the kernels and began the sprouting process.

If a thimbleful of kernels had been examined and too many sprouted kernels were found, the wheat from which that sample had been taken was declared chometz. The process of inspection went on until finally the purest and driest kernels were selected. In the selection considerable expertise was demonstrated, for instance when a kernel of wheat was bitten in two so its interior whiteness could be studied.

When the men had decided which wheat was suitable to be bought, they discussed the koshering of the mill; they considered how many poods of grain would need to be sifted this year. When they had come to an agreement, the men drank a toast and offered the hope that there would be no dearth of water for the mill in the season before Pesach, and we, the miller's family, expressed the wish that this year Jews might bake their matzohs in comfort. Having said that, all the men slapped their hands together as a sign of agreement.

Meanwhile, as the season advanced, more ice began to crack and shatter and the pile of snow before the house continued to dwindle. Pre-Pesach noises among the trees were well known to us all. And soon peasant wagons loaded with sacks of wheat arrived at the mill. Though the sun was out, the sacks had been carefully covered. The sacks were carried not into the mill, which, after all, was still considered impure for Pesach; they were carried into the house. Every one of us helped. Even the smaller children helped to carry a sack, pushing at one end as some adult hoisted it onto his shoulder. The sacks were piled in rows in the second room of the house. One sack burst as it was being carried in and wheat poured out on the ground, making it unusable for Pesach. The golden grains beckoned to us from the mud as if they were begging, "Gather us up; don't let us be impure."

Then it was time to make the mill kosher. Now there's a job for you! Though the mill had to be made kosher every year, when it actually came time to do it nobody seemed to have the faintest notion of how to begin. Just think of it. How do you make a mill kosher? How do you get rid of every fleck of a year's accumulation of flour so there'll be no sign of it anywhere? Think how much flour dust is shaken out by a mill in the course of a year. The walls of the loft where the flour was sifted through sieves of silk were overhung with a curtain of encrusted flour. There was not a nook or cranny, not a crack or a hole, into which, in the course of the year, flour (and by Pesach standards it was all impure flour) had not crept. From the threshold of the mill to the attic, there was flour dust everywhere.

Armed with knives, with goose feather dusters, with torn clothes and old rags, we all invaded the mill. Suddenly we hated flour dust; suddenly we were suspicious of each kernel that had wound up in some crevice. The first swipe of the feather duster, the first scrape of the knife—an expanse of plank cleaned. Fragrant wood shone through. We scraped and scoured; the millers ourselves were covered in flour, which on Pesach is not appropriate even for a miller, but the mill itself got cleaner and cleaner.

The great cleanup had its effect not only on the adults and the children; our ginger dog, Burtshik, was awed too. He could not understand why we were scraping and scouring so intently. He went about sniffing and licking and sneezing; he too wanted a part in the event. He saw how this time the people were covered in flour more than usual, and he wanted to mimic them. So he bared his teeth in a smile, then wriggled his way into the pile of scraped-off chometz.

Our black cat, envious of Burtshik though considerably more careful than he, also came into the mill, gazed at the people at work, sniffed at every corner where the scraping and cleaning was done, and started sneezing. She could not understand what was happening to the millers in their mill.

Arye the tailor, who all year long sewed crude coats for the peasants, also came to visit. Every spring, just before Pesach, when he knew we were koshering the mill, he came to sew the silken sifters with which we sifted the Pesach flour. The cloth we bought for him was a loosely woven, white transparent silk that, if you doubled it over and held it to the light, made shimmering circles. The usual task of trimming the millstones, which required that the upper millstone be turned bottom-side up, was now done with particular intent. Using pointed steel as well as flat hammers, ridges and little holes were cut into the stones so it would grind the Pesach flour with greater eagerness.

For three days and three nights, every member of my family was immersed in chometz as we worked to make the mill kosher for Pesach. When finally the mill was clean we turned to getting the house cleaned, tidying it up because the young rabbi of the town was expected. The word everyone hoped he would say after he had examined the mill was "kosher."

A holiday feeling pervaded the house. Yellow sand was strewn on the floor. The table was moved from its usual place; the curtains at the windows were smoothed out. There was a constant movement into the mill for a last quick checkup, to make a final swipe here, another scrape there, or to blow away the dust that was settling once more on the walls.

My father got the wagon ready. He repaired its ladder sides, strewed fresh straw on the floor, and created a soft place to sit. My mother covered that straw seat with a clean sheet. When the white horse was harnessed, my father, looking serious and thoughtful, drove off to get the rabbi.

Then it came, the wagon with the rabbi in it. All of us, the cat and dog included, peered out the window. My father leaped down from the wagon and helped the rabbi descend. He was not quite a rabbi. He was, in fact, a rabbinical assistant, because our old blind rabbi was still living. But of course one could not call a blind rabbi to examine whether the mill was kosher.

The young rabbi was a tall, lanky fellow with a sparse black beard and long, thick side curls. His face was pale; his eyes were black. He stood for a while beside the wagon and looked about the mill. Walking with care, he crossed over the permanent pool of mud before the threshold and went into the house. We all got to our feet. Everyone regarded him with reverence. He took off his long, black coverall and stood before us in his shiny black satin frock coat.

We wondered: How will the rabbi in such black satin clothing creep about in the hopper and the nooks and crannies of the mill? He knows he is about to kosher a mill. Surely he knows there is no way to get rid of every vestige of flour.

We had a freshly cleaned knife with a sharp point ready for him, and we handed him a brand-new feather duster—the entire wing of a goose. To give him more light we gave him a candle, and he started off slowly toward the mill.

The first thing he wanted to inspect was the large hopper where the silk screens sifted the flour. It was a huge hopper set on four legs—a whole room. So huge he would have to climb into it. Little by little, with the help of all the men in the house, he managed to creep his way in.

No sooner was he inside than his black satin coat was dusted with flour. Never mind that the miller's entire family had, for three days and three nights, scrubbed and brushed the mill. Holding his candle up for light he began to search every crack and crevice, testing them with his knife and feather duster until he succeeded in finding a single kernel of wheat in a crack. The kernel fell to the ground where it lay, silent and embarrassed. The rabbi picked it up and studied it. Smelled it. What he meant by that none of the bystanders knew. Each of them blamed the other: "It was you who left the kernel in the crack." Just then the rabbi found a dirty corner that had been entirely overlooked. He went to work now in earnest. He looked like a tall woodpecker as he wielded his knife, blowing dust or wiping it away with his feather duster. Pellets of dried flour fell to the floor.

We were dismayed. Three days and three nights of cleaning, and now here was the rabbi finding a whole nest of impure flour. One sensed he had some particular goal in mind that would compensate him for his trouble. No sooner had he discovered the hidden patch of impure flour than he grew calm. He stopped fussing and signaled to the men standing by that he was ready to come out of the hopper. Once again, and with reverence, they helped him out, though by now he no longer had the look of a rabbi. His satin vest was covered with flour. His skull cap had turned white; his black *peyos*—sidelocks—were dusted and his black beard too was floured over.

He went up into the attic, where the millstones now lay upended, with their faces to the sky. The heavy stones lay silent and cold—they had no inkling of the rabbi's approach. Nor did he have any idea what to do about them. Was he supposed to scrape the stone with his knife? That seemed to make no sense. He smiled and said to the bystanders, "I take it that you've been careful to make the stones kosher."

"Kosher, rabbi. As every year. Kosher."

The rabbi started down the stairs. He handed over his candle, his knife, and his feather duster. He had done what he had come to do. When, covered with flour, he came into the house, he smiled and did not know what to say. Everyone gathered around him, dusting him off, brushing him, shaking out his coattails. It was now very clear how tall and pale he was. His coat, dusted off, resumed its look of respectability.

When the rabbi had shaken the flour dust from his beard and side curls and wiped his face with his red handkerchief, and when someone had wiped the flour off his boots with a rag, there was a brief pause for consideration, after which he smiled and said, "May you have no lack of water this year. And may salvation come to the Jews. Kosher."

Then he took a genteel sip of the brandy that had been prepared for him in a little carafe and said again, "Kosher."

Once again the straw in the wagon was fluffed out and aired. My mother rearranged the sheet over it, and my father helped the rabbi climb back into the wagon. The rabbi was gone, back into town until next year. But he had left us with a single word: "Kosher."

Prosperity

Just after Purim the weather became milder. The ice blackened. Despite the optimism we had that the weeks before Pesach would be good for us and that work would be plentiful, that merchants in town would be sending their Pesach wheat to be ground in our mill because it had once again been declared kosher, there was now a new family worry. As the huge pile of snow facing the house began to melt, my father feared that a sudden spate of warm weather would melt the heavy snow too quickly and we would have floods. My grandfather, who had lain on top of the oven a lot that winter, had also been uneasy about the snow. He liked to tell tales of mills that were swept away by spring floods. "If the snows melt slowly, then no harm will be done. But God forbid if the melting is sudden. If we get warm rains, then we're in for trouble."

The shtetl grain brokers did indeed send their Pesach wheat to us to be ground. They hastened to do it before the roads became difficult. The sacks of wheat were stored in the second room of the house, where they were piled on top of each other until they reached the ceiling. And that was fun, creating piles on which we could climb. Even my father was pleased to see his children crawling up the sacks to touch the ceiling with their hands.

Little by little the peasants from the nearby villages also came, bringing wheat and rye to be ground. They left their wheat in the mill, storing it there until the weather turned milder. We all waited for the moment that would mark the end of winter and the arrival of the first warm rain.

Meanwhile I left the house early every morning to go to school and came home in the evening. I knew those were my last days as Mattes's pupil. Mattes, knowing my time with him was coming to an end, was nice to me. He was no longer the Mattes of old. I was studying the Song of Songs, and its melody as I sang it had a summer feeling. I wandered about the fields singing. There were days when I decided not to wait to be taken home in the evening. I even gave up going to my brother Binyomin Khayem's house to spend the night. Instead I ran home alone, reciting the Shema as, with my hands in my pockets, I made signs to ward off evil spirits. With a beating heart I passed the last house in town and the last barn and reached the darkened ditches and trees, now shrouded in night. I ran with all my might until, hot and panting, I burst into my house.

I always got home just as whoever was supposed to fetch me was getting dressed. Each time I came home alone my mother scolded me. She begged, "Don't do it again. Now that the weather is getting milder you shouldn't be walking alone at night."

Winter was really and truly over. The falling rains were so warm it was tempting to fling off one's clothes and stand under them. The pile of snow outside the house was visibly shrinking and sending a stream of water toward the mill. Still, every one of us, even my grandfather and I—my brother Binyomin Khayem too came over from the shtetl—worked to demolish it. We shoveled and hacked at it, throwing the large chunks of ice into the pond.

The ice on the pond turned black. The snow was melting. Both sides of the pond were now clearly discernible, as were last year's thick grasses at its edge and the low tree stumps that had been buried all winter. The trembling branches of the tall, dark willow trees sent the ice and hardened snow that still clung to them splattering down in showers. One could see the trees quickening. A spring breeze had woken them, and they waited for warmth to bring forth their green leaves.

We had hacked the ice away from the sluices so that the water, when it came, would be able to flow freely. From both sides of the bridge we examined the dam to see whether it was strong enough to hold back a large flow of water. We could see the water stirring under the cracking ice or spurting into the air to flow over it.

As warm rains poured down, the ground around the house turned slippery and the heap of snow around the house disappeared. We all said, "There'll be too much water this time. The mill will have to be flooded for a time. The wheels will be half covered in water." And then the water came. All the sluices were pulled up onto the bridge—"Go, water, wherever you want!" And with a rushing sound more and more water came. Everyone, everyone was outside. We recruited a Gentile miller who spoke Yiddish just like us; he was an expert in sluices. He also said the water would keep rising and it was dangerous.

We went to see the water level on the other side of the railway line that divided us from the meadows, gardens, and town. It was a terrifying sight. There lay a veritable ocean. Trees stood in water halfway up their trunks. The water was exerting pressure on the narrow bridge under the railway line. And water extended across the fields to the outlying barns. Earth and sky and water! If, God forbid, the flood should tear through the railway line, it would carry away our mill. It was clear we could not stay in it. So we harnessed our little white horse to the wagon and loaded it with all of our bedding and the smaller children.

When we reached the railway line we stopped, unable to go any farther. At dusk, when it began to grow chilly, our fear intensified. My father shouted toward the town; someone shouted back. We heard the yells as they came across the water. People in the town now knew Lippe the miller was in danger, but nobody came to the rescue. Night fell. We continued to hear people shouting at us from a distance. We took turns shouting back. I too shouted: "Help! Save us!"

All night long we stayed beside the railway line. By morning the water level had fallen, so we drove back to the mill. The water was indeed receding. Though the mill wheels were still half sunk in water, we were in no further danger.

Day followed day, and the water continued to subside. We could finally free up the waterwheels. We hung a large curtain across the middle of the mill to divide it in two. One half was kosher. That's where the flour for Pesach was sifted. In the other half the nonkosher mill stones turned.

Peasants from the surrounding villages began to arrive. Their wagons surrounded the house, as in a veritable marketplace. There was no way to take care of everyone at once, so many of the peasants had to wait a full day, or sometimes two or three days, for their turn. All of us were as busy as could be. Kalmen was our Pesach miller; my father and Moyshe ground the nonkosher flour. My grandfather, like everyone else, went about covered with flour dust. With the visor of his cap turned the wrong way around, he sang his red melody. The mill wheels clattered. The whole house trembled. The water beneath them and the water pouring through the sluices made a rushing sound under the house. The sun warmed everything. In the meadows last year's grass, black and wilted, peeked out here and there from under the melted snow.

Those peasants who had to wait for their wheat to be ground got a large cast-iron pot from my mother in which they cooked farfel. As a peasant who had his wheat sifted was leaving, he would contribute some flour to the farfel pot for those who still had to wait their turn. Those left behind squatted around the pot. Using wooden spoons, they served themselves portions of the farfel. While they ate they spat and told stories. My grandfather told tales of how it used to be long ago. The good old days when a man could buy a wagonload of poultry for a ruble and when a three-groschen coin could buy you the finest stallion. The peasants, gulping their farfel, agreed. "Yes, these are hard times. The little father, the tsar, presses hard on his people."

Just then the Gentile miller we had who could speak Yiddish came from the mill. Turning to us he told us, in Yiddish, that he was about to play a practical joke on the peasants. Turning to them he said, "Would you like me to show you a great trick? For one of you, I'll put half a dozen eggs under your hat. A sheepskin hat would be even better. Then I'll circle you repeating, 'Peep, peep, little chicks.' I'll circle you six times, after which six chicks will walk out from under the hat."

"Really? The hell you say."

"Really. Let's let the bastard do his trick," someone else said.

"Is it magic?" a third peasant said.

"Of course. He's in league with the devil. Look at him; he speaks Yiddish just like one of them."

"Lippe, sell me six eggs. I'll call the young devil's bluff. Let him do his damned trick."

This was said by a middle-aged peasant who wore a long sheepskin coat and a tricornered sheepskin hat. Having eaten too much farfel, he now moved slowly.

My mother brought out six eggs. The miller put them under the peasant's hat and made everyone stand away. Then he formed them in a circle so he could walk around the peasant as he recited "Cheep, cheep, chicks. Cheep, cheep, chicks."

There was a tumult in the room as people climbed onto chairs or onto the daybed so they could watch the coming miracle. The peasant pressed the brim of his hat with both hands firmly to his head, making sure the eggs were safe. His eyes bulged from their sockets; his face was flushed and anxious. Apparently he was scared.

The miller walked round and round the peasant, then he looked up at the ceiling. His eyes seemed to glaze over as he murmured mysteriously, "Cheep, cheep, little chicks." Six times he went around. At the seventh time he brought both of his hands down and smacked the top of the peasant's hat with all his might, breaking all six of the eggs.

There was noisy laughter. The yellows and whites of the eggs dripped down from the sheepskin hat onto the peasant's face and down into his collar. The peasant could not bring himself to be angry. "Jesus Maria." The other peasants laughed till their sides ached.

That's one of the ways we passed the time during the long evenings. Things got harder at night. When the mill got busy, it went night after night. We worked so hard we were on the verge of collapse. My father and Kalmen walked about unrested, red-eyed, hoping for the coming of Pesach, soon, soon, when we might finally catch our breath. But there was more and more work to do. There was no lack of water. I myself was turned into a little miller and was sent to check whether the hopper was running out of grain or to grease the steel axles on which the mill wheels turned. I could already speak with the Gentiles in their language.

One of the peasants wanted to know why I had been named Peretz, which in Russian means "pepper." "If only you had been named something sweet, like 'Cherry' or 'Gooseberry.'" Everyone in the household was delighted by the remark.

My grandfather said, "My grandson Peretz will be a rabbi one day. And it wouldn't be fitting for a rabbi to be called 'Cherry' or 'Gooseberry.'"

The peasants stared at me, shook their heads, and said, "Tsk, tsk." One of them picked me up and said, "He won't be a very strong rabbi. He won't be as strong as the Pope. A pope is fat, while a rabbi . . . ha, ha, ha . . . a rabbi is as thin as a dry stick."

My father and mother went off to Khone-Ber the yard-goods dealer to order some calico and cotton cloth for the children. The inexpensive cloth out of which kaftans were to be made for Moyshe and me had a fine smell and rustled wonderfully. I went with Moyshe to Motye the tailor, who lived in the circular marketplace. He took our measurements and promised my mother that the clothes would be ready for the holiday. "If I have to go without sleep, I'll have Peretz's kaftan ready by Pesach," Motye said.

At the time of the flooding all sorts of huge strange fish no one had ever seen before showed up in the river that flowed through our mill. They were remarkably easy to catch—it was almost as if they leaped into our hands.

"Fish are a sign of good luck," said my grandfather, "and if the fish come from far away that's an especially good sign. And that my grandchildren are growing—another good sign. If only we can get really good horseradish for Pesach, the real *maror*. Peretz, take a look behind the stable where there are large horseradish leaves. See if you can find some roots."

On the day before Pesach we purified the house. We cleaned

and scrubbed, applying a Pesach sheen to the entire place despite the fact that impure flour dust crept in from the mill. Our matzohs were baked in town—they came out better than ever. My father hoped that after Pesach he would be able to pay our landlord all that was owed to him for the entire year, with money left over to buy a milch cow.

Altogether we had every reason to expect a happy Pesach. Except that Motye the tailor, who had a great many clothes to sew, managed to get the clothes for the town children ready in time for Pesach but kept putting off sewing our clothes. "I'm just not fated to have things go right," my worried mother said, tears in her eyes. "Next year," she consoled me. "God willing, my dear . . ."

That was our only sorrow. Everything else went just swimmingly. Even the willow chose, in honor of Pesach, to display its new green leaves and bow its head toward the expanse of water in front of the house.

Zalmen the Scribe

In the days between the beginning and the end of Pesach, Motye the tailor delivered my new coat. My mother reproached him for having more respect for the pampered rich folk of the town than for us. Motye promised that next year, if we ordered clothes from him, he would have them ready for the children two weeks before Pesach.

Pesach was a happy holiday for me, particularly because my father was having discussions with old Zalmen the scribe about enrolling me in his school. Zalmen was not a native of Kleshtshel. He came from somewhere else and had become a teacher late in life. Zalmen the scribe did not beat his pupils, and he taught them how to write. He was called Zalmen the scribe because he knew how to write legal petitions and could address envelopes to foreign countries. Besides that he was a scholar and a warm-hearted fellow.

During the holidays, to please my father, I went to the homes of the richer members of the congregation and let them put Torah questions to me. My father, who stood by and watched me, had nothing to be ashamed of. One of my examiners told my father, "You're doing the right thing, Reb Lippe, sending the boy to a more advanced teacher. There's nothing more he can learn from Mattes."

Nevertheless, I had learned quite a lot from Mattes. His severity made an impression on me. It was Mattes who turned me into a quiet boy. His severity gave everything he taught a certain severe aspect. Mattes himself never sat down when he was instructing us. He walked continually around the table, looking over the shoulders of his pupils, keeping a watchful eye on each of them to see whether they had their eyes on their texts while another student recited.

His sternness was appropriate to the study of Gemara when he was explaining what a great wrong was committed when one man's ox gored another man's cow. The Gemara also taught the right ways to punish a thief. Mattes's severity was fitting too for the study of Humash, especially the book of Leviticus, where the rules for bringing sacrifices were explained or when we learned the curses Moses addressed to the people of Israel in the desert. During those readings, when Mattes slapped his pupils, his punishment seemed to parallel the text. But his rigor seemed out of place when he explicated, with a lilt, the Song of Songs or the Book of Ruth. Then a slap or a pinch seemed unrelated. Beating a pupil, pulling his hair or ear, was in no way relevant to a pupil's mistranslation of "I am the rose of Sharon and the lily of the valleys." At such a moment Mattes simply confused me.

I was very fond of the simple tales and narratives in the scriptures. We children had no notion of time or distance. We literally believed the Temple of Solomon had been set ablaze by fires laid around it by swallows and spiders, which is why we persecuted swallows and spiders. But it was all an uphill climb when we came to the Prophets. We studied the prophet Isaiah first. Mattes turned Isaiah into a fellow as severe as himself. When he came to Isaiah cursing the daughters of Jerusalem for their licentiousness, Mattes seemed to grow taller; his face was inflamed and he distributed slaps in all directions. At such times I was overwhelmed by fear. When, as we were reading the Book of Lamentations, Mattes slapped some child and tears sprang to the boy's eyes, we could believe the tears were being shed for the destruction of the Temple. But Mattes himself was of neither this world nor time. When, even as he was speaking of wicked Titus, who destroyed Jerusalem, he seized one of his pupils and clamped the boy's head between his knees and lashed him with his three-thonged whip, it seemed to me that Mattes was a direct relative of wicked Titus.

It was no wonder he turned me into a quiet boy, that he drove away any impulses I might have had to be mischievous outdoors. When I came into the shtetl and entered the synagogue or even the heder, I kept my childish thoughts and feelings to myself and stayed near the wall.

Which is why, when I came to Zalmen the scribe, who had his heder in a sunny room, my whole world suddenly lit up. Zalmen the scribe was in every way the opposite of Mattes. Zalmen was short. His beard was gray, and he had kind blue eyes that peered out at you through his spectacles. He had about a dozen pupils, some of them fairly grown. Once again I was the smallest and the youngest one in the class. Zalmen's habit was to sit at the table among his pupils. To the students he was one of their companions, sometimes a grandfather with his grandchildren.

Even so, Zalmen too had a thin stick with which, when he was provoked, he would hit a pupil on the shoulder. There was one boy who for no good reason loved to drive Zalmen up the wall. He had a way of propping his head on both hands so as to keep the boys on either side of him from sharing the text with him. Zalmen would ask the boy politely to put his hands down and to sit straight. When the boy refused, Zalmen moved the boy's arms away from the book, but the pupil put them back. It was shameful behavior. I wondered where the rabbi acquired his patience. The same thing happened with this boy at least once a week. It was as if the boy had been possessed by an evil spirit so he could torment our old teacher. The result was that we were all on Zalmen's side.

We studied Gemara and Tanakh with Zalmen. He helped me understand things much better than Mattes had. In his class we had time for study and time for going out to play. It was the first time I took pleasure outside the heder. The children were mischievous and invited me in too. At first I was afraid to join the other boys, but later I noticed that Zalmen stood at the window watching them with a look of deep pleasure as they had fun outside dancing and leaping. Although I could not manage right away to feel as free as the other boys around the school, one of the students taught me how to throw a stone all the way over a tall tree. I also learned various games using sticks and how to play hide-and-seek. And I grew physically stronger.

Once a week, on Friday, Zalmen the scribe taught us handwriting. Using a footstool as a blackboard, he had us sit on the floor in a circle around it while he wrote out the letters of the *alef-beys*. Each of us copied them out with a piece of chalk. I quickly learned to imitate Zalmen's handwriting. By the second week I was able to write my name.

That was the first summer when my daily trip from the mill to school and back proved to be a time of growth and blossoming. No one accompanied me on my way to and from heder unless they had to go into town anyway. From the time I started going to Zalmen's heder, I grew physically stronger and was no longer afraid of strangers. I even created opportunities to talk with the Gentile children I met on the way. They would look into the book I carried, amazed by its strange letters. Even our landlord, old Shrinski, would stop to talk with me. He wanted to know how long the Jews had been Pharaoh's slaves in Egypt. He knew Jews had eaten manna in the desert, which is why they now ate kugel on Shabbos.

"Do you like kugel?" he asked, laughing to himself. "You're a big boy now, Pertshik. Time for you to stop chopping down the young trees around the mill. And keep your cow from straying into my meadow. Yes, yes," he said, clapping me on the shoulder, "you're not going to be a miller like your father."

On Fridays I always had lots of time on my way home from school to visit my brother Binyomin Khayem, who lived not far from the rich man's mill. I would sneak up to the bridge that led to it and gaze down into the same river that flowed from there to our mill. And yet the river here looked different from our own. It looked citified.

This mill belonged to the only son of the rich Moyshe Podbilyer. It was completely enclosed, so one could not see the mill wheels, which in winter did not freeze. At this rich man's mill the very river seemed hostile. Not at all like our mill, which was surrounded by willows. The same water, but not quite the same. Here the water

belonged to the "only son," the son of the rich man Moyshe Podbilyer, so the water was full of arrogance. It was not until the water
flowed under the "only son's" wheels, through the tree-lined banks
along the meadows and under the railroad bridge that it looked
familiar to me again.

Once, when no one was looking, I tried drinking the water that
flowed through the "only son's" mill. I scooped it up in both hands,
and as I drank it seemed to me that it tasted different from our
own. It tasted of mud and fish. Though it was said that one could
grind better-looking flour in the "only son's" mill than at Lippe's
(which is why the shtetl's flour brokers had their wheat ground
by him), still as I left the "only son's" mill I was pleased I lived in
Lippe's mill. I wouldn't have wanted to live in the big house or to
have my father be the "only son" who always wore a black topcoat
and a black silk skullcap, which were never dusted with flour because he employed a miller who worked the mill for him.

My mouth retained the taste of the water I had drunk at the
"only son's" mill. When I had crossed the railroad line and neared
our pond and came to the ditch that flowed into it, I saw two stones
at the pond's edge—my stones. I knelt down on them and bent my
head. The water was so clear I could see my entire face reflected in
it. I could even see the little people that lived in the pupils of my
eyes. I put my lips to the lips that were reflected in the water and
drank and drank, tasting the loveliness of it all.

On my way home I followed the railroad tracks, beside which
clean yellow sand had been spread. I paused there for a while and
with my finger wrote out the entire alphabet in the sand. I imitated
Zalmen the scribe's florid script. Then I wrote my name, many times.
I stood for a while, admiring my handwriting. Then, so that no one
should step on the holy letters, I smoothed the sand out again.

I had time for a side journey into the woods to find out what
sorts of new trees had sprouted and whether last year's currant
bushes were in blossom this spring among the tree trunks. I peered
into birds' nests to see whether there were newly hatched chicks,
and if there were I would give them water to drink from my mouth.
I gathered stones along the railroad line and tried throwing them

over the tops of the highest trees. I had by then learned how to skip a stone across the water so it went skip-skipping and created brief spurts along the water's surface. I was delighted by it all, especially because I was doing all this at the same time as I was studying with Zalmen the scribe.

I thought, "Wouldn't it be great if I became as strong as my older brothers so I could carry heavy sacks of grain? So I could lift the millstones when they needed to be reshaped?" Because, though I was studying Torah in the town, I cared more than ever for the mill, where after a day at school I came home to my home and to my world.

Summer Flowers

A lyric summer passes now before my eyes. A summer in which an eight-year-old boy with rolled-up trousers runs about gazing at everything, perpetually amazed at the beauty of the world. It was a grand summer because everyone was in a good mood.

For one thing, my father rented a little garden plot from one of the landowners whose property I passed on my way from the mill to school. My mother planted potatoes, carrots, beans, beets, turnips, even cucumbers. And so every time I ran to school I would stop at the garden plot, where, fearlessly, I climbed the fence so I could regard the seedlings sprouting from the earth. I counted every potato tuber, every carrot, every little beet that thrust its first leaf out of the soil.

Then my father leased a bit of meadow that was near the mill. It was in a moist area where the grass grew tall. Of course, we would later cut the grass, form it into haystacks, and later still carry huge bundles of the fragrant hay home to our barn, where we would spread it out in the loft. It was fun to sleep on the haystacks in the meadow or on the fragrant dried hay in the loft itself.

Later my father led a red cow with a white spot on her forehead home from the market. She was an unruly creature who tossed her horns threateningly. Though to my mother's delight she gave plenty of milk, she had the habit of running away to the village where her first owner lived. A couple of times we had to drive to the village to get her.

There were frequent rains; there was work at the mill. So the mill was busy for several hours every day. The water clattered joyfully beneath the wheels.

All of the trees facing the house, all the trees on the pond and those on both banks of the river, were dense with leaves. The fish in the pond leaped toward the sun, frightening the swimming ducks. The ducks, their heads in the water, their tails in the air, grubbed in the mud with their bills. Under my mother's care, chicks and ducklings hatched. There was a brood under every sitting bird. But while the chicks were small, the ravens who had their nests in the high branches of the trees over the pond were a problem, swooping down to snatch my mother's chicks to carry back to their nests for their young.

"Children, I want those nests torn down. Otherwise there won't be a chick left," my mother said. I was by now a good climber, so I climbed up into a high tree over the pond and did what my mother wanted. In one of the nests I found some ravens' eggs, which I put into my pocket, but as I was climbing down from the tree I squashed the eggs and came home shamefaced.

Aside from the fine way things were growing all around us that spring, and the fact that our family had no concerns, our home life became more congenial because the children too had grown. Kalmen—pious and shy—was a sizable lad, very biddable around the house. "He is goodness itself," said my mother. It saddened us all to think that in a few more years he would have to do his army service. My brother Moyshe had grown into a considerable young man who could be trusted to run the mill by himself.

Meanwhile I was studying with Zalmen the scribe. I had my own inkwell with ink in it. I bought sheets of paper, sewed them together, and drew lines on them, making a notebook in which I wrote not only the letters of the alphabet but also row upon row of words copied from the models Zalmen wrote at the top of each page. For the first time there was an inkwell, pen holder, and pen in our house.

My sister Bebl was—all at once—grown. No one had noticed that her chestnut braids had turned thick and beautiful. That her gray eyes were wide and intelligent. My mother was delighted with her. "Bebl is like a lovely summer flower," my mother said. And indeed Bebl loved flowers and gathered them in the meadows. She gathered forget-me-nots and twined them into garlands, which she placed in bowls of water she set on the bureau in the large room. She put small flowerpots on the windowsill into which she placed flowers whose red bell-like blossoms hung down, as well as a horned cactus she got from somewhere. It grew and its horns grew too. If anyone cut their finger we pressed some juice out of the cactus and applied it to the cut.

Every Friday, when the challah had been baked, Bebl scrubbed the house. The floorboards gleamed yellow. Then she brought green reeds from the pond, which she shredded and strewed on the floor so the room smelled wonderful.

Bebl had girlfriends, town girls, who came to visit her on Shabbos afternoons. We sang all sorts of songs with them and danced all sorts of dances in the meadow behind the house. We danced the lancers and the quadrille; we danced in fours, in eights, and in twelves. Bebl directed the dancing, calling the turns in a clear voice. It was that way all summer, Shabbos after Shabbos.

My father was rarely angry. He always used Shareshevski's snuff, which cost six groschen a packet. That summer he began to use Dohrman's snuff, which cost eight groschen a packet. Therefore, when he took a whiff of the snuff, his blue eyes twinkled. He often gave me a kopeck or a three-groschen piece with which to buy something in town. My mother frequently suggested it would be nice if she could take a little trip to Meleytshitsh to find out how her parents, Grandfather Yossl Itzl and Grandmother Peshe Reyzl, were doing.

When she spoke of Meleytshitsh, the village where she was born and where her parents lived, a flush rose to her cheeks as if she were a little girl. I too wanted to see my grandfather Yossl Itzl, who had such a high forehead and whose gray beard was divided in two. I was no longer afraid of him. Now when he tested my learning he could ask what he liked—I knew he would be pleased with his grandson.

"Maybe at harvest time, God willing, he'll come over of his own accord. We should tell him to come over. He'd get so much pleasure from the family," my mother said.

My grandfather Yehoshua was the same as always. He went into town almost every day to say his prayers. He would occasionally miss a day in the middle of the week, but he never missed a Shabbos. When he walked along the dam he still seemed to be a tree among trees despite what had befallen him lately, something he could not understand or explain.

In the very middle of the day, and without any warning, one of his front teeth—a tooth from the very middle of his upper row of teeth—fell out. The tooth, though it had caused my grandfather no pain, had become loose before. My grandfather put the tooth onto the flowerpot on the window ledge. When someone came to the house to visit—a Jew or a Gentile—my grandfather displayed the tooth and, with a sibilant hiss, he would say, "Have you ever seen the like? That such a thing should come to pass."

Just the same, my grandfather still liked to sing his red, yellow, and speckled melodies. He sang the melodies clearly despite the fact that an upper middle tooth had fallen out of his mouth.

That year was the first in which I learned to appreciate summer's smells. Though our rented field was mowed by a Gentile of our acquaintance, we dried the hay ourselves: raked it, gathered it up, and formed it into stacks. When it was dry we carried it to the barn, walking up to our knees through the peat mud. The smell of the earth was fragrant; that of the hay was intoxicating. And when we had filled the loft in the barn with hay to the rafters, the smell of it reached the house. Each member of the household smelled of it.

Our garden in the rented plot of land gave a rich yield. No sooner were the potato blossoms visible than we could almost feel the young potatoes growing at the roots. One could nibble at a young carrot pulled freshly out of the ground. My mother plucked beet leaves and cooked tasty borschts. Because our garden was encircled with gardens belonging to non-Jews, I saw with my own eyes how the earth was good to Jew and non-Jew alike.

That summer I had an unexpected fright when, coming home one dark night, I was overtaken by a dreadful storm, with thunder and lightning rolling and flashing over my head. It was a summer evening. Clouds gathered from all sides, filling all parts of the sky. Suddenly it was night. Then there was a blast of wind that struck the barn door, flinging it open so our red cow with the white dot on its forehead, whose habit it was to run away to the village from which it had come, escaped from the barn, trailing a rope from her horns. Once out of the barn, the cow, her eyes blazing, headed for the open bridge and sped like an arrow across the meadows.

"Peretz, after her! Chase her! Catch the rope!" my mother cried. There was no one she could call. Fleet as an arrow, I sped after the cow. I chased her and she fled. Now she leaped over a high fence and landed up to her belly in mud from which, when she had extricated herself, she ran on. I had hold of the rope, but she proved stronger and quicker than me. She knocked me over and dragged me some distance through the mud. Then she got mired in a bog. I grabbed her tail and helped her get out of it. Then off she went, following her nose. When I grabbed her rope again, she shook her head, tossed her horns, glared at me, and was off and running once more.

I heard my mother calling, "Peretz, come home! Let the cow go ... come home!" But something compelled me to follow the cow, as if an evil spirit possessed me. Now it was really dark outside, and the cow disappeared into the dark. It began to thunder. Lightning went off above my head, and a sort of red heat touched my face. I fell into the deep, wet grass and looked about me in the dark. Where was I? Where was the mill? Thunder rumbled. The night itself was yelling, laughing with its thunder over my head, and I sat in the grass not knowing where our mill was to be found.

There was a gush of rain, and in a little while I was soaked to the bone. I became a river of my own. The lightning lashed the sky, lashed the dark night. Now, everywhere, the sky was ablaze. The thunder shattered the night. It was no longer a single night. Instead there were many nights racing about over the meadows.

They raced about me. Each of them touched my damp hair. Each of them whispered something in my ear.

I began to hear voices. Bebl called and shouted. My father called. My mother and Moyshe. All their voices came to me from one direction. I looked about, trying to discern the source of the voices, and I saw a small fire.

The lightning flashes were far, far away. The thunder too was now far away, at the very edge of the sky. I could hardly hear it. The rain came down in a drizzle. It was much warmer than the previous downpour.

I got up from my concealment in the deep grass and ran as fast as I could toward the sparkling fires, which seemed to be nearer and nearer. I ran and fell into a bog, from which I leaped out and ran toward home. The clouds drifted off somewhere. The dark blue sky overhead was brilliant with stars. The mill was now close by. Just the same, I kept running. And I felt a vapor rising from my clothes. I arrived at the door. Everyone was standing outside, staring into the night.

They grabbed at me, touched me to see if I was all right. "Who cares about the cow? Just as long as you've come home in one piece," my mother said, blowing any evil spirits off me.

In the house we celebrated my safe return. Fresh, dry clothes were fetched for me. I felt as if I'd come running from another world. As if far, far away I had been a guest of the night. It seemed to me the cow had deliberately tricked me into leaving home to follow her.

A few days later, when my father brought the cow back home—in fact he brought her home from her original village to which she had run on that stormy night—I regarded her with suspicion. She looked back at me with strange fires gleaming in her eyes.

When the loft in the barn had been loaded with fresh hay, Kalmen, Moyshe, and I went up to it to sleep at night. One night that summer, as we lay up there in the hay, I heard my mother uttering cries of pain at the top of her voice. My impression was that I heard her voice in my sleep. But in the morning I heard my brother Moyshe, who had been awake for a long time, calling to me, "Peretz,

Peretz! Hurry down! Mother's given birth to a girl!" Delighted by the news, I leaped down from the loft without hurting myself, wearing only my shirt.

That night my sister Soreh was born. Her coming was one more event in that lovely, melodious summer.

I Search for God

In the school run by the good Zalmen the scribe, there were boys who were eager to lead me into wicked ways. Because Zalmen was so kind, the mischievous children were able, on the sly, to do whatever they liked.

In Mattes's school the children had studied because they feared his beatings and whippings. If a boy had what Mattes called a "dense head," Mattes would advise the boy's parents to have him learn a trade. Though Zalmen kept a walnut stick at his desk with which he often tapped a boy on the shoulder, Zalmen's goal was to make good pupils by means of kind words. Because he was so gentle, the mischief-makers had an easy time of it, both those who were deceiving their parents and those deceiving the teacher in heder.

There was a ringleader among us who loved to play all kinds of pranks on the teacher. He also loved persuading the other children to assist him in his plans. Once, when Zalmen was not in the room, he got hold of his walnut stick and, with a sharp knife, cleverly cut round and round into the stick. They were very thin cuts, not easily noticed. Then when Zalmen came back into the room, one of the pupils, by prearrangement, provoked him by not wanting to look in the book so the teacher would hit him on the shoulder with his stick. When Zalmen struck the disobedient boy on the shoulder the stick broke into bits, and pieces of it flew about the room.

Yet the prank pleased Zalmen, who laughed and enjoyed the joke. He knew very well which of the boys had pulled the stunt, and he asked the boy to find him another stick because he could hardly be a teacher without one. The students brought him several sticks so he could choose the best one.

Some while later a couple of other disobedient boys thought up another prank. It was Thursday, the day on which pupils were expected to show what they knew by reciting individually from the Gemara. On Thursday even Zalmen the scribe was stern with his pupils.

What the boys did was this: they gathered up shards of a clay pot. One of the boys put the shards across his back under his kaftan. When it was the boy's turn to recite, he bent low and pretended to be looking for something under the table.

"Why aren't you reciting?" Zalmen asked.

The boy did not reply but went on as if he were looking for something under the table.

Zalmen lost his patience, reached for his stick, and landed a blow across the boy's back. The stick landed precisely on the shards, making a loud crack as if it had broken a bone.

"Ouch, oh, oh. You've broken a bone!" the boy wailed.

Zalmen turned white as chalk. He ran to the boy. As he caressed him and stroked his back the rest of the class broke out into hoots of laughter. The prankster took off his kaftan, and the shards fell to the floor.

I was inclined to stand off to one side while the children were planning things I didn't approve of. I was fond of Fridays because on that day Zalmen would write out lines in my notebook for me to copy. I studied the way he added flourishes to his letters, and I tried to model my letters after his. The writing lesson gave another pupil an opportunity for a prank. He was an audacious fellow who had once mounted a pig and rode off when it showed up in the yard. Now the boy caught a fly, dipped it in the inkwell, and let it crawl across a piece of white paper to make it write with its tiny feet.

We were studying Gemara, tractate Gittin. Though I had practically memorized the chapter, Gemara was still a strange world of legalities for me. While I half understood what was said about bills of divorce, the cases treated in Bava Metzia and Bava Kamma about injustice in matters of business and the punishments meted out for robbery and theft were more congenial to me. I was not at ease in the Gemara, though studying it along with the commentaries of Rashi and Tosafos sharpened my young mind.

Study of the Tanakh was not simple, but I understood it more readily. I learned many of the Prophets by heart. I could even grasp the prophet Isaiah, when he spoke in anger to God and to man. His harsh words directed toward heaven and earth echoed in my ears. The words of Koheles (Ecclesiastes) sent me creeping into the woods or into the high grasses, presumably to search for late currants but in fact so that there, in hiding, I could think about the difficult ideas to be found in that book. "Who then can know whether the soul of man goes up to heaven and the soul of the beast goes down to the earth if the final resting place of the beast is the final resting place of man?"

I tried to find the place where God liked to stroll. Sometimes I saw Him walking about our meadows when the sun was setting. Sometimes I saw Him high in the tops of the tall, dark alder trees when the wind stirred them.

We were also studying the Psalms in which King David speaks to God as to a fellow human, opening his heart to him and confessing his sins. When I was alone and lying awake in my bed, I thought about my own sins.

In the summer evenings, when I walked home from school, I no longer hurried. I deliberately made the trip last longer. One day, on my way home, I caught a frog and held it in my hand carefully so as not to squeeze it. I could feel how frightened it was. I could feel its heart beating and I saw the pulse in its throat trembling. I thought, "The frog speaks to me with a voice I cannot hear. It looks me directly in the eye and speaks to me, but I cannot understand it."

In the Psalms I learned a phrase the teacher translated like this: "Day speaks to day; night speaks wisdom to the night."

Of course. Each day tells the next one what it has seen in this sinful world. And of course I knew each night tells the succeeding one how mankind has sinned in the dark. After all, I knew our river was covered at night with a mist that crept under cover of darkness into the high grasses between canes and islets. At night the water sought a place in the dams through which to escape to the larger river that waited somewhere far downstream.

I could see how everyone in the house was fearful of our meditative millpond when it was enclosed in night. Even my sister Bebl—who could walk into the water up to her neck in order to gather the white water lilies—even she, if she had to get water at night, was a little fearful. Which is why I was afraid to go into the pond to catch fish or to put my bare feet into the water where the pond's edge lay hidden in shadow.

Though I was not particularly fond of the shtetl, still I enjoyed the excursions the shtetl folk made to our mill every Shabbos in the summer. They came because of Bebl and the other girls, who came out after the Shabbos meal to sing and to dance before the house. Their mothers too came out, bringing their younger children to carry their shawls for them because grown-ups were not supposed to carry anything on Shabbos. And since the mothers came, the fathers followed after to stroll about. With them came the smaller boys, who carried their handkerchiefs and snuff boxes.

The consequence of all this was that my mother, when she was about to bake bread, would set aside a portion of dough, which she used as a kvass starter. She filled a kneading trough with water, into which she put the starter. In a few days' time the dough began to ferment, and it was not long before there was a tasty bread kvass in the kneading trough. The men and women of the shtetl knew there was a kneading trough full of spicy kvass standing before the door of the mill. So they came in, wished us a good Shabbos, and drank kvass from a large, two-handled copper pitcher. On any given Shabbos, the townsfolk would drink up an entire kneading trough full of kvass.

My mother would bake cookies every Friday to serve to the little children who came with their mothers and fathers. The women sat on the grass in front of the house under a willow. You could hear a woman saying to my mother, "You have such reason—no evil eye—to be proud of your children. After all, the whole shtetl is talking about them. Promising children. Loyal and well-behaved children. If we live to see the day, we may still see one of Lippe the miller's sons become a rabbi."

My father was not pleased by the influx of people on Shabbos. It was the only day on which he could have some calm, when he could enjoy being quiet and out of doors. And now there were all those women from the shtetl, and there was nothing but talk around the house. "What makes them prattle so much? Why so much gossip, so much talk?" When the townspeople showed up and started to drink the kvass, my father had a way of disappearing. He made as if he had to go check whether our horse in the meadow was well hobbled or whether there would be pasture enough to last until the holidays.

My grandfather too disliked having visitors. He who so loved his melodies, he who had a specific name for each tune, he who liked to sing and clap his hands like a melodious child! One Shabbos during the day, at summer's end when a downpour had driven Bebl's girlfriends into the house, where they formed groups of eight, singing and dancing, four against four, my grandfather, who happened to be dozing on the oven in the middle of the room, crept down and, taking up the whip that was lying on the oven, drove the girls from the house, shouting, "Out, wantons! Out of the house! It's a sin to dance in a Jewish house."

Bebl wept. The girls did not come for several weeks on Shabbos, and the house seemed mournful without their dancing.

My father said I would fast on the next Yom Kippur. If not for a whole day, at least for half a day. My mother, as she usually did, pointed out to my father that the good Lord did not require little children to fast.

This year, when it was slichos time, I got up of my own accord. Not so much for the sake of the prayers but so that I could make the early morning trip to town. This time all of us went except Bebl, who stayed at home to look after my little sister.

It was a cold dawn; a white frost was on the grass. My grandfather, my father, Kalmen, Moyshe, my mother, and I were out in the cold dawn. None of us spoke so as not to disturb the early morning silence. Everything was still enveloped in sleep. The moon was already far away, on the other side of the forest, inclining to the west. In the east everything was hushed. In the streets where the Gentiles lived sleep still lay over the barns, on the fences, gardens, and houses.

Not till we came to the circular marketplace, which was surrounded by Jewish homes, did the dawn begin fully to wake. There were lights to be seen in many windows. Doors banged as people made their way to the synagogue through the darkened marketplace.

My mother was alert to every sound. "Do you hear, Peretz, darling? There goes an old man. Do you hear how small his steps are? Those other steps are those of a heavy older man. Do you hear how he puts one foot after the other? One, two, one, two. And now listen—there are two kinds of steps—that's a father walking with a young child. A heavy pace and a light one. Ah, how much life there is at dawn. A dawn like this is wonderful. I'm so glad you've come along."

On Rosh Hashanah I recited my prayers side by side with the grown-ups. This year I did not lie about nibbling the wings, gizzards, and drumsticks of the kapores chickens with the other little boys in the hay under the benches near the stockinged feet of the men. No, on this Yom Kippur I fasted for half a day and recited prayers from the holiday prayer book all day long, and when the praying men beat their chests with their fists as they murmured "For the sins that we have committed . . . ," I too beat my chest and thought about my sins.

I liked the Sukkos holiday better than Yom Kippur. My brothers Kalmen and Moyshe built the sukkah. When they drove the nails into the boards, I held on to each board to keep it even. Later we went into the woods and chopped branches of red fir with which to cover the sukkah. My sister Bebl and I brought whole bundles of red and green reeds from the river and twined it with the fir. We brought yellow sand from the railroad right-of-way and strewed it on the floor of the sukkah.

My mother, with a small child in tow, kept coming out of the house, taking pleasure as she watched her children at work.

⪻ Sad Tales

My sister Bebl reprimanded me for being too shy and not being mischievous like other boys. It was true. I did not have many friends among the boys at school. On the way from the mill to heder, I walked alone. I was getting used to being alone. And because I learned too much at my young age and my head was stuffed with Gemara, I tended to look up to the older men in synagogue.

I learned in the Bible that Jews had once had a land of their own. That wicked nations had destroyed their temple and driven the Jews into exile. In the Prophets I learned that the Jewish people were sinful. In the Gemara I learned about the laws a Jew must know and obey. A boy as young as I was learned about sins so terrible that people had been stoned, burned, or hanged for committing them. In my heart I could not condone that. The passages that were dear to me in the Tanakh, specifically in the Psalms, as well as in the Gemara, were those spoken by an individual to God as if He were an equal. It was there I learned that a man could pray to God, could praise Him and could also blame Him.

When I was alone somewhere in the woods, in the meadow watching our horse, or on Friday or Shabbos when I was at home, I spent time reflecting on why my sister Bebl was reprimanding me.

Zalmen the scribe had really taught me to write. About this time a man came to town who taught girls how to write letters. He was asked to come to our house once a week. Bebl, Kalmen, and Moyshe studied with him. Now that there was plenty of ink and paper in our house I too was drawn to write a letter, though there was no one to whom to write. We never received any letters, and so we never wrote any. There was no one for whom I could express my lovely thoughts on paper.

I noticed that people in the family were beginning to watch the train that ran past the mill. There were two passenger trains, one at dawn and the other in the evening, traveling north to south. Then one during the day and another late at night, traveling south to north. Each time one of the trains neared our district we heard its whistle. We looked out for each train. The passing of the trains stirred up hidden longings in us. When we saw the passengers looking out their windows, it seemed like they were gazing at us. "God willing," my mother said after musing silently over the passing of one such train, "someday you'll probably need to travel on a train like that."

My father bowed his head and was silent. Though he said nothing, I knew he was thinking the same thing. A couple of times lately they had talked about how Peretz would be sent away to study with a more advanced teacher.

It was about this time too that I began to wonder why my father was sad. Why he laughed so rarely. I knew he loved the children as much as my mother did, but he did not express it openly.

There were tales told at home about what had happened to him when he was still young, and in those stories I tried to find the explanation for his melancholy.

I heard these stories from my mother, from my grandfather, and sometimes from my father himself. It was not in Kleshtshel that it happened but in the vicinity of Visoke, where my father, who was not then married to my mother, had been in charge of windmills he rented from a nobleman. It was in the period when the Poles, trying to free themselves from the Russian yoke, revolted. So the tsar sent Cossacks to punish them. The Cossacks spread fire and ruin throughout the region, destroying every manor house in which a Polish noble lived. And the nobleman from whom my father rented his mills was a Pole.

It was spring, and my father had gone to the manor house to ask the nobleman for something. Just then a band of Cossacks came riding up, muskets on their shoulders and swords at their sides. They rode in and started to shoot at the estate. There was a brandy still on the property, into which my father and the distiller ran. They hid there, squeezed up against each other in a dark corner of the cellar, where they could hear the bullets whizzing above them. Suddenly a bullet struck the distiller right in the mouth, and since he was pressed up against my father his hot blood streamed into my father's face and onto his clothes.

Above, in the courtyard, there was silence. No more shots were heard. But suddenly the distillery in which my blood-soaked father was hiding was set afire by the Cossacks. My father could hear the crackling roar as flames engulfed the distillery on all sides. The smoke roiled through the cellar. When my father could no longer endure the heat he ran outside.

When he saw there was no one there he started to run toward home. Just as he was leaving the estate he saw the nobleman lying in the very middle of the road. A young blond-bearded man dressed only in a shirt, he was lying in a puddle of blood. The nobleman beckoned to my father to come near.

As my father bent down to hear what the wounded man wanted, a Cossack on a white horse loomed suddenly out of nowhere, his bare sword raised high and aimed at my father. My father fell to his knees and pleaded with the Cossack to spare his life, saying he was just a stranger passing by. The Cossack, with a sword thrust, finished off the nobleman, then told my father to go on his way.

Some while later, but still in those times, my father lived in a peasant village in which he was the only Jew. An eclipse of the sun was expected. It was summertime, and the people in the village were terrified. Just think of it: the sun would be covered over entirely, and night would fall in the middle of the day.

And that's what happened. In the middle of a bright day, the sun was covered over entirely. Stars shone in the heavens as if it were night. The cattle in the fields grew restless; then, terrified, they left the meadows and galloped home to the village. One of the oxen drove a horn right through the fence of the house in which my father lived.

The peasants decided that if the ox drove his horn through a Jew's fence, it was a sign that the Jew was to blame for the sudden appearance of night in the middle of the day. They hauled my father out of his house and nearly killed him, smashing him on the head with boards and stones. After that he lay ill for a very long time.

In that district, and in those mills, my father had a son named Yankev Mordkhe, a great scholar who was already engaged to be married and who went regularly to study in the Visoke synagogue. Quite often he would return home to his village on foot and at night. Now, one Pesach, when the snow had begun to melt, Yankev Mordkhe left the synagogue late at night and paused halfway back on his way to the village. On both sides of the road the melting snow gleamed in the moonlight. Suddenly he noticed Kozirik, a peasant whom he knew from his village, walking along with him on the side of the path. Simply meeting the peasant at night would not have mattered. The trouble was that Yankev Mordkhe knew Kozirik had died a week ago.

Yankev Mordkhe started to run—and the peasant ran with him! That was certainly Yankev Mordkhe's own shadow lengthened by the moonlight. But overwhelmed by a mortal fear, he continued running from the dead peasant until he got home, where he burst into the house more dead than alive. Shortly thereafter he sickened and died. My father mourned Yankev Mordkhe for a very long time.

My mother told me this all happened after the death of his first wife and after he had married her. Yankev Mordkhe died in my mother's arms. She often talked of what a fine student he had been and how much the townspeople had loved him. "Your father says," she once said while washing and combing my hair, "that you'll take Yankev Mordkhe's place. You'll become a great rabbi as he would have been if he hadn't had such a dreadful fright."

My mother lost seven of the eleven children to whom she had given birth. After my little sister Soreh was born, no more of my mother's children died. She once had four children with her first husband—all of them died. They were doomed, evidently, from the start. As a result a divorce was recommended. Now that I was studying tractate Gittin, I thought about how my mother's first husband had gone about divorcing her. And I learned from my mother how, as a young woman, she had cried her eyes out when one after the other her children died.

Only three of the seven children she bore after she became my father's wife died, and they were fairly grown at the time they passed away. So it is not surprising that my mother hovered over her surviving children. Even my father's children, the ones he had from his previous marriage, were as dear to her as her own.

Almost all of her children who died were taken by scarlet fever. The children who survived had also had the same sickness. No sooner did a child show the slightest sign of illness than my mother would feel about, examining the child's throat. "You have swollen glands, my child," she would say. "Come here. Let's put you into a towel so I can squeeze the glands down." With that my mother would climb up on the table. Then, after tying a towel under the child's chin, she would raise and lower him three times so the towel exerted pressure on the glands in the throat. Even when the children had grown to considerable size and it was hard for her to lift them, she still climbed onto the table to perform the treatment.

There was another household remedy. You put your head into the oven's chimney. Then, with your thumb in your mouth pressing against your palate, you exhaled three times into the chimney. After that my mother would put hot ashes into a woolen sock. She would rub the child's throat with soap and tie the warm, ash-filled sock around his neck, uttering this prayer at the same time: "Father in heaven, let me take on my child's burden. Punish only me, O Lord, for my sin."

Which is why the look on her face was a mixture of sorrow and joy when someone chanced to say, "Yes, certainly. When, God willing, the time comes, we'll have to look for a more advanced teacher for Peretz in some other city." Far-off Brisk was sometimes mentioned. They were thinking of sending me, a young boy, to Brisk. True, my older sister Frishke, my father's oldest daughter, did live there.

So it is no wonder that I too watched the passing of the trains from north to south with interest. Traveling from Bialystok to Brisk.

About that time, Uncle Avrom Tumener, the uncle who could drink up an entire jug of tea by himself, came to visit. By now we owned a yellow samovar, which was quickly made ready just for him.

Uncle Avrom had a girl with him who was just about my age. Her name was Sheyne, the same name as my mother's. She was a dark girl who could write very well and whose handwriting was even better than mine because she learned to write from a grandfather, her father's father, who lived in their home. From him she had learned to give her letters a flourish. We competed, she and I, to see which of us could write in a finer hand.

While my uncle sipped slowly from his cup of tea, Sheyne and I sat apart from the grown-ups, and I showed her my notebook and examples of my handwriting. Then she showed me what she could do. Of course I liked her handwriting better than my own. She wrote my name, "Peretz," putting an elaborate flourish on the final letter, *tsadek*.

There was some discussion about someday sending me to stay with Uncle Avrom. Uncle Avrom said it would probably be better for me to study in Visoke. There were better teachers there than those in Kleshtshel. The point was that Visoke was close to Tumene, where my uncle lived.

"Well, well, all things happen in good time," said my uncle. "We raise our children, and then, in good time, we send them away."

His words were at once pleasing and sobering. There was a long silence in the room after my uncle had spoken because my mother was unable to hide the tears his words had brought to her eyes.

~ Bebl Has a Suitor

As there was more talk of my traveling to Brisk to study with a more advanced teacher I grew quieter and quieter. I often felt my heart constrict and tears come to my eyes. There are no words to describe how I felt. Why was I to be sent away from home? How was I to keep in my ears the living clatter of the mill? How could I leave behind the sweet river water that was all the drink I knew? Or live far from home without seeing again the trees outside my window each morning?

I went about barefoot in summer. Even the snow in the winter no longer made my face and hands too cold. I was as familiar with our frosts as with our summer rains. Wherever I went, whether in the woods or around the pond, I recognized the young trees that had grown along with me. My path from the mill to my heder was familiar and well trodden. In summers, after a rain, I made clear footprints in the soft, black earth, footprints that lingered for a long time afterward. I recognized the very blades of grass that sprouted in the imprints of my footsteps. And the blades of grass knew me and looked up at me from my footprints, expecting to be recognized: "You see, we grew out of your steps."

That winter before I went to Brisk, things were already very different at home than the winter before. We stayed up later than usual. I now went home alone from heder, though my heart continued to pound until I was past the Gentile streets and arrived at the dams—but the fear was different now. I was at war with it. Every morning on my way to school I studied every stone, every protruding root over which, the evening before, I had stumbled and which caused me such fear that I had fled, running. And I saw that what had caused me to run yesterday was pure foolishness.

When I got home from heder I found everyone in the family still awake. Near the oven was a wicker cradle hanging from four ropes tied to the rafters. My mother sat near the oven plucking a chicken while with one foot she rocked the cradle with little Soreh in it. Bebl and Moyshe sat at the table playing checkers. The squares were drawn on a piece of white paper. The checkers were white or black beans. My father sat silently opposite them, his chin resting on his right hand, watching the progress of the beans moving across the paper. Sometimes when I came home I found Bebl and Moyshe sitting at the table fervently writing letters modeled on those they found in a sample-letter book.

That winter we had a frequent visitor from town, a dark and handsome young man who worked for my brother Binyomin Khayem. He was called Shmuel the dyer, and his hands, frequently stained red or blue, gave proof of his craft. He could write fine letters containing all sorts of elegant phrases. We all sat at the table demonstrating our skill, thinking up more and more curious handwriting flourishes. We exchanged the small wall lamp for a larger one; every night, Bebl cleaned the lamp. As a result, there was more light in the room. My grandfather often had to climb down from his place on the oven because the room was getting noisy.

It happened then that when I came running home from school, trying to escape the chill that pursued me along the dam, I was met with a blast of welcome, warm air. This was because the young man who visited us was also a skilled mason. And he had rebuilt our oven, putting a cooking range on it so that we could cook potato pancakes whenever we pleased.

The dark and handsome young man brought us all sorts of songs with lyrics that he taught Bebl and Moyshe to sing so that the house rang with music. In addition to my grandfather's red and speckled melodies we also got to hear "The plow brings blessing and luck" or "Whom do I see through the windowpanes, flying up suddenly like doves?" Shmuel the dyer told us these songs were written by a man named Elyokem Tsunzer or Elyokem Badkhn—Elyokem the wedding jester. My mother's eyes grew wide as she listened to the songs sounding through the house. Even my father lifted his head a bit higher when they sang "The plow brings blessing and luck." And he was pleased when I was able to sing along too.

I overheard that this young man was going to marry Bebl. That he would take her away with him. I thought, "How can Bebl possibly leave us? What will become of the family without Bebl?"

There was nervous talk too that a year from that fall Kalmen would be up for the draft. We were all afraid they might take him and make him a soldier. I could see how dejected he was from the way he kept his head lowered. He took longer than usual to recite his prayers and fasted more often on Mondays and Thursdays. When he recited the Psalms there was a tearful note in his voice.

On those winter evenings, though there was frequently joy in the house, I was occasionally sad. Sometimes when I came home and found them all singing, I would eat dinner, then afterward I would take my Gemara down from its shelf and look into it or I would take down the Tanakh and read the Prophets. At home the Gemara seemed to be my friend; at home, I wanted to absorb the words of the Prophets. I was very fond of the Prophet Jeremiah. I liked to turn to the page on which he says, "Blessed is the man whose faith is in God. He will be as the tree planted by a great river, which sends its roots to the waters and has no fear of the coming heat. Its leaves are green..."

"Do you know what, children?" my mother said. "It's a dark night. There is no moon. It would be good if you could scrounge some dried wood so I could set dough to rise for a loaf of bread."

I looked up at this. It was time for me to do something to please my mother. There had to be wood so that bread could be baked—real wood, not alder twigs. You could only gather such wood by taking a risk. Some distance away, near the railroad, there was a pile of old railroad ties that had been taken from under the rails so new, sound ties could be put in. These oak ties were as heavy as iron. Much too heavy for one person.

"Come on, let's all go," said the young visitor. "You come too, Peretz."

And so instead of going to sleep we got into our sheepskin jackets or quilted coats and crept out into the cold night. The young dyer, with my sister Bebl beside him, led Moyshe and me across the snowy, icy meadows. We sank to our bellies in the snow, but we went on. Tired though I had been when I came home from having spent the whole day studying in the stuffy heder, the cold winter night sent a surge of energy through me.

Quietly, quietly. There we were, almost near the tracks. Quietly, silently, though there was no one about. Still, trees could be witnesses. Clouds drifting across the sky could be witnesses. The snow under our feet was certainly a witness. The imprints of our footsteps were deep in the snow, and I could not help thinking how long they would remain there after we had gone.

Meanwhile, our hands moving about under the snow had already found the thickest of the oak railroad ties. We said, "The railroad ties belong to the government. The government is going to burn them anyway. So this isn't like stealing." It was a rationalization that made carrying the railroad tie easier. We hoisted it onto three sets of shoulders. I, the fourth one, thinking I was helping, grasped it with my hands and ran excitedly after the other three through the deep snow.

That was how we reached home with the oak railroad tie. "What a dreadful, heavy thing it is," my father said as he tried to budge it. My grandfather came down from his place on the oven and nudged the tie with his foot and agreed with my father that it had taken a lot of skill to drag that thing over such a long distance.

Then we took a saw to it. My father straddled the timber on one side and my grandfather on the other while Bebl and the dyer whipped the saw back and forth between them and the scent of vinegar rose from the oak. "Without a doubt, vinegar must normally be made from oak sap," my grandfather said.

There was no question of sleep anymore. Sleep was banished

from the mill. "There's blessing and luck in the plowshare" we sang. The samovar was put on to boil, and the young dyer told stories of other towns. Stories about Semyatitsh, his hometown, where there were even larger mills than our own. It was where our river flowed into the river Nurits.

And so it was night after night. It was not a very severe winter. The frost did not grip us too hard. As a result the train rushing by made more noise. And the trees—our strong, tall, dark alder trees— seemed to bow their heads in larger arcs so that their tops were all but interwoven with each other.

That year, before Pesach, I was measured again for a kaftan. Motye the tailor had promised it would be ready in time for Pe- sach, and this time he kept his word. As he was measuring me my mother told him I would be leaving home wearing the kaftan. That I would be going to Brisk. Motye therefore took my measure twice, and as was only right and proper, he prodded me to check where my shoulders began and where my stomach ended. He measured me for a kaftan that would allow plenty of room for me to grow.

"If he's going to Brisk, we have to let them see just how we sew here in Kleshtshel," Motye said, giving me an affectionate slap on the shoulder.

That Pesach, all of my friends in the synagogue knew—whether they heard it from Mattes or from Zalmen the scribe—that I would be leaving for Brisk after Pesach. My friends regarded me envi- ously. In fact, that Pesach did not feel very agreeable to me. When, during the seder, I asked the four questions, the members of the family bowed their heads, especially attentive to my words, and kept looking at me. My mother said sadly, "I hope and pray to God that a year from now you'll be sitting with us at this table."

My departure, then, was mixed with much joy and even more sorrow. It happened about a week after Pesach, when the road had dried to some degree. My mother spent the whole day getting me ready for my journey. She kept untying my bundle, which was wrapped in a white shawl, to put something else into it. I noticed tears in the eyes of the older family members. Even my father had tears in his eyes when I kissed the mezuzah on our doorpost as I was leaving the house. I couldn't bring myself to look into anyone's eyes, and I pitied my grandfather Yehoshua, who seemed smaller than ever. Perhaps it was because I had grown.

Now, for the first time, I observed that Bebl was a grown-up. That Moyshe was a fine youth. That Kalmen was, as always, very shy, keeping his eyes, even now, upon the ground.

I did not go to Brisk by train. I went, rather, in a wagon leaving from the shtetl that evening. Kalmen was supposed to go with me as far as Brisk, where he would turn me over to my older sister.

My father, my mother, and Moyshe walked Kalmen and me from our house to the shtetl. My grandfather, who would stay home, enjoined me not to forget about my home and to remember his melodies. Bebl, who stayed behind with my little sister, kissed me over and over again, her large, gray eyes welling up with tears.

It was a silent walk. We could hear the murmuring of the brooks among the trees and the quacking of the ducks paddling their way home on the pond. We heard the nightingale filling the spring air with song. But those of us who were walking the road from Lippe's mill to the shtetl walked in silence. Sometimes a tear flowed from my mother's eyes. And there were times too when I wept.

Never before had the dusk so enclosed me in its scarlet and green arms as on that night. I could hear the trees behind me whispering something to each other. I could sense the pond was saying something to the green reeds that were already sprouting along its edges. When we reached the first of the Jewish houses, I went to Arye the tailor's house to say my farewells. Rokhele the kasha maker wept. And my mother wept with her.

The wagon that was to take me to Brisk was already laden. It was a huge, open-sided affair to which a pair of bay horses was harnessed, and it was loaded with poultry: ducks, chickens, and geese. There were some calves and sacks of potatoes too. I was put between two calves so I might have a warm soft place to sit, because the journey would take all night. The wagon was ringed around by other parents who had come to see me off to Brisk.

When the wagon started to move my tears did too, but I swallowed them as I did the water from our river.

My father turned his face to one side; Moyshe wiped his cheeks with his hands so that, even from a distance, he could keep his eyes on me. I saw my mother's face soaked in tears.

In Brisk

A small person named Peretz arrived in Brisk. A small person in his eleventh year who had come to study Torah. He arrived in a ladder wagon, sitting between two red calves and two village women wrapped, despite the warm weather, in heavy shawls. My brother Kalmen sat on one side, dangling his feet, and the wagon driver, who did not live in Kleshtshel, cracked his leather whip over the backs of his two sweating horses.

There was yellow sand surrounding Brisk. There were low houses on both sides of its broad, sandy streets. And many Jews wearing long coats and hats and caps of all sizes. A broad, spread-out city atop the yellow sands. The sun made me warm.

It was nearly noon when we crossed a number of railroad tracks not far from a large train station, where we encountered many other wagons and horses of all shapes and sizes. Black horses, bay horses, white horses, street after street. As we moved we frequently asked, "Where is such and such street?" "Where is so and so's house, where Hershl the cooper and his wife Frishke live?"

What a spacious city, Brisk. No end to its streets and lanes. Just the same, if you ask a Jew a question, he is likely to reply. Among them there were those who could tell that here was a boy coming to study Torah. My peyos and my narrow face revealed the secret.

We arrived at my sister Frishke's house. It was a little old house with an attic apartment. Frishke, who had been looking out of her window, saw us coming and ran down to greet us. She kissed me and Kalmen on both cheeks. My sister's husband, Hershl the cooper, was indeed a cooper who hammered hoops onto casks. Outside the house were heaped piles of casks and hoops. He was a short man with a wide, red beard and hard, broad hands, whom I saw now for the first time. There were two young boys whom I was also seeing for the first time.

We looked each other over and little by little began to talk. "How was the trip?" my sister's husband asked.

"It was a good trip," my brother Kalmen said, speaking slowly. "Thank God. It was a good trip. Except that as we were driving along the road at night the wagon missed the road and turned over—its wheels in the air with Peretz and the calves under the wagon. Yes, they fell into the ditch."

My sister noticed then that I was smeared with mud. Everyone laughed and thanked God for the miracle, and it was suggested that we should recite the blessing of thanks for having escaped a great danger. God forbid, there might have been a disaster.

So there I was at my sister's house in Brisk. Soon the talk turned to my teacher.

"Yes. He's a very great teacher. I've talked with him. He's asking twelve rubles a term. He's a teacher with quite a reputation. After we've had some breakfast we'll go see him. He lives in the next street."

My sister Frishke was a talkative woman. In that regard she did not take after the rest of us. She was short and she squinted. But when she talked, it was as if I heard my father talking, or Kalmen or Binyomin Khayem.

"You'll sleep here, Peretz," my sister said, showing me a little couch set under the slope of the attic room. "He'll want for nothing—God forbid. I'll look after him as if he were my own child. He'll have all he wants to eat. God grant him health and a willingness to learn."

"So," said my brother-in-law, keeping his eyes on the ground as he listened to what Frishke said. Suddenly he smiled into his yellow beard and said, "So there really are no teachers fit for him in Kleshtshel?"

My brother Kalmen, his eyes on the ground also, said, "That's right. There are no fit teachers for him in Kleshtshel."

My sister treated me to a bagel. The bagels in Brisk were different from those in Kleshtshel. The Kleshtshel bagels were thin, smooth, and had larger holes. Those in Brisk were thicker and were braided with several braids. In Brisk the bakers also made flatbread sprinkled with onion, and my sister offered me some of that as well.

I did not have too much time to look over my sister's home. There was nothing else to talk about except my Torah studies. It would be dreadful if, God forbid, they should be delayed by so much as a day. As a result we moved into action at once. After a brief rest, my sister, Kalmen, and I started off to the home of the famous teacher.

Now, why is it I still remember all sorts of things that happened to me in my childhood years when I was but a speck on this earth, when my childish steps measured the distances around our mill? And yet an event as important as my traveling to Brisk to study Torah when I was an eleven-year-old, with so much Gemara in my head, soaked through and through with Torah . . . How can I have forgotten my teacher's name and what he looked like? Forgotten his heder and its pupils; forgotten even what tractates of the Talmud I studied there?

Is it, perhaps, because it was Brisk itself and not the teacher that was the major event in my life then. Not so much my arrival in Brisk as the fact that I had left Lippe's mill, where I was born, where I had grown, where like the currant and the mulberry trees I had my roots in the moist, dark, moss-covered ground.

I seem to remember that the pupils in the teacher's heder were a good deal bigger than I was. That the teacher—a restless man whose speech was not clear—paced the room distractedly. That the narrow and broad streets in the neighborhood of the school were unpaved, sandy, thickly inhabited by Jews.

I actually remember the poor, tattered women of Brisk and

their starving, restless children dressed in rags. The shouting of people, which had a life of its own in the sandy streets, still lives in my memory. I remember the Jewish drivers of the freight wagons loaded with heavy sacks snapping their long whips over the backs of their overworked horses.

Even in Kleshtshel I had heard of the great River Mukhavets in Brisk. A river on which there were no mills to be found because the flow of its current was so strong it would have swept a mill away like a matchstick. Log rafts, entire forests of trees tied together, were floated downriver to distant lands.

So I quietly went off by myself to where the Mukhavets flowed on its way. The river was easy enough to find since the people of Brisk drank from it. Water carriers were always going to or from it, carrying their big-bellied barrels and selling the water to the residents by the bucketful. I had only to watch them to find my way unseen with beating heart to the water's edge. That was during my first week in Brisk, at dusk, at the beginning of the summer.

Watching the great Mukhavets River with its low banks sent first chills then fever through me. The river gazed at me with its huge watery eye. Such a stern look. So angry. Then, abruptly, I remembered my own river from which I had drunk, in which I had washed myself and bathed.

One could see that the trees here and there along the banks were fearful of the river. They saw whole forests of rafts guided by steersmen with long oars floating past them downstream.

With my legs folded under me I sat at the water's edge and heard my own river speaking to me: "So now you've gone and left me, just when my banks are turning beautiful. The willows are green; the dark-trunked alders have fat, round leaves on their branches. Any minute now you could be putting one of those leaves over the tube made with your fist and then, slapping it with your other hand, you could make it explode."

Gazing at the irritable Mukhavets, I could hear the friendly *slap-slapping* of our mill. The water rushing under the waterwheels, making a musical sound. The quacking of the ducks on the river. The cuckoo calling. And the evening echo coming from the trees, "Cuckoo, cuckoo!"

Not far from where I was sitting, the water carriers, one by one, entered the Mukhavets, driving their horses belly deep into the water. The horses waved their tails and splashed water. The water carriers, standing on their wagons, drew the unclean water flowing at the feet of the horses and poured it into their barrels with a pail dipper attached to a long stick.

Who needs Bible study? Gemara? A teacher in Brisk? New friends? And what is Gemara if the heart yearns for the secrets hidden behind a tree on whose trunk a woodpecker is searching for grubs? When the heart yearns for a hiding place behind a tree on which the nightingale serenades the evening?

I had been a student with Moyshe Mordkhe, with Mattes, and with Zalmen the scribe and had learned whatever it was that I had learned. I had made my way along the path from the shtetl to my home. And on that path I had learned to understand the wind that blew among the trees. I grew up together with those trees, first crawling about on all fours, then getting to my feet and striding along. How lovely the path was that led over the bridge to our mill and from there to the narrow ditch into which cool water seeped from a hidden spring. It was good to throw pebbles into that ditch, scaring the little fish that had come into it from the river.

The huge Mukhavets also spoke to me, but I did not understand its language. The river's gaze was as unfamiliar as that of the big-city folk I saw bustling about in the unpaved, sandy streets.

Quietly I went off to the big Brisk synagogue, and there, during the early evening prayers, I saw the most famous rabbi in the world, Reb Yosef Ber. What a huge head, what a wide forehead! Salt-and-pepper hair and a not-very-large, forked beard. And two blazing dark eyes that seemed to penetrate anyone at whom he looked. He strode back and forth in the evening light of the synagogue, his hands clasped behind him. At one point he came near me. When he looked down at me I shivered as if with cold. Why was his gaze so penetrating? Was it the Torah that peered so shrewdly from his eyes?

My father wanted me to be a rabbi. And how could I be a rabbi like Reb Yosef Ber? Was I in any way like him? Was he ever really a small boy like me? Did he actually grow up in Brisk, in this sandy town among so many poor, hungry Jews? Among so many fallible people?

Through the windows of the nearby synagogues there came the sound of boys studying Gemara. Ah, how they sang. The sound of their voices penetrated every corner of the study house before it escaped through the open doors and windows. Their music moved me to tears. They studied alone, each one at his Gemara, at his own lectern, at his own book. There were no teachers there. No study partners. Ah, if only I could be like them!

To be like them, with my own reading stand, my Gemara, and my own corner somewhere in a study house, I had to become a yeshiva boy. I had to eat my meals in a different house in rotation; I had to sleep on a hard bench and not eat at my sister's house nor sleep there. What was written in *Ethics of the Fathers*? "Thou shalt eat bread and salt; and drink a measure of water; and sleep on the ground"—then you may study Torah. Then you will be worthy of studying Torah.

Between Brisk and Lippe's mill there was so vast a distance that I could hardly grasp it. Days came and went. The sun rose and set. A cuckoo called "Cuckoo, cuckoo!" and then listened as its echo replied from somewhere. What was I doing in Brisk? I yearned for home, though I hardly knew what I was yearning for. Though I had left the mill, and though I was in Brisk, I had not yet entered my new world.

And that is why I cannot now remember the name of my teacher, nor those of my fellow pupils, nor the Torah I studied in Brisk. It's because I had apparently never left home.

There is one thing I do remember learning when I was in Brisk. I learned to chew glass. Real glass.

It happened when I was standing by watching other children do tricks. One of them stood on his head; another tore a thick bit of rope with his hands. Still another filled his mouth with kerosene and then, lighting a piece of paper, he spurted kerosene on it, creating a burst of flame. Someone else walked on stilts he had made himself.

So, watching them, I said, "I can do a trick. I can chew glass without shedding a drop of blood." And with that I put a piece of glass into my mouth that was lying on the ground—glass from a broken bottle. I put it into my mouth and crushed it with my teeth. The children gaped, grimacing, as they watched. I spat out the bits of chewed glass, and indeed there was not a drop of blood to be seen.

"How can you do that?" the amazed children asked.

"I'm a miller. My teeth grind like the millstones in our mill," I replied, my cheeks ablaze.

I yearned for home. Endlessly, I yearned for home. At the end of summer, wearing a shirt and with a scarf around my neck, I was taken to the huge train station in Brisk, where I was put into a compartment and told to crawl under a bench so the conductor would not see me.

That was at the end of summer. At home the chickens and the roosters were regarding the tops of the trees with interest. They flew into the trees to spend the night because in the shtetl the shofar was already sounding.

Loneliness and Blaming God

Since I had come from Brisk a few weeks before Rosh Hashanah, my father wanted me to go to the shtetl synagogue to study during the week so that I wouldn't forget what I had learned in Brisk.

But I did not want to leave the house even for a minute. I had been away from home for an entire summer. I had left the mill just when the surrounding countryside was beginning to turn green. The yellow meadow flowers were peeping out of the grasses in the wetter places near the house. Now, with the summer nearly gone, everything around the mill had managed to grow without me. I could feel the trees in front of the house scolding me for having left them to grow without me all summer long.

Some of the young fowl around the house, which had been tiny creatures racing after the hen crying "Peep, peep, peep!," were now roosters crowing lustily, were now hens, brown and white, with red combs and earlobes. It seemed to me that the willows outside the window no longer looked toward the house but rather bowed their heads to gaze more intently into the millpond.

My family treated me differently. My mother kept trying to find out what I would eat. "Just think of it. Of course he got better food there in Brisk." This despite the fact that my mother could see I had come home much thinner than when I had left.

I did not want to make my father unhappy. Of course I would

have preferred staying in the mill, poking about among the wheels, looking at the millstones, getting into everything so I would emerge all covered with flour. And I still loved the smell of newly ground wheat. But my father wanted me to go to the study house. And my mother urged it too. She said, "Peretz, dear, go on. Please your father and go. Spend a couple of hours there, and then come right home."

I was distressed to see that my brothers and sisters regarded me as somehow different, as if I had suddenly become an adult, as if I had not grown up there with them at all. Even my sister Bebl looked at me without saying a word. My brother Moyshe, too, had nothing to say to me. I, on the other hand, asked questions about everything. I clambered about in the hay barn, delighting in the dry hay that had been prepared for winter.

Everyone at home was worried Kalmen would be examined by the draft board after Sukkos and might have to serve the tsar. It would be a hard service for him because he would not eat nonkosher food. So we worried while Kalmen went about with his head bowed.

Then there was my grandfather. Was it really true he had aged so much in the time I had been in Brisk? He seemed bowed, like a tree that has begun to wither. He made me unhappy when he said, "Brisk is a town full of Jews, Peretz. It would be well to die among many Jews."

To please my father I went off to the synagogue. But I went slowly. No teacher waited for me. And I wasn't going to school. So I came down off the dam and went in among the trees to see whether there were any late summer berries left. I was always very good at finding the last currant or raspberry. And I did indeed find some withered currants that had waited too long for me.

There were little places around the mill and on the way to town to which I always felt drawn. There were hidden springs surrounded by trees and high grasses from whose midst the water peeped out as if from a dark blue, limpid eye. On the surface of such springs there crawled all sorts of water insects and green frogs. I was afraid to drink from these springs, but I loved studying my reflection in their waters.

Now I was back from Brisk, and having stepped off the dam into the trees, I stopped by myself at such a spring, looked down at the smooth water, and saw my pale, narrow face and quiet eyes. I wondered, "Is this the Peretz from Brisk or the Peretz from Lippe's mill, who left his face behind on the surface of the water?"

Of course, a Jewish boy must study Torah. My father thought that if I stayed at home over the holidays I would forget what I had learned. How could I tell him I would not forget what I had studied? That I needed to stop studying for a little while so I could remember what I had learned even better?

How much better it would have been if my father had turned to me, saying, "Stop, Peretz. You've studied enough Torah in Brisk. You've spent enough time among strangers. Now that you've come home, take off those tight boots you wore in Brisk and run barefoot in the meadows. Or go to the woods and bring branches home with which to decorate our windows."

Ah, what I would have done in the mill if my father had spoken to me that way. Perhaps I would have shown him my skill at trimming the millstones when my brothers Moyshe and Kalmen lifted them for me, or I might have gone into the river and caught fish. Or I might have gone to gather dry wood, dragging it home in plenty of time before winter.

But my father wanted me to go to the study house. So I went, but I made sure to make the way there a long one. I went with deliberately slow steps through the town's circular marketplace, just as if I had been a stranger.

When I arrived at the study house, I did not at once take up a Gemara. Instead I chose the Book of Job, which I had not yet studied. A difficult book. I looked for explanations of the hard words in Rashi. The story was about a man in the land of Uz, an honorable, God-fearing man named Job who walked the straight and narrow way. Then Satan provoked God to test Job by heaping all sorts of troubles on him. God did as Satan demanded. He burned Job's house, killed his children, and inflicted boils on Job's body.

Then Job blasphemed fearlessly to God, indicting Him as a wicked God who values the wicked more than the just, which is clear because He has given the governance of the world into the hands of the wicked.

I sat there, confused by the story. The Days of Awe were coming soon. And here I was, who also had things to complain about, discovering the story of Job, a man who had absolutely no fear of God. Job, instead of lamenting, accused God of a whole list of evil acts that God had committed against a just man.

I could not help thinking of Brisk. I was not quite clear what the city's effect on me had been. Or why it was that my home and the region around it were wrapped in nostalgia for me. Or why the small store of language I possessed had disappeared within me. I saw with my mind's eye the study houses in Brisk, the young men standing beside their reading stands reciting melodic passages from the Gemara. They too were strangers in Brisk; no doubt they too had been sent away from their homes when they were young. Their fathers, like mine, had wanted them to leave home, to study in distant cities.

I looked around the synagogue in Kleshtshel and tried to compare it to the synagogues in Brisk. I thought, "Why could I not have been left to study here in Kleshtshel? I could have studied whole days at a time and gone home at night. There was no teacher for me here in Kleshtshel. So what? I could sit here and do my own studying. Why had I been sent to a strange, distant city?"

I looked at the books in the Kleshtshel study house: a number of Gemaras; various Talmud commentaries. I took down a Vilna Gemara, a huge book, so large that when I opened it, it obscured me from my chest to the tip of my nose. I looked into this Gemara as if for the first time. No. No matter how big the Vilna Gemara was, I was no longer a little boy. Mattes, the teacher, came into the study house. He recognized me and came over to greet me with the sort of greeting one gives to an adult visitor. Then he gave my cheek a gentle pinch, smiling a contented smile inside his beard. "I made something of you," he said, pinching my other cheek. "I know you want to be a scholar. I was the first to tell your father to have you study."

"Who is *this* Mattes?" I thought. "Didn't he used to pinch

my cheek hard? Didn't he try to beat me? And when he gripped my head between his knees, didn't I bite his leg? Is this the same Mattes? Is he really talking to me as if we were equals?"

"'Bread and salt shalt thou eat. A measure of water shalt thou drink, and upon the ground shalt thou sleep.' Do you remember that? You learned it from me. Now you know the true meaning of those words." He studied me quietly for a little while longer, then left the synagogue.

I made my way home at the same slow pace with which I had gone into town. Though I often ran in Brisk, here, in my own village, through my own streets and along my own dam that led to my mill, I felt as if my feet had hobbles on them. As if there were someone continually whispering into my ear, "That's forbidden. Running is a sin. Climbing the trees is wrong. Walking about barefooted is now also wrong."

Job had cursed God and had not been afraid of Him. If a teacher had been teaching me the Book of Job, he would have explained all that to me the way one explained the Song of Songs, in which everything was no more than a parable. An allegory of the Torah and its relationship to the people of Israel. Job too was nothing more than an allegory. But Job cursed God as well as the day of his own birth.

It was just before the New Year. Soon I would have to stand beside my father in the synagogue, reciting many prayers during the High Holy Days. More prayers even than last year. But I would never again weep as I said my prayers, the way I had last year. I thought, "Ah, if my father only knew that in Brisk I was not going to become as devout as he wanted me to be."

And I remembered how last year on Rosh Hashanah, when we had all returned from services, my mother had suddenly said, "I don't understand it. They have prescribed so many prayers for things I don't need. Left to myself, I would know what to ask God for, so I'm afraid He doesn't listen anyway to what we pray to Him for."

I remember the look of mute wonder my father turned on her. The whole family went silent. Now here I was, thinking that my mother had been right, though she had no idea of what I had

learned in the Book of Job, that God had more respect for the wicked than he did for the just.

On the way home I crept into the thick woods and gazed up at
the tall trees. The cold evening dew was already falling, and a number of leaves on the trees had turned yellow. The green leaves no
longer felt sticky to the touch the way they had at the beginning of
summer. The grasses too were turning yellow.

Just then a frog leaped out of the fresh moss. A greenish-brown
frog. I caught her and enclosed her in both my hands and tried to
keep my hands from pressing her too closely. She poked her head
out of the circular opening I made between my hands. She looked
me in the eye, and I could see her throat trembling. I could hear her
heart beating. The children in heder used to say frogs were humans
who had been cursed. They were turned into frogs and forced to
live both on land and in water because they had committed some
great sin.

"Listen, frog, did you know I was born here? That I was raised
here? And that I live in Brisk now? And that I've come home here?
Do you know, frog, that I love every bog just as much as you do? I
love the smell of the mossy earth, and I love it when my bare feet
sink into the soft moss and grass-covered mud. Do you know it
will be Rosh Hashanah soon? Can you say prayers to God? Are you
afraid of God?"

The frog pushed back with her hind legs, trying to leap out of
my hands. She gazed at me, but she pressed back with her hind legs.
She was like a small child who, though it cannot talk, has learned to
push aside an object it does not want too close. The look she gave
me was so human, so accusing, that I tossed her away over a thick
tree trunk so she would be out of sight when she fell among the
leaves and grass.

I crept out of the woods and vowed that during the Days of
Awe I would be even more pious than last year. That I would fast
all day on Yom Kippur even if my mother urged me to eat during
the interval when the Torah was taken out to be read.

My life was filled with yearning. When I thought about Brisk
tears came to my eyes. Not because I was longing to return to Brisk

but rather because after the holidays I was going to ask to be allowed to stay home.

But the fact that my home seemed to have turned its kind face away from me also brought tears to my eyes. The fact that an entire summer had gone by and I had not seen the birds building their nests near my home, nor the departing flight of the stork, nor the scything of the meadows, nor the blooming of the water blossoms on the pond made my heart ache.

My mother was aware of my unhappiness, and she said, loudly enough for everyone in the house to hear, "I'm not letting him go back to Brisk. Let him stay at home. How can one send such a young child away? Surely that's not something God commanded."

It was evening, and the sun was going down. The breeze sent white spiderwebs and moths drifting over the trees that were nodding their heads at the departing sun. I felt suffused by a sense of longing. I felt how a distant world was reaching its arms out toward me to tear me away from my home, from Lippe's mill. That's how I felt on my return from Brisk. It was a feeling I was too young to understand without anguish.

During the Days of Awe, I wept bitterly as I recited my prayers, but it was not because of my sins that I prayed so piously, nor was it the fear of God that made my heart ache.

⤸ My Grandfather and the Old Cherry Tree

Just as the gray dew that, rising from the river after sundown, drifted toward our windows, cooling the warm summer evening, or as
the rising sun at dawn drew the cool dew from the river and called
up the fish from its depths to the water's mirrored surface, just so
did our human sorrows call up joys in their turn.

The spaces around Lippe's mill, my home, called across long
distances. The house, which was divided into two longish rooms,
apparently grew too crowded for the natural joys that came with
the growth of children. My mother fussed around her young like a
hen around her chicks. My father searched for kernels. Stiff, long
feathers started sprouting from the young chickens' wings.

It also looked as if the house were stretching out its neck,
standing on tiptoes to look over the railway to the unseen roads
that lay far beyond meadows and bogs, forests and sandy areas.

It was the nearly youngest child who started it off by going to
Brisk to study Torah. Even though the child had come back home,
he reminded everyone of other cities. Not distant ones, but distant
enough that he had only to depart to be relegated to the imagination of his parents and siblings. And he carried in his own imagination the smell of the mill and the ground grains, the look of the
dark-trunked, erect alder trees and the bent, tall, reedy weeping
willows bowing over the pond opposite his home's windows.

Worries came up as quietly as the dew rises on summer evenings after a hot day, covering the tranquility of the river. Joys disappeared with the last specks of summer light upon the already yellowing grass.

Life, for the first time and unexpectedly, brought tears to my sister Bebl's eyes. This happened while she was still very young and because love came to her out of the familiar meadows only to be choked off in the fall darkness. The young man to whom she was engaged was called up to do his four years of military service. For a while thereafter there was no further singing in our house, and the town girls no longer came during the day on Shabbos to dance the lancers, the mazurka, the polka, and Cossack dances on the grass between the pond and the mill.

A little while after that my brother Kalmen went off to do his army service for the tsar, and there was one more anxiety to bear because we worried that, given Kalmen's piety, he would die of hunger in the army without kosher food.

My brother Moyshe reminded us more and more frequently that there was no way for him to acquire a craft living in the mill. He wanted to go somewhere else, where he could learn a trade of his own.

One day, when there was no work at the mill, my father took the wagon somewhere so he could transport cargo and earn a little money with the horse. But he twisted his leg so badly he had to be driven back and carried into the house.

So the sun started coming up mournful at dawn, and the nights became more restless and dark. And the seasons started to get mixed together—spring, summer, fall, and winter. The summer days seemed to crawl away somewhere. And we observed suddenly that there were now wrinkles on my mother's youthful face. And my father sat, engrossed in thought, looking toward the railway line as a train went by.

There was still an element of delight in the house. My prattling youngest sister Soreh, like all children her age, required ten pairs of eyes to watch her lest she fall into the river. My mother paid with frequent headaches and toothaches for the pleasure Soreh gave us.

Just after Soreh's birth my mother acquired a withered look and her eyes grew wider, deeper. She suffered fierce toothaches, and because there was no dentist anywhere nearby she packed snuff into the ailing tooth to soothe the pain. As a result my delicate mother, looking like a yellowed autumn leaf, often lay stupefied and dejected as she waited for her toothache to subside, after which she would get up to resume her household duties.

Since my time in Brisk I had overcome the fear that had oppressed me as I made my way from town to the mill. And since Brisk, where I had seen the huge Mukhavets River, I no longer feared the depths of our stream.

At home I was now treated as a grown-up. I noticed my father was pleased by how manually skillful I had become, and he no longer worried that my work in the mill would damage the store of Torah in my head. Sometimes my father or mother asked me to do the sort of work that not so long ago they would only have asked of one of the older members of the family—to bring a heavy log into the house or stop the motion of the mill wheel or get it started. And I was now able to carry a couple of poods' weight of grain on my shoulders to the loft to drop into the hopper.

My father might say, "Peretz, go catch the horse." What that meant was that I had to catch the horse whose habit it was to bite or buck people off its back when they tried to ride it. It was a white horse, and it had a great many bad habits. More than once he had bucked me off his back when I mounted him. Once, meaning to bite my head, he chased me and snatched my hat off with his teeth.

I went to school daily, but no one took me there and no one came to take me home. Going to school in Kleshtshel was a compromise of my father's and mother's to keep me from leaving home, where life had turned gloomy. My father knew eventually I would be taken from the local teachers in any case and sent away to study alone. That departure from home could not be delayed much longer, but meanwhile he was anxious to keep me at home, at least until my bar mitzvah, while I studied with the prominent local teacher.

He was a good teacher who did not beat his pupils. It mattered little to him whether the children learned very much or not. He would catch a little snooze a couple of times a day while the children turned the yard outside the heder upside down. When he was not dozing he told old folktales and stories taken from the Tanakh and Talmud, and by this means he kept the children bound to the table during the time they were in school. On winter evenings he told more stories than he taught Gemara. I think of him as my last and best teacher, and the one who most stimulated my mind. Furthermore, when he taught Gemara, he made it seem both clear and sensible. And all the while I was nourishing my own secret thoughts regarding God and the world, life and death, this world and the world to come.

Happiness, for a brief while, knocked once again at our door. In the annual army lottery Kalmen had been lucky enough to win a discharge before a year was up. He came home a little before the holidays, worn out and terrified, looking like he had aged in the army because they forcibly stuffed his mouth with pork. He was not allowed to recite his prayers or wear his tefillin in the morning. His fellow soldiers yanked at his young, blond beard.

Kalmen had come back home, but in the meantime he had also had a taste of the great world. On maneuvers he had seen cities and towns. The result was that he too, like Moyshe, though in a much quieter fashion than Moyshe, announced that there was no future for him in the mill, and he thought it might be well to look about for some way to learn a craft somewhere else, away from the mill.

My oldest brother, Binyomin Khayem, who was a dyer in town, had a child who was lame. Some while later that child's mother, Khaye Rivke, died. Her death touched our home, sending a thin, piercing chill of sorrow through it. There were now orphan grandchildren in town. New cares for my mother.

Winter, summer, and then winter once again. I've already described the old cherry tree growing behind our barn—our only cherry tree, near which there grew a plum sapling.

The cherry tree had twin trunks that united near the ground. It was an old tree. Even when I was four or five years old, I could easily climb up into it, though many times I cried for help when I caught my foot in the cleft where the trunks fused. Even before my time the tree had borne few cherries. There were times, however, when three or four of them, first green then red, peeped out from among the sparse leaves of its branches. In later years half of the tree began to wither. It grew so dry that the wind was able to break off many of its branches. Half of the tree was left dried out and leafless. We had little impulse to break off any of its withered branches and little desire to saw the dried half of the tree down.

It made me sad that each time I looked at the cherry tree there came into my mind the image of my grandfather Yehoshua, who was already 103 years old. Though he still had the blond hair of a younger man, he was now fearful of the coming of winter, and his melodies were stilled. One day he said to me, "Grandson, sing me the speckled melody." He always liked how I sang the speckled melody, which had a distant feel to it. It was the only one he asked me to sing. One had to begin it softly, softly: *"Dai-dai. Dai-dai-dai-dai. Oy, dai-dai-dai, dai-dai-dai-im."* It was a melody that seemed to get nearer when it was sung four or five times. Each rendering was a little more sprightly, warmer, until you had to tap your feet and clap your hands to keep time.

True, apart from losing one of his middle upper teeth a few years earlier, no other tooth had fallen out of his mouth. However, the days of his life took on an end-of-summer, twilit, clouded aspect. As spring came he was no longer able to shake the chill from his bones. On Shabbos during the day, even in the month of July, he would yearn for the warm oven on which toward evening he would lie.

Still, a hidden force appeared to blossom in him the way a branch on the old cherry tree would blossom to produce, later, a couple of cherries. My grandfather would occasionally take up the ax and make a decent little fire out of twigs. Or he would sit on the driver's bench in the wagon and wave his whip over the white horse's back.

The horse, knowing full well who was sitting there and whose hand was wielding the whip, showed no fear. "Ah, you son of a bitch. You think I can't handle this whip? You son of a bitch."

Gradually the distance from the mill to the shtetl became longer and longer for him. Leaving aside the impossibility of going into town to the synagogue for daily prayers, it was beginning to be hard for him to go there even for Shabbos prayers. To the family he justified his waning desire to go into town on the grounds that the causeway was muddy and that one could pray perfectly well at home.

Each day he slept a little longer on his bench beside the window that looked out on the willow trees beside the pond. And each day he cherished the bed itself a little more. In very good weather he would get out of bed and leave the house, but he never went any great distance, though he always brought back some sticks of wood for the household.

Often his glance would turn toward the shelves full of books over the window. "Peretz, pull down a Humash for me. Peretz, pull down the old prayer book for me, the one with the pages missing in front."

In the old prayer book over whose letters my grandfather's eyes, with spectacles or without them, had wandered over many years, there were yellowing pages on which the Psalms were printed in large letters, and it was toward those pages that he was drawn.

One overcast Shabbos, when the morning had made its leisurely way into the house and touched the cold oven, my grandfather, from his sleeping bench, announced to the family, "The sun's not going to come out today." Then, looking up at us from his bed with deeply frightened, unhappy eyes, he said, "Wouldn't it be simple justice to send for someone to heat up the oven?"

My mother took a jug down from the oven and poured out a glass of hot tea, which she sweetened for him with raspberry syrup. She held the cup to his lips. He took one sip, then another, and then would drink no more.

"What a foolish world," he said, looking out the window at the overcast sky. Then, with a smile, "Evidently, a man isn't truly turned to dust."

My father stood near him. My mother, and all of us grandchildren, watched him closely. He looked at us standing around his bed, then his gaze wandered from one corner of the room to another. He looked up at the ceiling and noticed a spiderweb in the corner facing him. "Strange. Until now, I never noticed that spiderweb. And a spider in the web. Ha. Never noticed it till now."

Then, his eyes on his grandchildren, he said, "Children grow-ing. The house gets crowded. You, Moyshe, you won't be a soldier. I'll see to it. You won't have to serve." With that abrupt remark he frightened Moyshe, who just then was wiping tears from his eyes.

For the next couple of hours Grandfather Yehoshua lay still. He slept peacefully, a look of great calm on his face.

We exchanged glances, understanding what was happening and at the same time not understanding that grandfather was getting ready to leave us, to leave the house, to leave the bench on which he had slept for so many years. Through the four panes of the window near which my grandfather lay the gray evening whis-pered, "It's the last time he'll be sleeping on that bed."

My grandfather woke once more before Shabbos ended. He looked at us sadly, his half-clouded eyes moving from one pale grandchild to the next as we stood gathered around his bed. Then he turned to look out of the window. As he gazed at the frozen wil-low trees by the pond, they stirred their branches for him. After that he straightened his limbs, sighed quietly, and closed his eyes forever.

🙠 I Become Bar Mitzvah

That summer we had guests. Uncles and aunts arrived to find out how we were.

The first to come was my uncle Moyshe Linever from Orle. With him came my aunt Blume Rokhl, my father's only sister just as he was her only brother. Though grandfather had lived to be more than a hundred years old, he had never had more than these two children.

This was the first visit my father had with his sister since grandfather's death. As soon as she crossed the threshold and my father saw her they were both gripped by a deep sorrow. They wept helplessly, like children, and sat for a long while broken down, sobbing occasionally, their heads bowed, their whole bodies trembling.

My uncle Moyshe Linever, that hidden saint with the heavy eyebrows and the long, graying brown beard, sat bowed as well, his eyes hidden beneath his eyebrows, while the rest of us, each in our own corner, shared their grief.

It was my mother who first broke the silence. "He lived like a holy man, and he died like one, going to sleep like a child. God grant us to live to his old age. He led such a decent life. He wouldn't hurt a fly. And then to die so peacefully."

All of us looked up at mother, whose face, as she spoke, seemed transfigured. The color came back into her cheeks, and there was a gleam of exaltation in her eyes.

We spoke of how the house seemed empty since grandfather had gone. Little by little, we began to talk about the health of children and of our nearest relatives.

The change to a lighter mood could be read in the changed expressions on our faces. Finally the talk turned to me and where to send me to continue my studies.

My father said, "There are no teachers for him in Kleshtshel. The time he spends with the local teacher is time wasted."

My uncle arched his eyebrows and said, "Orle would be good for him. Now that we actually live in Orle."

My aunt added, "I'd look after him as if he were my own child, of course."

My uncle, who was a leaseholder in the vicinity of Orle and who delivered milk to the town, had moved into the town itself.

This prompted my father to say that he liked Orle. But my mother observed that Orle seemed a bit far: fourteen versts from our town. "Yes, Orle seems a bit far."

It was easy to see that my mother was not pleased at the prospect of my leaving home. "We can discuss the matter when the holidays come around. God grant we live that long."

Later that same summer, my uncle Avrom Tumener, who worked a rented estate in the Visoke-Litovsk region, arrived. His dark beard was a little shorter, his peyos a little shorter than my other uncles'. As was his custom when he came to visit, he brought butter and cheeses, which my aunt Soreh, my mother's youngest sister, had sent. And as we always did when he arrived, we heated up the samovar so he could empty it as he sat drinking cup after cup of tea.

Looking me over, my uncle began by saying, "Of course, Peretz will have to go to some other city to study. Maybe he could come to Visoke. I'm there practically every week, so I could look in on him. Sometimes he could come home to Tumene with me for Shabbos. Sheyndl wanted to come with me on this trip because she wanted to see Peretz. She wants to see Peretz's handwriting. Her script is as beautiful as her grandfather's."

"Visoke is a bit far," said my father. "It's a full three miles and twenty-one versts. We almost never have any reason to go there."

"It's half an hour by train. All it costs is twenty-eight groschen," my uncle insisted.

A while after that my uncle Yoel Talviner, who lived in Semyatitsh, came to visit us for the first time. He was the husband of my mother's younger sister, Khaye Fayge. He was received as a great guest. Uncle Yoel was a tall man with a little blond beard. His side curls were twisted and long, like corkscrews. He walked about wearing white stockings and slippers. He was a Hasid and was talented musically.

Since in those days there were no trains yet to places like Semyatitsh, my uncle Yoel had never seen a train. He came to us in the evening riding in a rented wagon. The first passenger train of the day was due to pass our mill on its way from Bialystok to Brisk at six o'clock in the morning. My uncle Yoel didn't sleep a wink that night lest he miss the passing train. For his sake, the rest of us got up two hours earlier than usual to wait for the train, which would blow its whistle as it left the forest. My uncle became all eyes and ears. He stood outside the house gazing toward the embankment with his hand at his ear. The tension affected us all as if we too were about to see a train rushing by for the first time. When he heard it my uncle was transported into seventh heaven. He seemed to grow a full head taller; he stood on tiptoes, his mouth open, his little beard pointing out. As the train rushed by, my uncle recited a blessing in honor of the great wonder he had seen.

Uncle Yoel's advice was to send me to study in Semyatitsh because that's where Aunt Khayeh Fayge lived and because Semyatitsh was a town populated entirely by scholars. But Semyatitsh was far away, very far away, a total distance of twenty-seven versts.

None of us had ever been there, so none of us had ever seen Aunt Khaye Fayge. Nor had she ever come to us. As my father saw it, Semyatitsh was much, much farther away than Visoke.

It was already late in the summer when my uncle Avrom Hersh arrived from Meleytshitsh. He was the husband of my mother's youngest sister, Broshe. My uncle Avrom Hersh had been for many years a considerable personage among lumber dealers. He was a forest person who year in and year out studied trees. He was a slender man with a tiny blond beard and erect carriage, and he had the bluest of blue eyes. He seemed never to sit down but stood like a young pine tree, his head straight and a smile in his eyes.

He was a welcome guest. His advice was that Peretz should only be sent to Meleytshitsh. First because my mother's parents, Grandfather Yossl Itzl and my grandmother Peshe Reyzl, lived there. And then because my grandfather possessed a good little store of Torah himself that he could give me. While he, my uncle, and my aunt Broshe—never mind. Meleytshitsh! Only Meleytshitsh. No other option. After the holidays, send Peretz to Meleytshitsh.

The color came into my mother's face. She was delighted—no, enchanted—that the course of my life would take me to the town where she was born. She agreed at once. "God willing, after the holiday I'll take him there myself. I'll arrange meals for him with my old girlfriends. Why didn't I think of that before? To send him to Meleytshitsh."

In a very simple way a city came into existence that was, for me, far from home and yet not far from home. For my mother t seemed like a coincidence that she ended up having both her parents alive in her true home city. So everyone started making plans to send me to Meleytshitsh.

Meanwhile it was agreed I should stay at home until after the holidays. I would turn thirteen on the fourth day of Kislev. A month before that I would start putting on tefillin as required by religious law. So I would become bar mitzvah on the fourth day of Heshvan. That would be just the right time for me to leave home.

My father, in anticipation of that event, bought me a large pair of used tefillin from a bookseller. And I soon learned how to use them. My thoughts now turned to my departure, and I began to neglect attending the local school, but my father did not mind. He nodded when my mother said, "Let the boy stay around the house."

To please my mother he pretty much let me have my own way and looked on benignly as I wandered idly over the meadows or in the woods to gather raspberries for my mother, who wanted to make raspberry syrup. The syrup, used for medicinal purposes, was intended as a present for my grandmother. Though God grant she would have no need to use it in that way.

In those days and in those places where faith grew, as it were, like green grass by the wayside, becoming bar mitzvah was no small matter. Like the green grass, God was visible in every direction, keeping an eye on where people went and what they did. Until he became bar mitzvah, a boy was under the control of his parents. If the boy sinned, the consequences of his sin fell upon his parents' shoulders. And so he need not worry about punishment so long as he was in his parents' care. Though I did not think of myself as a particularly great sinner, I found it much easier to commit some prank or other so long as I believed God would not punish me directly.

That year, before I became bar mitzvah, on the fast days that come on the seventeenth day of Tammuz, when we commemorate the siege of Jerusalem by Nebuchadnezzar, and on the ninth of Av, when we mourn the destruction of the Temple, my mother secretly brought me food, so I fasted only for half a day. As she always did, she said, "Eat, eat, my child. Let the sin be upon my head. Just don't let your father see you eating . . ."

My last days at heder were burdensome to me. I was no longer content to sit among my friends listening as each one recited Gemara texts in his own fashion. Nor was I content to while away whole days in the company of such students, who were busy inventing new ways to trick our teacher.

The direction of my life was already marked for me. To go alone. To study alone. To rummage by myself through the huge mountain of books that was called the Talmud and all of its commentaries. To establish for myself that student's schedule we called "eating days." Seven days a week, to eat each day in a different household. How could I ever manage it? How could I sit at the tables of strangers, every day at a different table? I had been shy all my life, the way everyone was in my family. I was averse to getting help from strangers. I was particularly uncomfortable in other people's homes.

My mother would often pray, "Lord, do with me what thou

wilt, but keep me from having to depend on strangers." But how else was one to achieve Torah study? How else, except by "eating days," was a boy whose parents sent him away from home going to amount to something? For my father my destiny was clear: I would be a rabbi. It was by no means so clear to my mother. One thing she knew for certain: no practical good would come from keeping me at home beyond, eventually, turning me into a miller. She had heard, however, that no matter how disruptive it was for boys to live with total strangers, if they were sent away from home they might eventually become a credit both to God and man. So she was happy to think that from now on I would be living near my grand-father, Reb Yossl Itzl, whom she respected and in whose wisdom and way of life she had great faith. She excused his poverty as well as the decision he had made to not become a rabbi.

"God willing, after the holidays, I myself will take you to your grandfather. We'll go on foot, taking our time. We'll pick out a fine day and start out at dawn. If we go with a wagon, the trip will take three hours. God willing, we'll start out early and make a nice walk of it. It's been so many years since I've been home. Yes. Yes, we'll go on foot." Her face glowed like a young girl's when she described the journey to Meleytshitsh we would make together.

The holidays came and went. I recited my prayers alone, en-grossed in thought. There was a heavy pair of tefillin waiting to be used. The road my mother and I would travel on foot was waiting for me. Joy and fear jostled each other in my mind. Joy and fear and a profound longing that overwhelmed me as I wandered in the vicinity of the mill and watched the passing of summer. It was not my last summer under the weeping willows, nor was it the last time my life could be heard sounding together with the stream whose waters turned the wheels of the mill. But it was the last summer I would spend still guided by my father and mother.

⫷ On Foot to Meleytshitsh

The cold, thick dew that had lain for more than half the night on the fall meadows faded away under the purifying warmth of the young sun that rose above the leafless alder trees facing Lippe's mill. The illuminated millpond lay calmly reflecting the wooded banks. At the end of summer and after the falling of the autumn leaves, the mill, my home and birthplace, seemed more open, more exposed in every direction.

The whole family was gathered before the house. All of us, young and old, looked westward, taking in the yellow-green meadows that reached the horizon as if we were seeing them for the first time. Occasionally here and there we caught a distant glimpse of the dark outline of a few trees and low stumps clustered in a grove.

My father Lippe, then Kalmen, Moyshe, Bebl, and the youngest of us, five-year-old Soreh, were all trying to make out the path across the damp meadows, the shortcut that would make it easier to get to the highway that led to Meleytshitsh.

If one went into the shtetl and from there to Goshtshinyetz, one added three versts to the journey, but if one crossed the muddy fields toward the windmills near where the highway ran, the distance was shorter by a whole verst. However, if one walked due west, where the summer sun went down, one could reach the village of Prohobi, six versts from our mill, after which it was only six versts from there to Meleytshitsh. Besides, Urtshe Prohobier lived in Prohobi, and we could pause for a rest at his house. But that way was unfamiliar to us because there was no path from our house to Prohobi. We only knew we had to go due west, crossing meadows and muddy fields, and we would reach Prohobi and avoid the shtetl.

When we had explored with our eyes every trail made by herds of livestock and their herdsmen, or by barefoot walkers seeking a shortcut, when we had made imaginary maps of them with our hands on the blue air it was finally decided how we should head for Prohobi. Then everyone turned to look at us, the two barefoot travelers who would shortly start off across the autumn fields and from there to sandy Goshtshinyetz, from which we could reach Meleytshitsh.

My mother, Sheyne, and her bar mitzvah boy Peretz were about to start on their way. Since the days were already getting shorter, there was very little time to lose. And since the ostensible reason my mother was going with me was so she could visit her father and mother, grandfather Yossl Itzl and grandmother Peshe Reyzl, in Meleytshitsh, the family had managed to forget that this journey across meadows and bogs was the true beginning of the longer, uncertain journey that would take this bar mitzvah boy away from a life among trees and meadows to another life in the narrow confines of synagogues.

That lovely gift of a clear fall morning changed the expressions on the faces of the family standing there. Instead of looks of sorrow or longing there was an unexpected glow of excitement on every face.

I stood there barefoot with my shoes, tied together by their shoelaces, slung over my left shoulder. Over my right shoulder I carried a stick from which hung a bundle of clothes wrapped in a scarf—a few shirts and underwear, my tefillin, and a little winter coat with an astrakhan collar. My mother, standing beside me, was also barefoot. Her shoes too were tied together and slung over her left shoulder. Over her right shoulder, in a bundle tied to a stick, there was, among other presents for my grandparents, a bottle of the raspberry syrup she had made herself.

It was thus that we crossed the first ditch near our house and moved off with the meadows along the banks of our own stream. Behind us, when we looked back, we could still see the little cluster of family standing and gazing after the two travelers, who had by now climbed over a fence and were already moving along a dark path beaten down by the herdsmen and cattle that ambled about in the recently harvested fields.

It was late fall. Though the sun was shining, this early in the morning it did not have sufficient heat to warm the damp fields. When your naked foot sank into the wet turf you could feel a hidden icy cold that already presaged the coming of winter.

For a while we both walked in silence. Only then did we feel our throats constricting and a warm glow spread out on our cheeks. Only then did our hearts sink and our eyes cloud over as we passed through the district's wide expanse of green and yellow fields. For some three hours before noon we walked with the sun behind us, our faces in shadow. I wanted my mother to speak as a way of easing the fatigue that overwhelmed me as the distance spread its arms out toward us.

It was then I noticed how my mother's legs, bare to the knees, seemed to move restlessly, warily. She kept her anxious eyes fixed on the western horizon, her whole being focused on that direction like a bird that has left earth and whose attention is now fixed on the rim of the sky. Her cheeks were pale, her face longer and thinner than I was used to seeing it. As if her slender body had been seized by a wind, it strove westward leaving the mill behind, where Lippe the miller, Kalmen, Bebl, Moyshe, and little Soreh still stood looking after the wanderers getting smaller and smaller as they moved farther away, looking now like a couple of uprooted trees on their way to the place where the summer sun sets.

My mother heaved a deep sigh. She said, with a worried look, "If you are tired, my child, we can sit on this dry little hill for a while." Without waiting for my reply she sat down to catch her breath on a hillock covered with yellow growth. It was clear to me that neither her fatigue nor mine had anything to do with walking. We had not, after all, gone so very far. What accounted for our fatigue was our leaving home. Surely my mother had lain awake the last few nights before leading her child away from home. I had also lain awake. It made us both tired.

She studied me now as if for the first time. Wiping the sweat from my forehead with one hand, she removed my cap with the other and stroked my hair. After an interval, she said, "Of course, child, we could have taken the trip by wagon. It would have been much easier. But I hope we'll arrive in Meleytshitsh today. Do you see, Peretz, how tiny our mill looks from this distance?"

I could think of nothing to say. I liked that we were making the trip on foot, though I could see it was hard for my mother. I could not understand her excitement. She went on, "We're sitting here, my child, as snug as can be. Didn't even have time to get any news from Meleytshitsh. It's nearly ten years since I was last there. Do you see what a wide world is spread out before us? There is no end to the distance, and yet we're as far away as ever from the edge of the sky. Strange how tired I've gotten. Let's get moving again." Her cheeks were flushed, a touch of color encircled by an ashen, emaciated pallor.

We got up and resumed our journey. We skirted Lapinski's mill, which shared the same river as our own. We crossed a fairly deep ditch, wading up to our knees in reddish mud. From time to time we startled a bird sitting hidden among piles of earth. The bird flapped its wings, rose into the sky, and disappeared into the morning calm.

"When I was young, my child, I too felt the pull of the wider world. But without wings one spends one's years in the same place. Yes, things might have been different. And yet I get to see a child of mine climbing his way out of the mire and into that wider world. I hope you'll do well away from home."

We came out upon a hard, narrow strip of overgrazed field—an unfamiliar area with stiff, dry, spiky grass that stabbed at our bare feet. In the distance rows of geese etched white lines on the field. A cool eastern breeze toyed with their feathers. Along the entire length of the field was a loosely constructed three-railed fence.

Off to the west some yellow-brown thatched roofs could be seen. There were still a couple of versts to go before we would come to the village of Prohobi. My mother suggested we should rest a bit longer behind the fence so we wouldn't have to stay too long at Urtshe's house in Prohobi. "Truth be told, I'd just as soon not stop anywhere. But we must stop at Urtshe's for a while."

Urtshe of Prohobi was a relative of my father's. Though we had never been to his house, we knew Urtshe, a sturdy villager with a wide, red beard who, when he came to Kleshtshel, walked across the boggy fields in his bare feet the way we were doing now. When he came to our mill he would wash his muddy feet in the river, then put his boots on and come into the house to say good morning. So there was no way that, passing through Prohobi, we could avoid his house. But my mother did not want to stay long enough to eat anything.

So we sat for a while longer behind the fence. My mother took a piece of rye bread out of her bundle and some pickles. We "washed" our hands by rubbing them in the grass, then refreshed our flagging spirits. A rabbit darted out from somewhere and stopped quite near us, stunned to see us sitting there behind the fence. He twitched an ear, then scooted back to wherever it was he came from.

My mother laughed. "He's afraid of everything. If he had come closer we'd have given him some of our bread."

My mother, feeling better because she had eaten, turned garrulous. She told me how hard it had been for her to divorce her first husband. "What was there to be done, since so many of my children died? Four were born, one after the other, and all four died." She said she'd like sometime to visit Mezritsh, where her first husband lived. She also wished she could visit Semyatitsh, where her sister lived. She told me about my father's son by his first wife, Yankev Mordkhe, who died of fright and whom I was said to resemble.

"It's a good thing you'll be staying with your grandfather. It won't be as if you're entirely among strangers. He'll love you. I just know he'll love you." We didn't stay long in Urtshe's house. Urtshe was not at home. His wife, a heavy woman, and a daughter who resembled her oohed and aahed over us, expressing amazement at our walking barefoot. "All the way to Meleytshitsh on foot. Oh my ... oh my ... Well, if children give joy, one can fly for their sake."

When we left the local dogs accompanied us some distance from the village. We barefoot travelers were a wonder that roused their ire. The dogs excited me too, and as in the good old days I showed them the way back to the village.

At this point, having passed Prohobi, we were half the distance to Meleytshitsh. From here on we were on the broad, sandy Goshtshinyetz road. Here and there were pine trees, a wonder to us both because there were no pines anywhere in the vicinity of our mill.

"What a fine smell the pines have. Just like in Meleytshitsh. Just wait till you see the Meleytshitsh forest. It's right next to the town. I hope you'll go into the forest, dear, the way I loved to do."

The sand was warm, so it was not as good walking in it with our bare feet as it had been crossing the wet fields. The way ahead seemed very long. A new fatigue assailed us, rendering us both silent. Then, as we approached Meleytshitsh, my mother's eyes widened. Her appearance changed. Her face looked younger, as if she had shed a great load of years, as she approached the shtetl where she was born.

"We'll have to find some sort of water near the shtetl so we can wash our feet and put on shoes and stockings."

We found just the brook we were looking for; my mother remembered it from when she was a child. As we washed our feet and our faces and stretched our legs, I began to feel some of my mother's excitement. Suddenly I felt very warm.

We put our shoes and socks on and were ready to go. My mother said, "I see you're warm. I am too, all of a sudden ... We're here in Meleytshitsh, my child. Let's rest for a while on this stone. When I was a girl I used to come for a walk this way with my girlfriends. We used to sit on this very stone." And there, on that stone, my mother took me in her arms and pressed me to her. I could feel the swift beating of her heart. Mine too beat wildly.

The sun was going down, and the shadows of the Meleytshitsh houses stretched in our direction. It was hard to get to our feet. It was as if we had taken root in the stone. I looked about, taking in the strangeness of the place. My mother's gaze encompassed the shtetl where she was born and where her youth had blossomed.

My Mother Meets Her Childhood

My mother's excitement infected me. I felt as if hot winds were blowing over my nerves. The stone on which I sat seemed to glow. The shtetl of Meleytshitsh and the dense pine forest were gazing at us. We had trouble getting to our feet.

My mother was not yet old. She was hardly forty. But in the interval since she had left her native shtetl and her present return to it, she had lived some very hard years. She had buried seven children before their time. How often had I heard her murmur, "Lost. Those years are lost, fallen in the mud like autumn leaves."

The sun had gone beyond the pine forest and descended to the left into the shtetl, illuminating the tops of the trees. A cool, easterly breeze blew thick above the autumn ground and reminded us it would make sense to finally set our eyes on Meleytshitsh for real.

Now, almost in Meleytshitsh, my mother's slender body trembled. Her eyes glowed as from behind a mist. "Ah, here it is, dear. The pine forest where I used to run about among the trees when I was a child. It looks like they've cut down a lot of trees since then. And the forest looks a bit older. How long has it been? It seems as if it were only yesterday. And now I'm taking you to Meleytshitsh. In the summertime nothing can compare to this forest. It's a health-giving forest. Sick people come here in summer and get well."

We dusted off our clothes. We had already put our shoes and socks on. My mother had taken out my warm, black coat with its astrakhan collar. She smoothed out its wrinkles and told me to put it on. She patted smooth her thick, dark-brown hair. She adjusted her head covering and the shawl on her shoulders. Our bundles were now in our hands; the sticks on which we had carried them were thrown away. With considerable screwed-up courage she turned her face and her steps toward town. I anxiously clung to her side.

"It's strange. I wonder if I'll meet any of my old girlfriends in the street and if they will recognize me. Yes, it's very strange to see how the shtetl will look."

I remembered the Book of Ruth and how Naomi and her daughter-in-law returned after many years to Bethlehem and how Naomi recognized her old friends. They recognized her too and skeptically asked, "Is that Naomi?"

Just as we turned into the lightly paved, sandy main street bordered on both sides by low houses, some with thatched roofs, a middle-aged woman carrying an empty pitcher came toward us. Evidently she was on her way to the well for water. The woman, seeing us and our bundles, stopped, blood rushing to her face. My mother, who was leading me by the hand, stopped abruptly, as if someone had struck her. Both of the women stared.

The woman dropped her empty pitcher and my mother dropped her bundle. They flung themselves into each other's arms. They wept and laughed. In their eyes and faces there was a sudden bloom of youth.

"Sheyne, Peshe Reyzl's daughter! I can't believe it."

"Do you see, Peretz? This is my old friend with whom I used to go into the woods every evening in the summertime. And this is my youngest son, Peretz. He's named after his aunt Perl, may she rest in peace. I'm taking him to his grandfather."

The stranger looked me over. A look of maternal tenderness came over her fair features. She took me into her arms and hugged and kissed me. "He's so pale, Sheyne. They say you live in a water mill. Isn't there anything to eat in a water mill?"

"What a fuss you're making." My mother caressed my cheek.

"Even if we fed him nothing but honey cake his face would still be pale."

"Yes, yes. You're all like that. How are you? And how is Bro-she? Oh my, if your mother and father only knew you were already here."

My mother turned sprightly, awake and filled with fresh energy, as if under the stranger's gaze she had been born again.

"No doubt he'll be studying in our study house. And he'll need eating days," the woman went on. "Let him eat his first day with me. Let him eat with me on Shabbos. It'll be a pleasure to have him in my house on one of his days. I'll tell my husband about it right away."

"Yes, of course he'll need eating days. But his grandfather will undoubtedly want him on Shabbos."

"Well, then, let it be Friday. I don't mind what day it is."

And that was how I was provided with a Friday at the moment of my entrance into the town. That care for me made my mother glow. We strode along the street on our way to my grandfather's house. She was hardly recognizable as my mother.

The evening was beginning to darken; men were making their slow way to the synagogue for the evening service. We arrived at a long, low house that had a garden behind it in which green cabbage heads looked out at the evening.

When we neared the house my mother, like a little girl, ran toward it. It turned out that at my grandfather's they had known we were coming and had been staring their eyes out for days watching for us. My mother had sent word to my grandfather via several passing Meleytshitsh residents who had come to the Monday market in Kleshtshel.

My grandfather, who had several grown students sitting around the table with him, sent them home the minute we arrived. My grandmother, a tiny bundle of goodness, ran from one corner to another, confused about how to greet her guests. She flung her arms around her daughter. She wanted to pick her grandson up, but that turned out to be too hard to do. My grandfather shoved his skullcap back on his head, revealing his broad, shiny forehead. The twin tips of his gray beard fluttered in the breeze.

"What a strange notion, to come on foot. Can't one get a wagon to Meleytshitsh? And what kept you from harnessing up your own horse?"

Indeed, it was hard to explain why we had walked such a great distance.

"I couldn't have managed it," my grandmother said, touching me all over. "To take such a tender chick and lead him such a long way. I have to run over to tell Broshe that Sheyndl and Peretz have come."

At that moment a white goat with a long white beard came into the house through the open door. Shaking its beard, it looked the guests over, sensing the unusual excitement in the room, then turned its attention to a flat sheet of rolled-out noodle dough that was on the bed. Putting its forelegs on the bed, the goat seized the sheet of dough in its teeth and ran off with it.

"Oh, the Lord preserve us. Yossl Itzl, she's snatched the dough again! Run and catch her. Maybe you can still save the noodles . . ."

My grandfather laughed heartily. We laughed along with him, but he did not chase after the goat. My grandmother ran after it and came back a minute later, empty-handed. She grumbled, "That goat is sucking my blood. And my husband thinks it's funny. What doesn't a goat eat? The minute I roll out dough for noodles, the goat appears. I need ten eyes to protect it, and he thinks it's funny."

My grandmother had sent someone to tell my aunt Broshe that Sheyndl had arrived. My aunt Broshe, even more diminutive than my mother and with an even narrower face, darted into the house and clasped my mother to her. The two women, who had not seen each other in some ten years, were both transformed into little girls in their parents' home. I found it wonderful to watch my mother here within the walls among whose shadows she had grown.

When the women had eased their hearts—sometimes with tears, sometimes with laughter, informing each other of recent babies and recent deaths, while silence was taking over from laughter and cries of joy were taking over from sighs and sorrows, my grandfather, sitting beside the table near the long shelf filled with books, turned his attention to his grandson who had come on foot to visit him in Meleytshitsh. Stroking my cheek, he said, "They say you're a good student on your own, so it looks as if you'll be studying in the study house without a teacher. If you're diligent, you'll do well in Meleytshitsh."

My eyes ranged among the books on the shelves. I could see there were more than just Gemaras on them. There were commentaries as well. I had often looked into such books and had difficulty understanding the main issues in them. I was amazed to see my grandfather owned Maimonides's *Guide for the Perplexed*.

My mother recounted how she had met her friend in the street and how she had insisted that Peretz must eat with her either on Shabbos, or at least on Friday. My grandmother and my aunt Broshe would not hear of it. "What are you talking about? You're going to let Peretz eat days in Meleytshitsh? He'll eat with me," my aunt Broshe insisted.

"He'll live here and he'll eat here," my grandmother maintained.

Slowly my grandfather explained the tradition of eating days. He spoke of the passage in *Ethics of the Fathers,* "Thou shalt eat bread with salt . . ." To eat days was not the same as begging; it did not mean being dependent on others. There was no shame in eating days. On the contrary, the Torah enjoined it. "If one sincerely means to study Torah, he ought not to live in luxury." What was the point of bringing Peretz to Meleytshitsh? There was plenty to eat at home, and Kleshtshel had a synagogue with books in it. And yet his mother had brought him here. That's because the only way to make something of a boy is to send him away. To make him eat days; to make him sleep on a bench in the house of study.

My mother, who had utter faith in what my grandfather said, was silent, thereby giving her assent to his words. My grandfather was right. Meleytshitsh, not my grandfather's house, was my mother's goal in bringing me here.

"His best home is away from home," my grandfather went on. "Home? Grandparents? Uncles, aunts? He doesn't need them. On Shabbos he'll be with us; Fridays with you, Broshe, and five days of the week he'll be with others."

There followed a silence. It seemed to me that my grandfather's house, the house in which my mother was born, was now also a part of that near yet distant world called "away from home."

✍ Among Strangers

My grandfather, Reb Yossl Itzl, did not become my friend. He was the exact opposite of my grandfather Yehoshua, on whose lap I had often sat and with whom I had often sung his melodies. Grandfather Yossl Itzl was an erect, stern, learned man with a thin-lipped smile. He had very little use for the real world. He wanted to be beholden to no one, not even his own children. He taught Torah to several older boys. He interpreted the biblical text with lucid intelligence. He made the Gemara seem simple and clear. He seemed to me to resemble a living, rigidly bound book that moved about with measured steps.

My tiny grandmother, Peshe Reyzl, frequently had to put up with my grandfather's "Leave me alone!" Particularly in the matter of the goat, which he hated to see come into the house though it gave four glasses of milk a day. He always ended up laughing when the white goat, shaking its beard, came into the house. He didn't care at all that the goat slipped in and snatched up a piece of dough from the kneading trough or a sheet of noodle dough from the bed.

He was a tidy man. Though he took snuff, the two tips of his white beard never showed any signs of tobacco. Perhaps my mother inherited her skepticism, her minimal piety from him. Who knows? In the synagogue he had very little inclination to be with the people at the eastern wall. He recited his prayers without pretense of any kind. He always had a sharp word to say whenever the conduct of any of the shtetl folk displeased him.

It may be that my grandfather thought that no particular good would come of my becoming a study house inmate, a bench sitter. He talked with more affection of his sons and grandsons who lived by the labor of their own hands.

My eating days were easily arranged. My mother, who a few days later went back to Kleshtshel by wagon, arranged a couple of them for me herself. My grandfather introduced me to the shammes of the synagogue. He was a Hasid with long, curly black peyos, a black beard, and blazing, dark eyes. He was kind to me and showed me the place in the synagogue where I could settle to do my studying, and he arranged the four eating days that I still needed. Besides that, he offered me a job that would net me six groschen a week.

"Since the books are pulled down from the shelves every morning and left lying about, your job will be to gather them up at night, when everyone has gone away, and put each one back in its proper place."

I liked that. I took the job not so much for the six groschen as for the opportunity to put those hundreds of books in order—volumes of the Talmud in all sorts of sizes and bindings. And I had the chance to look into each of the books before I put them back into place. I kept the volumes in fine order and more than earned my six groschen. Every Friday the shammes paid me my wages as he caressed my cheek. In the synagogue, my spot was closer to the stove.

I began to live on my own, with my own silence. To me the atmosphere in the synagogue was a bit too much like a marketplace. In Kleshtshel, when I went to synagogue to pray with the older family members, I had my home outside of the synagogue. In Kleshtshel, none of the members of my family was too fond of the shtetl or the people who lived there. We thought the shtetl was too tumultuous. Whenever any of us went to the market on a Monday, they returned home exhausted. On Monday evenings, after she had come back weary from the market, my mother would say, "I'm not going next week. I don't care if Elijah the Prophet is waiting for me there with a fortune." Home was where all of us found peace. I too found peace there.

Now that the synagogue was my home—apparently I had found no true second home at my grandfather's house—I observed with my very young eyes the people who came into the synagogue three times a day to pray and the clamor they created every morning, afternoon, and evening. The marketplace atmosphere came with them. The worshiper rushed in distracted; he grabbed a book from the bookshelf, scanned the text, sang a couple of phrases from the prayers, and glanced at a tractate of the Gemara. I quailed watching them. The moment the congregation arrived I made my way to the stove near the door, repelled by the frightful way they leafed through the large pages of the Gemara. To keep from watching them I kept my eyes fixed on the pages of my Tanakh text.

Still, there were two people I watched with special interest. One of them was the rabbi of Meleytshitsh, with his long, snow-white beard that covered his chest. His blue eyes had a genial glow. He walked so gently as he came in it seemed the books on the shelves murmured as they noted his quiet arrival. His image lingers in my memory.

I remember too the image of his son-in-law, a yeshiva student from Volozhin with pale, transparent features, a thin little beard that was so black it looked blue, and eyes that were dark and thoughtful. The rabbinical chair of Meleytshitsh was waiting for him. He was already contributing to the journal *Ha-Melits* (*The Advocate*). His pen name was Ehad Ha-Rabanim Ha-Margishim, which means "one of the concerned rabbis." His moral stature was later to make him the most famous rabbi of his age. The rabbi and his son-in-law looked at me kindly. The old rabbi greeted me, which unsettled me for a while. The son-in-law sometimes patted my shoulder, and once or twice, without saying a word, he caressed my cheek.

But I felt like a sapling that had been plucked out of the earth by its roots. Many of the roots had survived the sharp tug from the ground, while many had been torn. The remnants remained in the earth, feeling pain. In my solitude, some part of me was suffering.

I felt diminished in my own eyes. I was a small Jew in the midst of grown, restless Jews who came hurriedly into the synagogue three times a day to pray.

And what is there to say about eating days in Meleytshitsh? Every day I was in a different home. It was not good to cross a different threshold every day and then wait for some member of the family to take notice of me, to reply to my "Good morning" or "Good evening." I did not feel that it was like being invited to dine in someone's home. The feeling I had was that I was an impoverished youngster who had come to a stranger's door to beg a meal. At the beginning I had trouble saying anything at all or picking up a spoon, taking the food from the plate, and bringing it to my mouth. One day a week—on Shabbos—I ate at my grandfather's house. On Fridays, at my aunt's. The five other days of the week I was in the homes of perfect strangers. There were all kinds of homes in which I ate and there were all sorts of people in them.

There was one home where the mother of the family practically hovered beside the door waiting for the yeshiva boy to show up. She had water ready for him so he could wash his hands, and the table was set as for an honored guest. She brought the plate of food and placed it reverently and affectionately before me, after which she stood nearby watching to see whether I was enjoying my food. The little children of the family, who had already eaten, stood near their mother and regarded with wonder the boy eating in their house. In a home like that it sometimes happened that, as I was leaving, the mother of the household would slip me a couple of groschen so I could buy some little thing for which my heart might yearn. One never saw the father of the family during those mealtimes. There was a mother, and that home was pervaded with a mother's goodness.

In another home, the minute I crossed the threshold I was met by gloom. The gray walls regarded me and denounced me for coming uninvited. Playing children ignored the stranger who was a yeshiva boy and who would have been more than willing to do some playing himself if the heavy weight of the Torah had not burdened him. Though a mother or an older daughter served it, the food was, as it were, thrown on the table, which had not been set and was dirty. Neither the plates nor silverware were washed. Once the food had been set on the table, whoever had served it left the room and was not to be seen again. In the meantime I swallowed down the food along with the tears that gathered in my throat. Then, leaving half of my food uneaten, I rose and, saying "Good day" to the household, I went out.

There was, too, a home where the father of the family took the responsibility of seeing that the yeshiva boy was fed. He was disturbed by the pallor of the boy's cheeks. A boy, even a boy who was studying Torah, needed strength.

"Why don't you see to it that the boy looks better?" he might say to his wife as he clapped me on the shoulder. "Eat, eat," he urged, "so you'll have the strength to study Torah. You'll have more energy if you leave nothing on your plate."

It was not a feeling of shame that caused my food to stick in my throat, nor was it shame that made my spoon tremble in my hand. I had entered into a world that was utterly strange to me, a world whose dimensions I could not understand. Just as our river back home had its own bed from which it could not wander far, not even in spring when its banks were too narrow to accommodate the surge of water, so it was, evidently, with my life, which took on a specific direction from my earliest years. It was not my father who had defined that course for me. My life was bounded by Jewish ways that moved from one mist-shrouded corner to another. With many others like myself, I was thrust onto a path that had been trodden before me by the generations that preceded me. "Protect the children of the poor, because Torah goes forth from them." It was a well-intentioned sentiment.

I did not come from a poverty-stricken home nor from a home that had any conception either of wealth or of poverty. And yet crossing the threshold each day of a stranger's house to get meals that were sometimes better than those I got at home made me feel poor and small and shrunken.

At the beginning I felt ill at ease in the strange new synagogue despite the fact that it was destined to be my true home in the years to come. My longing still had to dig, to gnaw deep down into myself, to reach hidden sources of energy and uncover hidden powers by whose means I was enabled to strengthen myself so I could live that life in the synagogue whose sounds, and even whose silences, were unusual, nothing like the silences in nature.

I had to get used to the light of the yahrzeit candles that were so often left burning on the synagogue's reading desk or the cantor's podium. I had to learn to control my fear of the shadows that crept out of corners the moment I found myself alone on some rainy or blustery fall night. I had to drive away the fear that assailed my heart at the new existence into which I had been plunged while still in my childhood.

Before my eyes I had the sight of hundreds of volumes on their shelves, volumes I was expected to approach with the sort of care with which I might have approached an unfamiliar spring from which I was meant to drink knowledge and wisdom.

More than once, when I came to the synagogue after one of my shame-inducing meals, I would stand before those bookshelves, staring at them, expecting any one of those books to start talking to me in a human voice, or in the language of the birds that flew around our mill, or in the language of the waters that flowed beneath its wheels.

The First Night Alone in the Synagogue

My grandmother was against my sleeping in the synagogue, though when I slept in her house it was on a board from a sleeping bench that had been laid across two chairs. Such a bed did nothing to compensate me for no longer being at home. Instead it made sleeping in the synagogue more attractive. "Will you be sleeping on that hard bench in the synagogue all by yourself?" asked my grandmother. She shrugged her shoulders as she looked at my grandfather, who simply smiled at her.

Most of the time I was alone there at night because that winter there were no other yeshiva students in Meleytshitsh, though there were the local Jews with a hunger for scholarship who slipped into the synagogue during the day to look into a book.

But I never tired of being alone. I was drawn to the solitude that can only be achieved in the course of long winter nights. I was alone with the shelves of books, with the lamps and chandeliers, with the great wall clock, and with the endless *drip, drip* of the ritual washstand near the door.

At the beginning I was an object of wonder to the Jews who came into the synagogue. They'd say a few words, wanting to know where I came from. I was able now to observe more closely than ever two unique and separate worlds within the synagogue. Rich Jews, who had seats at the eastern wall, condescended to me. The ordinary Jews who sat near the stove regarded me with paternal affection. I was drawn to these simpler Jews, who in the course of their work week snatched time to come into the synagogue to take part in the prayers and who, on Shabbos mornings, sang sadly into the pages of their Psalm books. I felt closer to the shoemakers, tailors, blacksmiths, harness makers, wagon drivers—all those with rough hands, heavy boots, and craggy faces who sat around the great stove in the synagogue between late afternoon and early evening prayers. Their speech sounded like what I heard at home, and their gestures, too, reminded me of home.

The curious came into the synagogue to listen to the strange discourse that took place around the stove, where winged speech transformed reality into dream and turned the ordinary into the wonderful: "Hmm. Hmm. Just think of it," they murmured.

The essence of my being was drawn to the human knot around the warm stove. Though my eyes were on my book, my ears registered their words. Harsh words, tender words; words like the pinecones children stuck into each other's hair around the Ninth of Av. Words steeped in childishness and childlike belief.

I came to love my place near the stove. I could lie awake or go to sleep at night near it. The bench there was so friendly, worn smooth by the constant rubbing of hard buttocks so that the grain of the pine shone through. Really, why not sleep here alone and be the first to rise and greet the dawn?

I began to notice too the maternal glances from behind the grate on the second floor that separated the women from the men. There were mothers there who no doubt wished as a son a little scholar like myself. And there might have been mothers who grieved that such a young boy had been sent away from home to live among strangers.

The first night I spent in the synagogue was a Thursday. It was a *mishmer* night, when yeshiva students or ordinary Jews of scholarly bent spent the whole night in study. And yet I ended up spending the night alone, in company only with a huge yahrzeit candle burning near the podium. It was the sort of first night that foreshadowed the coming of many, many others when I would resist the effects of sleep and, with an inflamed wakefulness, navigate the waves of the Talmud sea. My voice sounded different on such a night; my steps made a different sound. The ticking of the clock had a more serious sound, and its pendulum moved back and forth with a strange restlessness.

At the washstand near the door water dripped into a copper basin underneath. The sound of that dripping reminded me of the water under the mill at home. It seemed to me that the water from the washstand was in distant communication with the water in our pond, telling it about me, Peretz, Lippe's son, who was moving about here all alone among the shadows the wax yahrzeit candle created from the tables, the podium, and the brass chandeliers and hanging lamps.

I had not yet chosen a new Gemara tractate to study. Earlier I had made up my mind to restudy all I had learned from my teachers throughout the years—to reexamine and reevaluate everything I thought I had understood with their help. Now I chose a difficult tractate, Bava Basra. Under the tutelage of my former teachers I had learned it practically by heart. But having undertaken to study the difficult Gemara portion on my own, it seemed to scowl at me as if at an urchin who was brash enough to want to become the proprietor, as it were, of his own days and nights.

On that first Thursday night, when my melody sought to find its way out through the wintry, frost-covered windowpanes, I opened the book to the tenth folio, a jam-packed couple of pages that deal with charitable acts and the relationship between man and his world.

In the name of Rabbi Yehuda it is taught: "Ten extremely stubborn things have been created in this world. The mountain is hard and strong, but iron can conquer it. Iron is hard, but fire can soften it. Fire is strong, but water can extinguish it. Waters are strong, but clouds can scatter them. Clouds are strong, but winds can drive them. Winds are strong, but the human body can contain them. The body is strong, but fear can break it. Fear is strong, but wine can weaken it. Wine is strong, but sleep overcomes it. Death is stronger than them all. And charity can conquer death. As the wise man in the book of Proverbs says, "Charity will save from death."

What else did a childish heart need among the shadows all alone in the middle of a winter's night? Who cared about the world outside the synagogue? The whole town slept. All except the thirteen-year-old Peretz, Lippe's son, who did not sleep. The mountain is strong; iron can master it. Everything, everything can be mastered, except death.

It was hard for me to understand the promise that charity would conquer death.

Drip. Drip. Drip. The water dripped from the washstand, carrying my thoughts back home to my native river, which was now wintering under the ice. I could hear the gushing of the water, the snapping and cracking of the ice. The water was alive underneath. The breaking ice always used to rouse me from sleep; it had always spoken to me of the strength of gushing waters. As a child I had always feared the water hidden under the ice more than I had feared the open pond in summer.

And now the dripping of the washstand made me uneasy. I was sure that even if I snuggled up to the warm stove, the *drip drip* of the water would keep me awake just the same. Why did a washstand have to drip? I went up to it meaning to stop it. No luck. A half-filled washstand. With the water dripping one drop at a time, it would not be emptied overnight. Nor would it be smart to let all the water out of the washstand at once because then the shammes's assistant would have to draw cold water out of the well to fill it again.

"Make peace with the drip-drip!" I followed the command of my now-awake mind. I began to study aloud. My thin little voice created an echo that returned to me from above, from the women's section of the synagogue. A lovelier voice. Mine, and at the same time not mine.

Was anyone thinking of me at home? Were they all sleeping as peacefully as they did when I used to sleep with my mother, who would soothe me when I woke during the night?

I did not want to admit I was scared, that fear surrounded me. A fear that filled the huge vault of the synagogue, including the women's section, where my echo replied to me. It seemed to me that death and sleep were corporeal brothers. Sleep produced sobriety. But what did death produce?

What good did it do me to be afraid? Would I leave the synagogue to go back to my grandfather's, knock on the door, and call, "Let me in because I'm scared?" I was not about to do that. It would be best to conquer my fear. There was no way for me to leave the synagogue for a soft place to sleep. The hard bench would befriend me if I befriended it. As for the hard but warm stove, how many dry, cold hands had caressed it, warming themselves? How many tired, aching shoulders had it eased of their rheumatic pain? I sat beside the large, crudely built but warm stove. There was so much humanity within it. It was tall and broad-shouldered. When I stretched out on the bench beside it, I was only half its length.

It was after midnight. Maybe I would fall asleep. I put an old tallis under my head and lay down, fully dressed, curling up under my winter coat with its astrakhan collar. Cuddling down into it so my body would take up the least room.

I closed my eyes. I tried imagining the dimensions of the synagogue, to see the niche in which a wax yahrzeit candle was burning. What a huge world the synagogue was. With tables and reading stands and benches and shelves full of books. A midnight world in which a single candle was burning. Its flame crackled and emitted sparks, and the water dripped from the washstand. *Drip, drip. Drip, drip.* And the wall clock went *tick, tock* and *bong, bong* when it sounded the hour. Midnight had sounded long ago. Soon there would be a single *bong*. One o'clock.

It wouldn't be so bad to be alone if it weren't for the way my own likeness was doubled. One Peretz, Lippe's son, lay scrunched down on a hard bench beside the stove, and the other Peretz was everywhere. He had already been to Lippe's mill, seeing if he could find a place to rest, looking for somewhere to sleep between its narrow four walls, but all the sleeping spaces were taken. Evidently the mill had become too crowded for Peretz, who needed an entire synagogue to accommodate his thirteen-year-old body and an entire synagogue stove for his own use.

"No point in scrunching yourself up under your coat, in making yourself smaller and smaller. Even the bench and the stove are laughing at you. Get up! Shake your bones a bit. Go to the wash-stand and wash your eyes—your whole face—with cold water. Take broad strides, back and forth, from the stove to the Holy Ark. Don't be scared. Go on upstairs to the women's section of the synagogue and see with your own eyes that there's nobody there. Day and night, this place is now your home, so crawl out from under your winter coat with its astrakhan collar."

That was how Peretz, Lippe the miller's son, reprimanded Peretz, the yeshiva boy.

I did as I was told. I washed my hands and face at the wash-stand. I lit a candle and went up to the women's section of the synagogue and saw it for the first time. Empty! Nothing there. No shelves of books. A dreary emptiness. Here and there, on the empty benches, some pages had fallen from Hebrew prayer books. Here and there a page from a women's Yiddish prayer book.

With the same candle lighting my way, I went back down to the synagogue and began to examine the books on its shelves, books with which I was familiar because every night I gathered them up from the tables on which they were scattered and looked into each volume before I put them back. The books recognized me. We were familiar with each other. The leather spines and gilded book titles of the Gemara and its commentaries. Each letter seemed to smile at me. Each of the titles poked fun at me because I had intended to stay awake, to study the whole night long, and had ended up being assailed by fear. The books said, "Aren't you really one of us up here on the shelves anyway? If you aren't yet entirely, you soon will be. Because what is the old rabbi if not an old volume of the civil law? His son-in-law is also a code of law, although a bit better bound and with new, not-yet-stained covers. Lippe's mill? What does Lippe's mill have to do with you now? You were born there; so what? Where were we born? Certainly not in Meleytshitsh. We're happy here on the shelves. And you're the one who keeps us in order; you keep the dust off us."

"We are the repositories of eternal life. Death is not stronger than sleep. Sleep here and we'll look after you. The water is dripping from the washstand. When the last drop of water has dripped, it will be quiet here."

In a deep bass voice, the thick Talmud tractate Bava Basra that lay open on the table beside the stove said, "Go to sleep."

I was drunk that night—not on wine but on the solitude of my first night of living alone within the confines of the synagogue. It was a drunkenness that sleep finally conquered. I know I heard the clock strike two. I fell asleep, not stretched out beside the stove but with my head sunk into the open Bava Basra, as sleep rose from it to rock me to rest.

✍ An Unearned Slap

All of a sudden, one day I had a feeling of revulsion against the shtetl in which my mother had been born. It happened entirely unexpectedly and despite the lovely summer, when sleeping in the synagogue was such a pleasure and despite the fact that the books on the shelves to which I often spoke at night had become my friends. Without warning, young as I was, I was exposed to shame.

It was precisely because of the books on the bookshelves that the offense so unexpectedly came my way.

Almost from the beginning of the second week since I had come to live in Meleytshitsh it had been my task to gather up the books from the tables and put them in order on their shelves. Punctually every Friday, the shammes paid me six groschen for that labor, which I performed to his satisfaction. I created order on the shelves: tall books side by side with tall books, short books beside short books.

One day the old rabbi stroked my right cheek and said, "How nicely you keep the books in order, my son."

The shohet, a tall, gray-bearded man, nearing eighty but erect and energetic, was always in an irritable mood when he came to the synagogue. It was said he would not give up practicing his craft, even though his hands had begun to tremble. He was the only one dissatisfied with me. He had several times complained angrily because I had imposed a new order on the arrangement of books, and he had trouble finding his volume of tractate Berakhot, which, if I was in the synagogue when he arrived, I usually handed to him.

One day at the beginning of summer, at eleven o'clock, I came back from eating breakfast at one of my "days." As I opened the synagogue door I found the old shohet waiting for me. I had no sooner crossed the threshold than he slapped my face. It was a ferocious blow. "You young scamp. You've done it on purpose. You've hidden my Gemara so I can't find it. There! That's what you get."

Not only my cheek was on fire. My eyes, my ears, my entire head were aflame with resentment and shame. I felt as if my legs had been sawed out from under me, as if my whole being wanted to weep out loud.

I went up to the women's section of the synagogue and hid my face behind a lectern. My whole insulted life burst into tears and protested inside me. My world was suddenly dark. If I had been able, I would have run off barefoot across meadows and bogs, over ditches and across fences, and back to the mill. Not to the Kleshtshel synagogue but to the mill. Never again to have to see another of these pompous, arrogant shtetl men.

But that was not possible. Not now, before Shavuos, six months after I had left home and come to Meleytshitsh with the idea of studying there for several years. How, under those circumstances, could I run off? Would I be able to explain that I had run away because the old shohet had slapped me? And that was why I no longer wanted to study in the synagogue?

One way or another I would have to get through the summer in Meleytshitsh. To swallow my shame and hide my pain. I must not even tell my grandfather about it. Because no one must be permitted to know how profoundly insulted I had been in my mother's birthplace.

For the rest of that day I could not see the letters in my book. They seemed to leap about and leave the glossy white pages. No matter how hard I tried concentrating on the Gemara, I could not drive from my mind the memory of what had happened. I raised my voice louder than usual as I recited the passages, shouting with anguish the words of the tractate I was studying. And the synagogue itself became a vast emptiness for me. Until the shammes came in.

By then it was time for the first of the evening prayers. Usually when he came in, he would come to the lectern at which I was studying, pat my cheek affectionately, and say a kind word or pass on a friendly greeting from someone who wanted to praise the diligent young yeshiva student.

"You'll excuse me," I began, "but I'm not going to gather up the books anymore . . . I just can't anymore . . ."

My eyes filled with tears. I told him what had happened to me that morning when I came back from breakfast.

The shammes was enraged. He offered me ten groschen a week if I continued to keep the books in order, but I refused. Even when, the next morning, the old shohet caressed my cheek and said he forgave me, I remained stubborn. I no longer gathered up the books. Their order on the bookshelves had changed. I regarded them with sadness from a distance, wondering whether they were aware of the insult to which I had been subjected.

I was afraid of the beautiful pine forest behind the town, the forest in which the trees stood like sentinels and about which my mother had spoken with so much tenderness to us children. The forest in which her youth had bloomed. When, sometimes, I quietly walked among its trees, each of them seemed to regard me with a sort of green gloom.

The Meleytshitsh forest was famous throughout the district. During the summer, consumptives from Brisk and even more distant places used to come to Meleytshitsh to drink goats' milk and to sit in the shade of the fragrant, dry forest. Sick men and women lay in braided hammocks and strolled under the trees. Sallow faces, twisted bodies, coughers, spitters, and groaners inhabited that forest during the summer. I was grief-stricken when I saw these sick folk who had come to occupy the healthy pine forest.

I had come to know practically everyone in Meleytshitsh, which is why the summer visitors who frequented the forest felt like intruders. They caused me to imagine a world where everyone—men, women, and even children—was sick with diseased lungs and ravaged hearts. Illness was their way of life.

But Meleytshitsh looked forward to the coming of these ill folk. The townsfolk waited impatiently for the winter to pass, for spring to come, but not because they longed for the first appearance of green grass to enliven their spirits; instead they awaited the coming of the first tuberculars, who would rent apartments there. It was from them that Meleytshitsh derived its income, and that troubled my mind. Fragrant pine trees, and among them people who struggled to breathe as they choked on the blood that welled up in their throats the way pitch wells in a wound in the bark of a pine.

That was why I sought the open trails behind the forest through the rye and wheat fields that led me into a spacious and healthful world. My way led to the place where the sky and the land came together. As I looked back at the distant forest it seemed to be enshrouded in perpetual shadows.

Late in the summer a book peddler came to Meleytshitsh. A pious Jew with long peyos. A ginger-bearded, talkative fellow driving a horse and wagon. He unharnessed the horse in the square before the synagogue and began to unload packages and boxes of books. Inside the synagogue he laid them out on the long table beside the stove. He mostly had volumes of the Humash, prayer books for the New Year, sets of the Mishna and the Tanakh and commentaries on the Talmud. But on the same table he also had a section of unbound storybooks written in "jargon"—that is, in Yiddish—which he laid out next to the Yiddish prayer books written especially for women.

It was the first time I'd ever seen such storybooks, each of them by a particular author: Shomer, Oyzer Bloshteyn, Ayzik Meyer Dik, and Yehoshua Mezakh. I noticed that older people looked askance at these storybooks. Others smiled as they turned their pages. During the day girls came by who paid the book peddler a small deposit to ensure they would bring the storybooks back intact.

The book peddler spent the night in the synagogue. In the evening, when we were alone, he invited me to look into his storybooks. I opened one of Shomer's books. I couldn't understand it. I couldn't get interested in those princes and princesses. All those books of wonder made no impression on me.

Just the same I paid him several of the groschen I had saved for a volume of Elyokem Tsunzer's poems. The book had the well-known songs "Good Luck and Blessing Are Found in the Plow" and "Return of Zion." I bought the poems and hid them among my things. Occasionally, secretly, I would look at them. I understood that these songs needed to be sung, so I tried to invent melodies for them. It was something of a riddle for me, how a bookseller who was a pious Jew and who went around selling prayer books and copies of the Humash could also sell such secular books, and in the synagogue at that.

At night, when the bookseller and I were alone in the syna-gogue, he told me the authors of those books were still living. And that these books were intended only for servant girls. The book dealer himself sometimes looked into the books written in "jar-gon" and smiled into his red beard or laughed aloud.

When he rode away, he left me with a new yearning. There he went, with a wagonload of books, riding behind his horse from town to town. He had by now, undoubtedly, been to many towns. How good it would be to load a wagon with books and travel from city to city, from shtetl to shtetl. And, like him, to unpack the books and to lay them out on a long table beside the stove for people to inspect.

Before the bookseller drove away I quietly asked him, "Are there other towns in the world in which yeshiva boys study?"

He considered me for a while from beneath his brow and said, "My son, the world is large. There are Jews and synagogues in ev-ery town. No Jew, anywhere, is ever lost."

Visiting Home

I left Meleytshitsh twice to visit my home, where I was looked upon and treated as a guest. Little by little my home had become "someplace else" and my birthplace like an inn.

It was destined to be that way because I was growing up among strangers. Though I was nearly fourteen years old, I was a slender sprout, nothing more. My roots had not yet been entirely plucked out of the wet soil around Lippe's mill. But now, living among strangers, I was learning to discern how their homes could be welcoming. Homes in which hardworking fathers and harassed mothers made room for an outsider among their own children, providing him with food one day each week. Putting his plate before him with family affection, delighting to see the visitor enjoying his meal.

However little I liked going to the homes of strangers each day for my meal, and no matter that sometimes the food stuck in my throat or was washed down by hidden tears, I learned to understand it was among strangers that such a green rootlet as I was could learn to dig deeper and find enough nourishment to grow. Though I had not yet found my calling, now that I was able to choose on my own the tractates and commentaries I would study, I began to discern the outline of those shores of the sea of Talmud that had hitherto been shrouded in mist.

In the course of time, slowly, I became bleakly aware that there was a huge world beyond Lippe's mill. What I was beginning to understand as I looked into those books that I put daily into their places on the shelves of the Meleytshitsh study house was that there was a Jewish people who had lived for thousands of years. And that I was a tiny particle of that people, who had been scattered throughout the world.

Young as I was, I often wondered whether I would grow into one of those idle scholars who lived apart from the world like those I saw when I first began to live in the synagogue.

Or I wondered about those other simple folk, the overworked Jews who lived in the side streets of the shtetl and who came into the synagogue to sit around the stove. In my mind I compared them to my family. I would have preferred to be rooted among them, and I wondered how I would ever make a living taking the path onto which I had been thrust.

That was why I came home from Meleytshitsh with a hidden grief that would not leave me even when I wandered among my favorite places. There was a difference in the way the water sounded: shriller, almost angry. The water had acquired secrets of its own. It had found new places toward which to flow under the grassy banks. There was now a certain distance between me and my family, a distance they enlarged at my coming home. It was hard for me to tolerate the respect with which my parents and the people in the household regarded me or spoke to me.

"You're already an assistant rabbi," smiled the Gentiles who lived on our street. I felt that I had indeed become something of an assistant rabbi. And I was diminished, therefore, in my own eyes.

I seized eagerly on all sorts of tasks in the mill so my delicate hands could go back to being a little rougher, so I could have callouses on my hands like the rest of the family. I got blisters from whittling a hard, dry piece of wood for too long. I found places where repairs were needed in and around the mill. Here there was a paddle missing from the waterwheel. There a part of the ground by the mill had sunken. The chicken coop would not close tightly enough; the fowl were able fly out whenever they wanted. And there was even a little dry wood, a few branches to drag together in the house.

That made my mother extremely happy. Bebl was pleased I had not become overly refined. I had grown a little bigger and could now lug a heavy load. I was already helping to trim the millstones.

But my father did not like it. In the synagogue the men asked pointedly, "So what is your Peretz up to? Is he out catching fish?"

That's what some man or other asked, and it humiliated him. Lippe the miller knew Peretz was an assiduous student in Meleytshitsh, and he knew he was beloved there for that. Every Monday my father ran into Jews from Meleytshitsh at the market: shoemakers or hatmakers who came to Kleshtshel with the goods they produced. These were Jews from Meleytshitsh who gathered around the synagogue's stove and kept an eye on the pale yeshiva boy. These men gave my father good reports about his son.

Nevertheless, if some Jew from Kleshtshel went and asked my father, "What's your Peretz doing? Is he catching fish?" my father wanted to prove that his son studied Torah. His Peretz was not growing up to be a fisherman.

He had a talk with my mother. She persuaded me to go into the shtetl for a couple of hours each day to study at the synagogue. I did it a few times, but I found it odious. I didn't like the study house in Kleshtshel. The spirit of learning didn't take hold of me there. The books on the shelves looked at me with unfamiliarity and coldness, as if they were looking at someone who had become estranged from them.

To compromise I brought a few books home with me from the synagogue. At home I sat and studied with the true chant of the Gemara. I liked doing that at home. I realized my father didn't completely understand. It didn't seem natural to him that the Gemara melody should keep time with the noise of the water under the wheels or with the rush of the wind among the trees, with the knock-knock of the mill's paddles.

I brought Elyokem Tsunzer's poetry book that I had purchased from the bookseller in Meleytshitsh as a present for Bebl and Moyshe. For them it was as if I had given them a precious stone. Bebl's fiancé was the first one to sing Elyokem Tsunzer's songs for us.

Now Bebl would sing songs out of the book and dissolve into tears. My father looked into the book with astonishment. It was impossible for him to understand how such songs could be printed with the exact same letters with which the holy books were written. For my mother and the children the book was a sort of greeting from a melodious world in which even Jewish children lived. But wherever and whenever that was, their imagination could not take them that far. Now that I had finally seen a bit of the world myself, I understood the separateness of my home and my family to whom I was attached with so many fragile roots.

On a number of occasions we sat at home not saying a word, and everyone's gaze was focused on me as if they wanted to hear something from me. My mother wanted to hear about the city of her birth, for me to unwind the years of her past, to spread out before her the fields around Meleytshitsh, to place in front of her the forest she loved so much. My father was hoping I'd recite a bit of Torah, which would fill the house and drown out the banging of the mill on the other side of the wall.

The children loved me to tell them about the people away from home. How they looked, what they were like, how they spent their days and nights . . .

My mother wanted to know how I was received at the houses where I ate. She wanted to know how mothers who were strangers spoke to me, how they looked upon her child and if they were sincerely unbegrudging with that bit of food they placed before him one day a week.

"If I could invite a yeshiva boy once a week, I would bring him a plate from heaven." My mother was looking for someone to reward for the good that strangers were doing for her child. If a yeshiva boy came to her once a week, he would receive quite a good reward. But in the shtetl there were no yeshiva boys from elsewhere for now. And what boy would walk so far twice a day to eat?

My father harbored a silent resentment because they overlooked me in the synagogue the way the children of simple parents are overlooked. He didn't demand much of the shtetl landowners and proprietors. But a boy who had become bar mitzvah some time ago, who was visiting from out of town, and who was a deft learner to boot—they could at least call him up to the Torah for an aliyah. A boy from a rich family who came for a visit would have been offered the coveted reading from the Prophets. But Lippe's son . . .

On Simchas Torah, when the portion of the week was read several times so that everyone—absolutely everyone—could be called up to the Torah, when they would find a bit of Torah for the young boys who would put their father's tallis on and recite the blessing in a resounding voice, why, even then, when it came to Peretz, Lippe's son, was he was still shoved in among all the boys, among some twenty rascals, children of the poor, of penniless craftsmen and other laborers?

That's what they did to me when I came back from Meleytshitsh. They shoved me, a fourteen-year-old boy, in among a pack of huge eighteen-year-olds under a single old tallis, and there I had to pronounce the appropriate blessing so the Torah reader would recite some of the weekly portion on our account.

My father regarded that as a dreadful slap in the face and did not know who to blame first.

My mother let him know, without ambiguity, how she felt. "Do you see why I hate this stuck-up shtetl?"

By then we were already thinking of a city to which, after the holidays, I would go for further study. Visoke-Litovsk was frequently mentioned. The city of Orle, eight versts closer to Kleshtshel, was also considered. But it was the train that determined that I should go to Visoke. The train went there twice a day, and the whole journey took altogether some forty minutes. Though the family went to Visoke less frequently than to Orle, and though my pious uncle Moyshe Linever lived in Orle, it was nevertheless decided I should go to Visoke.

I myself was drawn to it by a secret feeling that had to do with the fact that, seven versts from Visoke, on a rented farmstead, lived my uncle Avrom Tumener. My uncle, on one of his visits to us, had promised me that if I should choose to study in Visoke he would invite me occasionally to Tumene. He had a daughter, Sheyne, who was the same age as I was. She was the one with the beautiful handwriting. She had sent me a note written in a script filled with flour-ishes inviting me for a visit.

My mother was set on me going to Visoke to study. Visoke it was then. This time I traveled by myself, found the synagogue by myself, expected the shammes to know who I was and to arrange my eating days.

This time my family bade me a lighthearted farewell, though in fact the train would be taking me much farther away from my birthplace. Compared to the journey on foot to Meleytshitsh with my mother, my trip now to Visoke—that was a great distance. The noise of the train wheels under the cars, the panting of the locomo-tive ascending the hills, made me feel like someone who was being carried, against his will, into a distant and strange world.

✍ Visoke-Litovsk

Did I then sense that I was entering a world that was already in decline? No. That was not clear to me. Though I did have a nearly hidden notion that a hand was leading me away to a world somewhere on the other side of the study house.

I was a diligent student who swam ever deeper in the sea of Talmud. Just the same, I was beginning to lose respect for the God to whom everyone prayed. I secretly stopped praying. I took occasional glimpses into Maimonides's *Guide for the Perplexed*. Though it was hard to understand everything in it, nevertheless I did see that the concept of God was not entirely clear to Maimonides. In the Talmud I found laws and judgments, and I tried to make a rational link between what was in the Talmud and real life as it is lived. I accepted some of the laws and in my heart I rejected others.

What most disturbed my peace of mind was the unfamiliar world that came toward me as I left my birthplace and turned toward strange places. Three years ago in Brisk, when I was a mere eleven years old, I had been displeased with the way city Jews lived their lives. "Vanity of vanities" is how that pulsating life in the sandy streets of Brisk appeared to me. And my solitary life in Meleytshitsh, where I slept alone in the study house, had made me much older than my thirteen years. Night after night alone with the shelves of books. I hadn't found a way to interpret my young dreams because I wasn't really trying to. I hadn't uncovered any secrets because I didn't yet have a clear approach to them.

What of Meleytshitsh? Had I left my mother's birthplace and agreed to go to Visoke-Litovsk only because the old shohet had slapped me for mislaying his tractate Berakhot when I arranged the bookshelves? It was not clear to me what waited for me in Visoke-Litovsk, the larger city.

One thing I did reflect on: "In Visoke, it would be good if someone offered me lodging every night. Occasionally on a Thursday I might spend the whole night in the synagogue, of course. But to sleep alone there night after night! No. Not again."

In one of the synagogues in Visoke I found a shammes who busied himself on my behalf. He arranged for a full seven eating days and also found a place for me to sleep in the home of a furniture maker.

By pure chance, that arrangement worked out well. It was my good fortune each night, when I came home from the study house, not only to be greeted by the friendly faces of the family, beaming with health, but also by the marvelous smell of pine and oak shavings that cushioned the floor.

The various articles of finished or unfinished furniture greeted me in the same friendly fashion: clothes chests, beds, and tables made of oak and pine, intended for young couples.

The family was made up of the young furniture maker, his wife, and their child. And always, always—except on Shabbos and holidays, when I came home late at night—I found the broad-shouldered apprentice at his task. A youth of twenty who earned all of thirty rubles for the whole winter and who worked from five in the morning until eleven at night.

I slept on the workbench, so I always had to wait for the apprentice to finish his day's tasks. It was then that my mattress was laid down on top of the bench. It was a straw mattress through which, nevertheless, I was able to feel the sharp edges of the workbench.

Every morning at five o'clock the apprentice knocked at the door and his master let him in. I was up by then and went off to the study house.

That sleeping place was dear to me. I felt close to the family. I felt close to the wood too. Sometimes in the evening I would come home a bit early on purpose so that, at first a bit shyly, then later more boldly, I could take up the plane and make an effort to smooth out some hard piece of oak. Or else I might try, using a narrow saw, to cut a board. The members of the family watched me, wondered at the dexterity of their yeshiva boy, and checked to see if the wood, when I was done with it, was straight. I would make a leg for a chair or plane a board that would later be used in their work.

When, finally, I lay on my mattress, I lay there a long time in the dark house breathing in the pitchy odor of pine or the acidic smell of oak.

Some of my eating days were not very congenial to me. When I entered those homes I felt like a tramp who begged from door to door. It seemed to me that in those homes they deliberately served me my food on dirty dishes or flung it onto a dish as if they were serving a beggar. I felt that what I was given had been put together from food left on others' plates. I often vomited up my food as soon as I left those homes.

I freed myself from one of those days. I searched for a convincing excuse and found it.

It was winter. There was a burning frost outdoors. Twisted into a knot by the cold, I went for breakfast to the house I did not like. I generally ate two meals a day there. I said a quiet good morning to the family. The woman of the house handed me an empty pitcher and told me to go fill it at the well so that I'd have water with which to wash my hands. It seemed a fair enough request. What was wrong with bringing water into a home where, once a week, I was fed? If this had happened to me in a home where my food was handed to me with some show of generosity I'd have gladly done it. But this was happening in a home where the minute I crossed the threshold I was made to feel inferior.

I took the pitcher and went out to the frozen well, which was quite far from the house. I filled the pitcher and brought it back. Then, before the woman, who was in another room, had time to return, I stole away and went back to the study house. I felt like one who has committed an ugly crime. I was afraid someone would come after me to ask me to go back to eat. But nobody came.

That day became a day of fasting for me. I didn't tell anyone what I did. The shammes never found out about it. Very seldom, if I had a groschen or two on me, I would secretly buy something to eat.

That was a good reason for me to start looking forward to the end of the term, when I could go back home and never come back to study in Visoke. Besides, I was repelled by the fanaticism of Jewish life in Visoke. The winds of piety from Brisk blew strongly across Visoke, whose Jews looked to Brisk as if it were Jerusalem.

There was a young son of the rabbi, a boy more or less my age, who befriended me. He used to look secretly into secular books. It was in his hands that I first saw a Hebrew grammar. And I soon understood why he was edging away from his rabbinical upbringing. I could see he would not follow in his father's footsteps. Inwardly, I envied him.

Torah and work still seemed to me the best formula. When I came to my lodgings at night I was refreshed by the smell of oak and pine. The apprentice sent the plane across a long pine board, his whole body bent over the work and the wood shavings curling off the wood with a whistle, piling up around his hands. At such times I could, in my mind's eye, see how I, a grown man, would one day rise from a book in which I had been immersed and, extricating myself from some difficult case, go to my worktable near the window of my room and, taking up the plane, begin to plane away at the fragrant pine boards. In my imagination I could still see Peretz the miller. Of course, he would be a miller in a larger mill beside a larger river using French millstones and rollers that ground a finer flour. He would be a master of all sorts of skills and at the same time he would have a lucid head, steeped in Torah and wisdom.

"Could there be anything more lovely than to do one's studying at the top of one's voice over the rushing sound of the waters under the mill wheel surrounded by the smells of flour and ground kernels, the smell of oak and pine boards?"

Uncle Avrom Tumener, who had a leasehold on part of an estate that belonged to a nobleman some ten versts from Visoke near the village of Tumene, looked me up a couple of times on his trips to Visoke. He left me with a couple of silver coins so I could buy myself something.

Once he took me home with him to Tumene for Shabbos in a horse-drawn sledge whose shaft was set with bells in the aristocratic style. On a frosty Friday afternoon we drove across fields deeply covered by snow. The drowsy blood in my veins seemed to wake up. I was eager to see his Sheyndl, who was my age and who had once sent me a beautiful letter filled with noble thoughts and written in an embellished script.

I was treated as a very welcome guest by my aunt Soreh, even though I was the youngest compared to her four children. No small thing! Her sister Sheyne's child, a yeshiva boy.

It was a comfortable world, the expansive wintertime world that surrounded my uncle's home. Stables and coops for cattle and barn fowl. Haystacks and bales of straw. Milk, butter, sour cream, and clabbered milk—all of it smelling delicious. No poverty here. No scarcity. All of the children—the oldest who was already grown, another son, then the oldest daughter—were good to me and were glad to see me.

Gladdest of all was Sheyne, the youngest child. She clung to me. No matter where I went, there she would suddenly be. And I could see her attachment to me pleased everyone.

The old grandfather, my uncle's father, lived with them in the house. It was he who had the decorative script and had taught it to Sheyne. He was a tidy old man. Though his hands trembled when he wrote, I felt, as I regarded his thin, aristocratic fingers, that they had been born to write. He could write Russian, and he could write using German letters. Sheyne too had already mastered various alphabets.

Sheyne wanted to know what sorts of things I was studying. She was not happy to learn I was going to be a rabbi.

"Why not, Sheyne?"

"I don't know why not. But I want you to learn how to ride a horse. To be a healthy, powerful man. I want you to study but not to become a rabbi. Rabbis are such faded people."

She thought for a while, then she said, "I'll tell you what, Peretz. I'll study Gemara too. When you become a great scholar, you'll teach me how to read the Gemara. I've asked grandpa to teach it to me. I want to know everything you know. It doesn't matter that I'm a girl."

She led me about that Shabbos all day long, and I followed after her. I climbed up into the hayloft, where she introduced me to the fragrant odors of hay and sweet clover. She took me with her to the cows in the stable and pointed out which of the cows would soon be delivering calves. And she showed me, too, just where the unborn calves lay in their mothers' bellies.

She could not understand why I was living away from home. How I could eat in a different house each day, and how I could do that for seven days a week.

"It's true. You don't look very strong. You look, as a matter of fact, very pale. Your cheeks are thin, sallow," she whispered as she kissed my cheeks.

Then Shabbos was over. I felt joy warming my veins. Cheerfully, I moved through the white, snow-filled fields.

That night we pretended to be writing letters. Sheyne wrote me a letter in which she told me how huge the lovely world was. How brightly the stars shone in the heavens; how all the trees waited for the coming of spring, which, when it came, would wake them to life with its warmth.

I wrote to her about the profundities that were to be found in the books I studied. How the Torah was like a great sea into which all sorts of streams flowed.

"Do you know, they call me *Sheyne*—beauty—the same name as your mother's? They say a young man can't marry a girl who has the same name as his mother."

She said this very softly, and a look of distress appeared on her narrow features. Her dark eyes sparkled like a couple of stars.

I returned to the synagogue on Sunday. My uncle had taken me back to Visoke in the same sled whose bells rang melodically.

That Thursday night was one of those all-night Thursdays. The thoughts that raced through my mind that night came to me from across white fields in a sled drawn by a couple of brown horses. I kept hearing the jingling of bells.

My voice as I recited passages from the Gemara could not overcome the melody of the bells sounding across the snow-covered fields.

Learning and Labor

When at Pesach time I left Visoke to go home, my intention was to stay there until the summer ended. But I didn't discuss the matter with my family. I waited until the end of Pesach.

As always, there was plenty of work to do in the mill. Pesach grain. An abundance of non-Pesach flour to make. There was plenty of water too. It was easy for me to help out. My mother found me some of Moyshe's old hand-me-downs, which I wore to work.

As soon as I arrived I felt an oppressive sadness at home. The older children were poised to leave. Kalmen was engaged to be married to a young woman who lived in the nearby shtetl. He would be married in summer, and so he would be looking for work there. A contractor who painted all the railroad's various posts, signals, and the iron bridge that crossed our river had promised to hire my brother Moyshe that summer. And so he would become a painter. Bebl's fiancé was expected back from the army at the end of summer. No doubt she would be married then and would also leave the house.

I foresaw how the family home would be emptied. My parents would be left alone with six-year-old Soreh. My father was not a very skillful miller. If something went wrong in the mill it would have to be repaired by strangers. The grief in my parents' eyes was visible when they spoke of their children's departure. Which is why I felt how important it was to stay home that summer while the older children were still in the house. Moyshe would be working not far away, so he could come home for Shabbos from time to time.

But there was a deeper reason that kept me from leaving. Secretly I was not satisfied with the progress of my studies in Visoke. It seemed to me I was feeling about in the dark. I had not, even in the earliest years of my education, been able to imagine myself wearing a rabbi's fur hat. But then I had not had any other outlet for my youthful searching except the study house. I was not eager to attend some distant yeshiva, though there had been some discussion about sending me to Lomzhe or to Damir, where there were yeshivas that would take young scholars like me. Later I would go to Slobodka or even to Volozhin—the great yeshivas. When those cities were mentioned, my father's eyes lit up.

My instincts were to be alone. To study alone, to undertake my life's quest alone. To seek, in some other place, the silence in which I would find the dimensions of my own being; the kind of stillness that had nurtured me at home. The silence that had accompanied me daily on my way to heder.

In Visoke I had become a skeptic. There, as in Meleytshitsh, I had been unable to abide the shtetl-dwelling Jews who brought the atmosphere of the marketplace into the synagogue. When I left Visoke I still felt unfulfilled. The occasional visits I had made that winter to the home of my uncle Avrom Tumener, where his youngest daughter had whispered into my ear tales of a different kind of world, had dampened my enthusiasm for eating days. And it was unimaginable that I could study in strange shtetls without having to eat days.

That Pesach, in the course of the seder during which we eased our overworked limbs onto the pillows of our chairs, I, as the youngest boy, had asked the four questions and then recited the Haggadah in a ringing voice. After we had drunk wine and mead twice, a conversation began whose theme was how wonderful it was to have all the children sitting around the family table.

It was my mother who made the suggestion that I should spend the summer at home and devote a few hours each day to pursue my studies in the local study house. It was a plan my father approved.

What pleased him especially was that now the local community would see that his Peretz was a diligent scholar who could hold his own without a teacher.

Once again I resumed my walk from the mill to the shtetl, this time without leaping and dashing as I had done when I was a boy. I was an adult now. I had been eating days for more than a year and a half. I had spent many nights sleeping alone in the synagogue, absorbing the sound of the *drip, drip* of the washstand beside the stove. While my walk to town was still accompanied by the murmur of the waters flowing in the ditch along the path, I noticed that the saplings that had been growing out of the roots and trunks of the older trees when I had last walked by had grown, as I had, and were now firmly rooted trees. But I was in the process of uprooting myself from my home while they seemed to be growing closer to the trunks of the older trees.

I made the acquaintance of the books on the bookshelves of the shtetl's synagogue. I looked through each and every volume. I found what I needed—and I found, too, a place beside the stove. Former friends of mine from heder who had remained in the shtetl also came in to study. The sound of our thin voices singing the Gemara melody curled upward and wafted outdoors through the open windows. They went into the streets and alleys to tell the world that we were there immersed in learning and worship.

But the mill was always in my thoughts. It followed me into the study house, and though I sat there my mind was in the mill. What I had to do was to work out a way of being both in the synagogue and in the mill, to allocate hours to them both but avoid being seen as an idler.

Fridays, however, belonged to me. Even the most devoted scholar studied only half a day on Fridays. It was then that I caught fish. I waded into the pond with a net, crept in behind the hidden islets where I had once been afraid to explore. On Fridays too I went into the woods carrying an ax as I scrounged for firewood to drag home.

I had learned something useful in Visoke from having my lodgings at the furniture maker's. I had acquired, almost without knowing how, considerable skill at woodworking. I could handle a saw and a plane. I could mark a piece of wood and cut it along the mark I had made. When a paddle was missing in the waterwheel it didn't turn evenly and made an irregular clatter, sometimes fast and sometimes slow, which seemed to pierce my mother's ears. It made her very happy when I cut a paddle and repaired the wheel. She thanked me and kissed me, saying, "How nice it is when a wheel turns properly. I can't bear it when it rattles."

That summer my brother Moyshe left home to become a painter on the railroad line. Kalmen got married and went to live in the shtetl, where he opened a little shop.

Little by little my father and I had become pals. Seeing me get ready to trim the millstones he said, "You know something, Peretz. Let's lift the stones together; then you can try your hand at trimming them."

I needed no further invitation. Imagine! Working alongside my father. Though he had more strength than I did, we lifted the millstone together, using wedges and rods. Together we strained at the task; the blood rushed to our faces. The rods bit into our shoulders as we lifted the millstone and turned it over. Covered with flour, I sat at last on the millstones. Using a small steel flat-head hammer I chipped away at the crossbars, and using a hammer with a pointed tip I cleaned out the grooves. It was a joy to feel the chips of stone spurting up from the work, flying into my face, striking my hands.

Later, when the stones had been trimmed, my father and I replaced the upper stone over the lower one. The two had to be set precisely over each other. We set them carefully in place; we turned the wheels. Sparks flew out from between them and there was a burning smell. We adjusted the stones so they were flush. When there were no further sparks we knew they were properly aligned.

My father stood down in the mill, ready to drive the wedges under the beams that would move the stones to the right or left.

I shouted down to him, "Give the wedge a tap to the right . . . a bit to the left . . . a little more to the right, Papa." And my father did it. He tapped the wedge the way his son, the scholar, told him to from above. Then I saw that my father and I were friends. I noticed how his gaze rested on my arms.

"Don't strain yourself. It's so heavy. You could hurt yourself." But I could see it pleased him that I could handle a heavy load. After all, I was my father's son. The son and the grandson and the great-grandson of millers.

From time to time I visited my uncle Avrom Moyshe, the miller. I was drawn there by his windmill at the same time as I was attracted by his workshop and its tools. There were all sorts of saws hanging on the walls and various planes on his shelves. He too had shelves filled with books that enticed one to take them down, to look into them. I'd noticed his books years ago, when I had not understood what was in them. There was *Tower of Strength*, by Moshe Chaim Luzzatto. I once had not understood if the content of this book was secular, profane, or sacred.

I took the book down from its shelf and opened it. My uncle lit up. His eyes brightened in his flour-dusted face as he undertook to reveal its true meaning. "See how the Song of Songs is at once a secular and a holy work? Both truth and imagination. And that's how it is with *Tower of Strength*. Love is truth. Love can be at once earthly and at the same time belong in the highest spheres. If one wishes, one can bring down the heavens or one can raise the earth to their level. Love is love. What matters is how you interpret books like Song of Songs or *Tower of Strength*."

My way home from his mill took me through the bogs. I had my trouser legs rolled up above my knees and enjoyed the pleasure of feeling my feet sinking into the soft ground. I walked a long while thinking about Luzatto's drama, *Praise for the Upright*. But thinking even more about my uncle Avrom Moyshe, who told me how, with love, worlds could exist between heaven and earth. He had revealed the secret of the sacred and the profane. How what was commonplace could become Divine if one's essence and one's soul were sanctified.

That summer proved a turning point. I stood before two paths, but I could not decide which one to take. I had learning and labor before me. I had already begun to unite the two. My mother, who demanded nothing from me—neither wealth nor greatness—would certainly have been pleased if I continued to unite them.

I heard it from her often enough. Each time when I came home from the synagogue and was sitting at the table eating the meal she had prepared, she would look at me from a distance and say, "God keep us from the charity of strangers." And I understood what she was referring to. She was distressed by the thought that I might have to eat days again if I went away from home.

Another time she would say, "Children, I can see no point in your staying on at the mill." That thought nagged at my gentle mother, who asked for so little from life. Moyshe had reached his goal: he had learned to apply red and white paint on the road signs and iron posts here and there along the railway line. A couple of times that summer he came home for Shabbos. Now, instead of flour, he had paint on his clothes and he smelled of paint. That pleased everyone in the family. No one wanted to see him dusted with flour again.

That same summer my mother received news from Meleyt-shitsh that her father, my grandfather Reb Yossl Itzl, was sick. She left at once for Meleytshitsh. Her heart told her that her father's life was in danger. He was seventy-five years old. She loved him and never stopped talking about him. She stayed in Meleytshitsh for a couple of weeks and came home only after the required seven days of mourning.

His death had completely transformed her. Her face was narrower; her eyes seemed to be gazing off into space. Her sorrow was immense. Never before had she spoken so much. It was as if she was trying to shout down her pain with words. She was afflicted now with all sorts of doubts. Instead of telling us what my grandfather's last hours were like, she talked philosophy. My father was amazed.

"It's all foolishness, children. Foolishness!" she said, gazing off into the distance while we swallowed our grief, unable to console her.

She began to deny the truth of things in which she had always believed. "Children, I saw what they did to my father. How they put him into the ground; how they covered his eyes with shards;

how they covered his grave with earth. And then—nothing. Not a sound. The spadefuls of earth fell on him. And he ... not a sound. I think it's all nonsense. I don't care if they bury me behind the cemetery fence when I give up my soul. It doesn't matter where one lies. Dead is dead. Enough! No one has ever come back from there."

With her return from Meleytshitsh she was even more convinced than before that there was nothing to be gained by staying in the mill. Hard as it was even to think of it, she would willingly have left the mill herself. She who had always hated shtetl life suddenly felt she wanted to run off somewhere—even to some shtetl. Where else was it that her imagination was aiming for? Listening to her talk like that was hard on us.

But her words encouraged me to think again about my own departure. It was a sad end to summer.

I Find My Friend

That gloomy summer's end spurred me once again to think of leaving home. I no longer felt the need to see the river covered by ice, nor to doze off for the winter in company with the trees around the mill, nor to sink into silence in the course of the long winter evenings. Summer's end struck me like a sudden gust of wind blowing through my home. Soon I would be fifteen. I had lost my boyhood treble and now had my own voice.

I had to leave.

It's true, our river water was still the best I'd ever tasted. The sounds of the water rushing under the mill wheel could be heard above the sounds of my Gemara melodies. The flour dust on my face and hands still felt good. My shoulders yearned to carry heavy loads and my hands longed for an ax, a saw, a plane. The smell of grass; the look of autumn colors; the feel of bare feet on frozen ground.

But I had to leave.

I left, but not to any very distant place. I went to Orle, some fourteen versts away, whose Jews came to the Monday market in Kleshtshel. Orle was near where my pious uncle Moyshe Linever and my aunt Blume Rokhl, my father's only sister, lived.

I went off to Orle a few weeks after the holidays with a wagon driven by a Jew from there who had come to our market.

Orle had two synagogues, the old one and the new one. The two faced each other across the same street. The semicircular synagogue yard, surrounded by buildings, closed off the old walled synagogue. Behind it was the cemetery. I chose the new synagogue, whose north-facing windows looked out on the old one.

On my first day in Orle, the shammes arranged all seven of my eating days.

"Just think! Moyshe Linever's his uncle." He found me good days and a good bench to sleep on beside the stove.

It was now late fall. The earth was lightly dusted with snow. Orle was a shtetl like all the others, with a circular market, large shops and small, streets and alleys leading away from the marketplace.

There were no other visiting scholars in the study house. A couple of local boys came in during the day to recite a couple of pages of Gemara. I found myself a lectern in the northeast corner of the synagogue. The scholar in me asserted himself as I sang out the Gemara melody in my nearly mature voice.

From the old synagogue on the other side of the street came an echo of my melody. No, not an echo. A voice all its own. There was another scholar there singing a melody that was an older brother to my own. A scholar with a deeper voice that had considerable sweetness to it.

I cast a quick glance out the window. Who was studying over there in the old synagogue?

I saw a boy of fourteen or fifteen years old standing at his reading stand right beside the window. He stood erect, keeping his eyes on the book that lay before him, precisely the way I was used to studying. His head, tilted a bit to one side, moved up and down, the way mine did.

How did it happen that such a young boy could have such a deep voice?

The shammes of the new synagogue was a tall, lean, black-bearded, middle-aged man who limped heavily on his left foot and who spent his free hours in a corner of the synagogue making leather coin purses, pocketbooks, and billfolds. He always smelled of leather.

At the end of the day, I asked him who was studying with so much diligence in the old synagogue.

He said, "That's Yitskhok, one of the dead Rabbi Sender's sons. He has a keen mind. A genius. He would have surpassed his father, but he went astray somehow. Then he went to London. No one knows what he did there. It's suspected he yielded to temptation. Then, not long ago, he returned, and as you see, he's a dedicated scholar. Day and night his voice rings out. But nobody knows how long it will last."

"But he's still very young," I said, amazed.

"He'll soon be old enough to be conscripted, small as he is. He lives with his mother, the rabbi's old widow, in the second half of the old synagogue, which used to be the rabbi's house. The community turned it over to them in honor of the dead rabbi. Reb Sender was a very great rabbi."

The shammes sighed and went away.

I returned to the Gemara. But my thoughts were turbulent. The shammes had both revealed and not revealed a mystery to me. Yitskhok had left the straight and narrow path—and was at the same time a dedicated scholar. He'd gone to London, and now he lived with his mother in what had been the rabbi's house.

The mystery himself walked into the synagogue, moving with firm steps that did not accord with his size. Yitskhok, the rabbi's son, came in, strode around the podium, then walked around and around the synagogue, glancing at me as he went by. Then he went out.

It was as if he had left a tumultuous wind behind. I reviewed what he looked like. In height he was shorter than me, though I was not myself as tall as I should have been for my age. His head was round under the soft black cap he wore shoved back over it. He had a broad, luminous forehead and fine lines in his face.

What did his sudden appearance here mean?

The sound of his voice reciting Gemara was once more at my window. Again the lovely melody but with more energy now, more enthusiasm.

Then, as if I had been loosed from a chain, I sang out with my own melody. My turbulent thoughts would not leave me be; I want-

ed to shout them down with my Gemara melody. I felt that Yitskhok and I, though we were in separate synagogues and reading separate books, were studying together.

That evening, just before the early service, he appeared again,
in the same hurry as before: he strode around the Torah table,
then, coming close, turned abruptly to me. Thrusting out a delicate
childlike hand, he said, "Hello."

"Hello." Now that he was close, I studied him. Large, deep blue
eyes. A small, neat mouth. A tiny blue vein throbbed in his pale
forehead. There was a shallow groove on each side of his nose. But
what purity there was in those blue eyes of his!

"You're going to be studying here, in the new synagogue?"
Yitskhok asked.

"Yes."

"Throughout the winter?"

"Yes."

"You've found eating days?"

"Yes. For the whole week."

"Where will you be sleeping?"

"In the synagogue."

"There's a bed for you in the rabbi's house, where we live. If you
like, I can talk to my mother about it."

Unable to take my eyes from his face, which had the look both
of a grown Talmud scholar and of a child, I thanked him and said
yes. What else could I have done?

That very night Yitskhok came into the new synagogue and,
without much said, took me to his home in the second half of the
old synagogue. The rabbi's widow was in her fifties. She had a rosy,
refined, aristocratic face. She stood at the door and greeted me. I
could see how closely her son resembled her.

The rabbi had died not long before, and his house could easily
have been a small synagogue on its own. Nothing was missing. There
was a holy ark, shelves full of books on the walls, two long tables with
benches alongside them, and lamps hanging over the tables.

At the north window a bed had been made up, where I would
sleep.

The rabbi's widow asked me a few questions about my parents and my brothers and sisters. Yitskhok said nothing. Not long afterward, both of them disappeared into a side room.

I looked around at the bookshelves. I took a book down and looked into it for a while. Then I turned down the flame of the lamp that hung over the table near my bed. I got out of my clothes and into bed, where I let my body get used to this new place.

I had trouble falling asleep. The silence of the dark house sounded all around me. A wall clock ticked too loudly.

Maybe in this bed . . . maybe Reb Sender had slept in this bed his whole life. As for the rabbi's son? A living mystery. The shammes had half revealed some things about him. And here I was, in his home, lying in a strange bed. How had this all happened in a single day, contrary to all of my plans? I had counted on sleeping in the synagogue. It had seemed a good thing to do in Orle. And suddenly here I was in a soft bed. I had lowered the lamp too early, before I even had a chance to examine the walls.

My head crawled with thoughts.

What had Yitskhok done in London? Such a huge city, said to have millions of people. Why had he come back? And why had he wanted me to sleep here in the rabbi's study? He had said not a word but had gone off, leaving me here. If only I had known the dead Reb Sender. It seemed to me I could hear him walking about silently in the dark house.

I thought once again about my own home. So near, so familiar. *Slap . . . slap . . .* the slap of the paddles in the waterwheels against the water. Before I left home, I had made my mother happy by replacing many of the paddles myself. I imagined myself carrying a sack of wheat and the good feeling of the weight on my shoulder. I was carrying the wheat up the stairs to the hopper. My body was sturdy. I was pleased by the weight I was carrying. Yes, the river would be frozen by now. At dawn ravens and magpies would be walking about pecking for food in the snow.

Then the mill disappeared, and I felt the presence of the holy ark. I tried to guess how many Torah scrolls were in it. I imagined that the letters had left the parchment and were dancing around inside the darkened ark. They escaped quietly through a crack in the door and were dancing on the floor, dancing under the table near my bed.

And then I was at home again. It was summer, and I was teasing my little sister Soreleh. We were playing tag. She tried to tag me, but I climbed up the willow tree that overhung the pond. Soreleh started to cry because she was afraid I'd fall into the water. And then there was my mother, just returned from my grandfather's funeral in Meleytshitsh. She sat in the house talking while everyone else was silent, wiping the tears from their eyes. My heart went out to my mother, who had suddenly become an orphan.

Suddenly there was song. Restrained song. The voices of two men. Both voices very sweet. The song was right there, near me. I recognized one of the voices. It was Yitskhok's. It had rung out that way during the day as well. I did not recognize the second voice, but it too was very sweet.

The melody seemed to enclose words in a circle. Words from *Duties of the Heart*, second chapter, where the author says, "Though understanding and wisdom vary from creature to creature, there is only one essential source of understanding. Just as the sun in its essence is one and singular, yet its light varies according to the color of the glass through which it passes."

The words, led by the melody, drifted over me, over my closed eyes. The music was not very loud, but loud enough to keep me awake and to rock the night like the waves a breeze makes as it blows through a flowering wheatfield.

I opened my eyes. Yes, I was awake. It was he, Yitskhok, the rabbi's son, and beside him a bearded young man. They sat close to each other, an open book before each of them. Two lighted candles in brass candlesticks, one before each of them. The flame of the candles elongated the singers' shadows so they reached all the way to the walls.

The clock struck four. Evidently, I had slept three or four hours. Perhaps they had been studying together since midnight— and all the while I'd slept. I followed their recitation with my mind. I was familiar with *Duties of the Heart*. I had sought its truths many times. But until I heard their melody together, the words of the text had not made any deep impression. There was much about the book I had not understood, that seemed alien. I liked my body. I cared for it as for my soul. But there in *Duties of the Heart* the body was considered unclean. My body was pure. As pure as my soul. Right now my body was sensing the softness of my bed and yearning for the hard, planed surface of the bench I was used to sleeping on beside the stove. My body knew the feeling of stone and was on good terms with it. It sensed the water and the sand along the banks of the river, the green grass and the ice-cold dew that covered the autumn grasses at dawn. No, my body was pure.

Their melody was worth much more to me than the words they sang. Just as the melody of my Gemara recitation was sometimes dearer to me than the content of the passages themselves. It was not a good thing that melodies went along with words, no matter whether they were wise or foolish. Maybe now, with these two, the melody was the heart of the matter. The melody surging at my bedside.

The gray light of dawn woke me once more. There was no one in the room. Not far from me, two pale candle stubs protruded from the candleholders on the table. No. It had been no dream. They had really been there during the night and had roused it with their sweet song. Then they had gone away.

The next night—the same thing. During the day, Yitskhok said few words to me. "Is there something I can do for you? Maybe your bed isn't soft enough." That's all. But at night, the melody. The same thing, night after night, all week long, until Friday during the day, when the under-shammes, sweeping the study house, kicked up enough dust to drive me away to the rabbi's rooms for a couple of hours where, until that moment, I had only come to sleep at night. It was there, then, that Yitskhok and I had our first real meeting, which produced first recognition and then intimacy.

ᔥ Torah and Haskalah

Friday, during the day. My first Friday in Orle. I had never seen such a huge pile of trash as the old under-shammes swept up from around the benches of the eastern wall and piled before the door. By now it was so large he could not move it with his long-handled twig broom.

"Go to the rabbi's house while I clear this away," he said, smiling. "You've studied enough this week. Go get some rest in honor of Shabbos until I've cleared out the trash."

In the rabbi's study, there was Yitskhok, as if he had been waiting for me. He gave me a welcoming smile. His mother gave us tea and some egg kikhl.

I noticed Yitskhok was surrounded now by a pile of books that were strangely different from the ones he usually read. His handsome, clever head was uncovered. He seemed more relaxed. He asked me to sit near him.

"Do you know this one?" he asked, pointing to a thick, bound volume.

"No, I've never seen a book like it."

"It's the annual *Ha-Asif* (*The Harvest*) of Nahum Sokolow. The poems of Heinrich Heine, translated from German, are published here. Do you know them?"

"No."

Then, with almost the same ecstatic and pious melody with which he recited the Gemara, he sang, "If only the flowers knew how deeply my heart is wounded."

Though it was the beginning of winter, in my mind's eye I was transported to the springtime meadows around our mill. And now I saw the yellow marsh marigold blossoms and the forget-me-nots. They knew about my cares and sorrows. I could see my sister Bebl gathering them and braiding them into garlands. They knew her cares as well.

"And here you have Yehudah Leib Gordon's poems. Read them when you have time. Do you know Perets Smolenskin's *The Wanderer in the Paths of Life*? And here are Brandstetter's stories. Or perhaps you'd rather read some books in Yiddish. Here's Linetski's *The Polish Boy*."

My head, as if it were doing a circle dance, was spinning. It was as if a barrel organ were playing somewhere outside the window. I saw the mill wheels sparkling before my eyes, and the spray of water cooled my flushed face. Yitskhok's diligence at the Gemara was only a veil to hide his real behavior. That was what the shammes meant when he said, "He's a genius. He could have been greater than his father, but he wandered from the straight and narrow path." Apparently he wanted to lead me off the straight and narrow too.

"Have some tea. Later, you can look at these books," his mother said. She was not pleased to see her son opening a door for me through which, if I went, I would be led astray. She did not openly protest it, but her feelings were apparent.

"Here is Yehudah Leib Gordon's famous poem 'The Tip of the Yud,'" Yitskhok said. "It's the poem in which he pokes fun at the foolish laws that relate to writing a bill of divorce." And he began to sing, "Ah Jewish woman, who understands your life? / You are born to darkness and in darkness live."

The rabbi's wife could no longer stand it. Her face flushed, she stood up. "It's not true, my son. Your Yehudah Leib Gordon is lying!"

Yitskhok did not reply. Instead he sang the Heine poems that had been translated in *Ha-Asif*.

"Will you let me copy the poems? I'll put them into a notebook.

Of course I know I can't have the books themselves because—"

"By all means, copy them. Writing them out will be very useful to you. It'll give you a sense of each poet's style."

As he spoke, his eyes lit up. The difference in our ages was more evident now. He was twenty and I was fifteen.

The difference in knowledge, in enlightenment, was much greater. Still, the difference in our ages was no impediment. I felt a warm intimacy between us, though at the same time he was even more enshrouded in mystery.

I returned to the synagogue. It had been cleaned. There were new candles set in the chandeliers, ready to be lit. All the glass lampshades had been polished. I went to the bookshelves searching for some book. But my mind was no longer on any of these books. I thought, "Has he actually found his course in life? Is his heart at ease? In the study house, he is a scholar. Every night after midnight he gets up and piously studies *Duties of the Heart*. And then, on Friday, just before Shabbos, he reads the poems of Yehudah Leib Gordon. Poems that are mockingly contemptuous of everything that he, Yitskhok, studies all week long in the synagogue."

I felt a secret desire stirring within me. I wanted to speak with him. Not now. Not immediately. But I would have to talk with him sometime. He would have to explain himself to me.

But when I came to him ready to set forth my doubts—even as I was still struggling to find the right words with which to begin—he asked me about my home and how I had spent my earlier years. It pleased him that I was a miller's son and that I had acquired manual skills. He had noticed how handily I was able to move the long table in the rabbi's study and how, all by myself, I was able, by taking hold of one end of a bench, to put it where I wanted. He liked the simplicity with which I explicated a difficult subject in the Gemara and the ease with which I extricated myself from the twists and turns of the Prophets.

But perhaps it was not necessary to talk with him. Perhaps there was no need to ask him to explain his behavior. Instead, it might be better just to follow his lead without question. He was a scholar. So was I. He studied works on morality; so did I. He had introduced me to the world of secular books. Well, I would look into them. Certainly I was familiar with *Duties of the Heart*. To purify the soul, to purify the body. That was everyone's duty. Without question, the books to which he had so unexpectedly introduced me were disturbing. I would not give them up. When the time was right, he and I would talk. When the time was right, I would find the words with which to express my thoughts and the doubts that pressed against my mind and produced such an ache in my heart . . . yes, the time would come when I would talk with him.

On that Friday it was as if I had been reborn. My eyes had glimpsed a world that seemed enclosed in a rose-colored mist. My days long past in the mill, my days in Meleytshitsh and Visoke, and my wakeful nights in the Meleytshitsh study house passed through my mind and danced in that mist.

It was hard for me to feel just then that my earlier days had been spent in darkness. My days at home in my father's mill . . . those were after all the days of my natural growth. Even though I had been so often bent over the Gemara, and despite all the contact I had with a number of rabbis, it had never occurred to me that I might one day be one. I had already begun to trim my peyos, and I no longer twisted them between my fingers. Though I still put on tefillin and recited some of the prayers, my mind was on other things. The prayers had nothing to do with my spirit.

My life in the Orle synagogue was easier than it had been in the other places. I was not scrutinized as closely as I had been in Visoke. The Orle populace was not as pious as the one in Visoke. In the new synagogue where I was studying, the congregation was made up of simple folk, manual laborers. As were the households where I ate days.

I often visited my uncle Moyshe Linever and had a chance to study him more closely. Like my brother Kalmen, he rarely raised his eyes. Nor did he speak loudly. He was never disputatious. My aunt, my father's sister, was like him. She respected him and he respected her. They never raised their voices to each other and never demeaned each other.

He had been a tenant farmer and had lived in a village from

which he delivered milk to the city every day. Now he owned a tiny grocery store. But he did not himself work in it. He hated measuring and weighing things, and his wife was not much better at it. As a result they were very poor. They ate little and spoke even less. They had one son who was just like them, so when I came to visit them I hardly opened my mouth except to answer questions. My aunt looked pleased when I came to visit. Just think! Her brother's son was a scholar! My uncle showed no emotion. On the other hand, it seemed to me he understood that, in some way, I was deceiving myself. It was clear to me he did not like my sleeping in the rabbi's quarters. "Pious people think Yitskhok is possessed by the devil. He doesn't fool them with his diligence and his Gemara singing the way he does the mothers who pass by the yard in front of the synagogue."

My uncle, no doubt, was among those who were not deceived by Yitskhok's lovely voice. Especially this uncle of mine who could not understand why my kaftan was buttoned from left to right. "How come?" he wanted to know. "'The right must govern.' The right side must rule the left."

The kaftan had been resewn for me and had been turned inside out so the buttons and the buttonholes were reversed, and that was why they buttoned from left to right. Yes, an uncle that observant must have had grave doubts about the wisdom of my sleeping in the rabbi's quarters.

Once my uncle told me, "The fault lies with the old rabbi, Reb Sender, of blessed memory. He did not keep an eye on his children. And he never noticed they were becoming undisciplined, a disgrace to the Torah."

I bought ten double sheets of paper and folded each sheet into four. Then I sewed myself a booklet that had eighty pages and copied into it the poems that, secretly, I had learned by heart. When no one was listening, I sang them aloud using the melody of the Gemara. I slipped the verses of new songs into my Gemara melody. The echo that sounded in reply came from a distant world.

✍ In a Blizzard

Was I going astray? Was I taking the path of darkness?

I had restless thoughts and was overwhelmed by doubts. In *Duties of the Heart,* in the "Gate of Submission," it is written: "A man must make his every limb subservient to God. Because that way he will not raise his voice too loudly. His mouth will speak no unworthiness. He will look upon the world with modest eyes. He will control his own spirit. Submissiveness, that is the wise course for a man on this earth." I studied diligently, bent over the Gemara. My days were consumed in the fire that raged in my blood and whose flames I fanned. I caught glimpses of how profoundly I was linked to times that were hidden in a corner of eternity. My voice reciting the Gemara was a spiritual thread entangled with those past generations that had endured martyrdom.

And here was Yehudah Leib Gordon. Such a wise man. Whose voice was so strong and so smooth. His verses were forged of silver. And he laughed at what I and tens of thousands of young people like me were doing. He said expressly that we were all enfolded in darkness. He said expressly that we were abandoning our lives. Wasting our days and years. That we were trying to grind air in a mortar. And that the broad, open light of the world that lay outside of the synagogue had been obscured for us. Perets Smolenskin did the same thing, though he pitied the fate of those who, like me, wasted their youth to decay in a dark, imagined world and who traveled paths that were both thorny and deceiving.

It was for this reason I spent several all-night Thursdays in the synagogue. I wanted to be awake. To see if I could not find some bridge between my present world and the one I had so unexpectedly discovered in the strange books I was reading. I understood one could only reach that unknown world by means of enlightenment. By studying foreign languages. By learning new forms of wisdom, for me as yet unknown. By going to secular schools where one wore uniforms with bright buttons.

There was no direct bridge to that world. For people like me, the way there was neither straight nor easy.

According to the wisdom I had imbibed from the ethics books, what I ought to do was to stay at home. To help my father run the mill and, in my free time, study Gemara. Study and behave according to the precepts of those books with which, for the time being, I was intimate. To be humble was a virtue. To practice solitude. To be alone with the Creator. Ah, how easy that was!

But on such solitary nights in the study house I was nevertheless encircled by fears. My thoughts made my head whirl.

I could see the old synagogue through the east windows of my synagogue. The famous old synagogue of Orle with its vaulted roof and its high, carved ark of the law. Just behind the old synagogue lay the cemetery, several hundred years old. On those silent Thursday-night vigils, it seemed to me that even before I was overtaken by fatigue, even before my voice reciting the Gemara was stilled, I could hear secret voices from the old synagogue. That from under the fallen gravestones there rose the spirits of the dead and that they came to stand invisibly under the windows of my synagogue. They recognized the pale youth who sat behind the Torah table and faced the holy ark. They knew his thoughts and were amazed to see such a pale lad alone in a synagogue in a tangle of turbulent ideas.

It became disturbing for me to be there alone. Even as a boy two years younger, I had slept alone in the synagogue in Meleytshitsh. Now with confused thoughts, I was looking straight over the forbidden fence with eyes that had already perused forbidden teachings, heretical books. Now I could feel how alone I was in a strange world, where terrors were lurking around me.

After one such miserable, wintry vigil night, when dawn had peeped through the frozen windows, I decided I would walk home for Shabbos. That I would start on my way just after the recitation of the first of the morning prayers. It was fourteen versts from Orle to Kleshtshel—a five- or six-hour walk. It was practically a straight road that passed through a couple of villages. Though my uncle tried to dissuade me from the trip because of the cold, the deep snow that lay on the road, and the shortness of the winter day, and though the rabbi's widow and Yitskhok, who could not understand my determination to walk home for Shabbos, also tried to talk me out of it, I went anyway.

What kind of demon had picked me up and set me on the road to Kleshtshel on a freezing cold winter day?

I put my tefillin and a notebook containing the copied poems of Yehudah Leib Gordon and Mikhah Yosef Lebensohn in my inside coat pocket. To keep my feet from freezing on the road I wrapped a couple of burlap sacks around my boots and tied them on with twine so they wouldn't fall off. My aunt and uncle shrugged their shoulders as I scanned the road before me, but the sun, which since early morning had been shining brightly, persuaded them to let me go. I tied a scarf over my head to cover my ears, put on woolen gloves, and started on my way.

Sheer momentum carried me over the first few versts of the frozen road. The expansive, snow-covered countryside under a lowering gray-white sky drew me on. I ran to keep myself warm. When the sun shone I sang at the top of my voice. The road, banked high with snow, was stained yellow by the passage of horses and the manure they left behind. I dodged a couple of peasant sledges pulled by small horses going back in the direction from which I had come. Two other sledges overtook me, traveling in the direction I was taking toward Kleshtshel. I skirted a village. A couple of dogs that tried to follow me understood quickly that they must not get too close. When according to the position of the sun it was noon, I knew I had reached the halfway point.

But what was that steel-blue cloud coming toward me?

The cold was not any stronger. None of my limbs had been affected by it. And I had not forgotten to touch my nose or those parts of my face that were uncovered to check whether they might be freezing. Everything was all right.

But all at once there were snowflakes. At first they fell more or less at random. Here a snowflake, there a snowflake, falling lightly on the road, on my clothes, and on my face, where they melted pleasantly.

Suddenly there was a wind blowing strongly from north to south, bringing with it a stinging snow that covered the footsteps of men and horses and the marks made by the sledge runners.

It did not become colder, but now it became a bit harder to walk because the wind had playfully heaped up mounds of snow or whirled the snow to create deep drifts. My right foot sank to the knee, and my boots began to fill.

I had a thought: "Keep walking just as long as you can still see the road. So long as you have strength enough. Do you have strength to run? Try to run, because there can't be more than six versts left to go. See, there's the village of Dasze. From Dasze to Kleshtshel is five versts. Run as long as you can. And now that you've run this far, and you're so close, wouldn't it be only right to rest a little? Yes, here. By the side of the road. Here, on this soft pile of snow. Your whole body is warm. It won't hurt you to rest a little."

I sat down on a freshly formed hummock beside the road. I heard the wind driving snow to my right. The snow was sticking to my right side. A sweet sorrow, a sort of misty fatigue, enfolded me. The fatigue and the sorrow must be emanating from me, and that's what's helping the snow arrange itself on my body. It won't hurt to take a little nap. Especially now that I was so warm. My ears were warm; my feet were warm. A nap. To take a nap. Last night I had kept a vigil. Slept perhaps for an hour, not more. That was a mistake. If I planned to go on foot to Kleshtshel for Shabbos I ought to have slept the night through.

"How come there are tears falling? Tears welling from your eyes and falling—on whose head? The north wind is piling the snow on me. The earth—how soft it is. I ought to be resting; instead, tears are running down my snow-covered cheeks."

"Readiness is all. To be submissive," is what *Duties of the Heart* recommends. When a man is submissive his voice becomes still as a matter of course. His whole being yields to the Divinity that has created everything.

"To whom ought I now be submissive, when the snow is covering me like a quilt and the wind is rocking me to sleep?"

It's the *rattle-rattle* of the mill that I now hear under the sound of the wind. A bit of water had come into the pond. Tomorrow is Shabbos, when the mill is stopped. And my brother Moyshe, who has come home for the winter, has chopped the ice away from the wheels, put a quarter bushel of grain into the hopper, and started the mill. That way it will draw some water away from where it is swelling under the ice. Let there be rest on Shabbos. In winter, the mill turns only three days a week. The wheels turn so slowly. *Rattle, rattle.* Not so steadily. The wheels are frozen again. It would be well if I could get home before they stopped the mill from turning. It's been more than three months since I've enjoyed the mill.

"Ah, perhaps they are trimming the millstones today, and I'm not there to help. Who knows? It may be that my mother has intuited that I've started home for Shabbos on foot, and here I sit, practically covered with snow. I want to sleep and am afraid to fall asleep. Maybe she'll make them harness the white horse and send them out to meet me because it's storming outside.

"Hey, you're sitting still. Is that the way to get home for Shabbos?"

Howl . . . howl . . . The wind whirled and howled. *Howl!* Going home on foot on such a winter's day. *Howl!*

I got up and felt a stinging sensation in my toes, a stinging sensation on my face. I rubbed my face with snow. I leaped about, trying to leap out of the snowdrift that had covered me. And with unnatural energy I started to run, escaping from the place where I had taken the sad rest that had rocked me to sleep.

The stories of people who had died in snowstorms that my grandfather used to tell during long winter nights came to mind.

I was frightened, and I seemed to fly ever closer to home. Now I passed the village of Dasze. Dogs came toward me, spurring me on. I was so warm sweat ran down my face and vapor rose from my body. But I did not flag.

Then I saw the hunched village. I caught glimpses of the Gentile cemetery. And there were the spires of the church in the middle of the market square.

I decided to go around the shtetl. I could take a shortcut through the Gentile streets. Mostly I did not want to see the marketplace. I did not want anyone in the shops to see me. And so it was that I arrived at our fences and our frozen trees. I heard the *rattle-rattle* of our mill in action. And now here was the house. On Friday it was well heated, the ice on the windowpanes had melted.

"Look! Look who's here!"

There was a joyful tumult. No one could believe their eyes—to think I had come on foot. Alone—like a dog that had strayed and then found its way home again. My body was overwhelmed by such joy. Such joy.

The familiar Friday warmth enfolded me. A real joy. And I had earned it.

Between Heaven and Earth

My visit at home did not last longer than three days. I had no patience to endure the long winter nights there. That Friday excursion, that nearly fatal experience in the storm, was, finally, not really worth it. Then, because I could not be sure where the energy had come from that had enabled me to run home through the storm, I decided to go back to Orle in one of the wagons that had come to the Kleshtshel market.

In Orle I was so restless even my sleep was disturbed. Too often I went back to spend the night in the study house, where I immersed myself once more in secular books that described the world outside. I felt aspects of that world within myself. I heard sounds occasionally that did not have anything to do with a study house or my solitude in it.

Though he was so much older than me, Yitskhok, the rabbi's son, was my friend. It was clear too that he was not at peace with his thoughts. In that fervent singing of his I could sense he was trying to drown out a cry of pain. To ease an unspecified anguish that I also felt. Faith and reason. Faith and experience. The two concepts were openly at war within me. I had no rest. It was faith that had compelled me to take my tefillin when I set out for home during the snowstorm. The need for knowledge compelled me at the same time to put into my breast pocket the notebook into which I had copied the secular poems of Yehudah Leib Gordon.

Experience taught me to read through the entire Tanakh once again. To reexamine many of my earlier interpretations. To reexamine the Song of Songs, Koheles, and Job. I did not this time find that the Song of Songs contained songs that transcended all others. The songs King Solomon addressed to a shepherd girl pertained now to my experience, to the meadows I knew and in which I had spent my childhood. The songs came to me out of familiar groves of trees. From the edges of our pond overlooked by willows.

Job accused God of too much respect for the strong and the rich. Of oppressing the poor and withholding justice from them. Though I had found it written somewhere in the Talmud that Job never was and never existed, that he was untrue, was merely an exemplum and nothing more—still I no longer regarded that as a sufficient explanation. I agreed with Job. The words of his friends and God's reply to him revealed nothing to me.

The doubts in Koheles were also near to my heart. The last chapter, in which Koheles finally advises us to fear God, seemed not very persuasive. I wanted to find my own way out of the encircling doubts that had me in chains.

It was well to be a scholar. It was good to swim through the waves of the sea of Talmud. Good to recite out loud when you are all alone in the synagogue and you hear the echo of your voice coming back down to you from the women's section. It was good to pour out one's soul into the night when the clock struck twelve, when the dead rose in the old Orle cemetery behind the old synagogue and climbed out of their graves to rummage about under my windows. It was my song that brought them reluctantly out of their graves. And it was my song that set them a boundary beyond which they could not approach.

Usually, during the recitation of prayers, I sat beside the stove with a copy of the Tanakh open before me. The man beside me was a Hasid, the owner of a store whose wife looked after the business. He had time. He was a Kotzk Hasid, a fanatic with flaming dark eyes. He had coiled peyos and a fine forked beard. Under his mustache lurked a little smile.

He often studied the others at prayer. "Oxen, horses," he remarked. "An opponent of Hasidism is a horse in harness. Not a crumb of exaltation. He chews straw day in and day out. Dry as hay. Say what you will, he understands nothing of Hasidism."

The fact that I was sitting beside the stove reading the Prophets seemed to be what drew him to me, what made him willing to tell me how he felt. He recited his prayers according to the Hasidic form, but in fact the prayers seemed to be an afterthought. His mind, his essence, was truly carried away to a world somewhere above.

I could not understand why, when the second congregation was reciting the Eighteen Benedictions, he chose to tell me the following story:

"The opponent of Hasidism does not understand why, on Friday evening, we are obliged to have a drink of brandy before we eat the fish and a second drink when we have eaten the fish. According to us Hasidim, it is intended as an allusion to the book of Genesis. There, as you should know, we are told that Adam ate vegetables and herbs. Now the story is that he was weakened thereby and could not do any work. So he went before God and complained, 'I don't have any strength. I can hardly drag my feet on the diet you've given me.' God looked him over, then said, 'Fool, go catch fish.' So Adam went off with a net to catch fish in the River Hiddekel. Well, as you know, in those days even the fish could speak. And when Adam had cast his net, one poor little fish complained and wept bitterly, 'What's this? Don't I have a right to live? I beg you, let me live . . .' So Adam, seized by pity, went back once more and complained to God. 'Give me proper food. I don't have any strength. The fish have scolded me, so I don't have the heart to catch them.' God smiled and said, 'Fool, have a drink of brandy!' Well, when Adam had drunk his brandy, his heart was fortified. The little fish wept and begged and pleaded, but Adam's ears were stopped. And that's how it was. He caught fish and brought them to Eve, who made a fine fish stew for him, and he was well pleased. But the problem was that after he ate, the little fish in his stomach cried out again to scold him, 'How can you do this to us? What is this?' The same thing over again. So Adam was seized by regret once more, and he complained immediately to God. God looked at him and smiled and said, 'Fool, have another drink of brandy.' It stands to reason then that after the second drink of brandy Adam became a whole new man. All was well with him. He wanted to dance for joy..."

Looking into my eyes, the Hasid smiled under his heavy mustache and said, "It's not too late for you to become a Hasid. You're just right for it. You have the voice for study. And you could find a dance melody in yourself as well."

The Hasid was not a particularly practical man. It was whispered that he left his wife to look after the store while he spent time dancing and drinking brandy. Inwardly he danced a secret dance. Several times he stayed up on Thursdays in the synagogue during the long winter nights; he sat beside the stove with a book in his lap, singing a wordless melody. Sang up to the vault of the synagogue. There was no practical point to that. It both pleased and displeased me, as when such melodies rose in me as well, and I too danced an inward dance.

With Yitskhok's help I undertook secretly to study Hebrew grammar. This helped to open my eyes so I understood more clearly the new books I was studying. And it made many nebulous passages in the Tanakh clearer to me. I tried writing; I tried crafting all sorts of rhymed verses. Simple things I had already grasped suddenly turned strange and distant. I was fixated on what was incomprehensible and hidden.

Because of my reading in secular books I discovered a Jewish people who lived in the here and now and to whom contemporary poets spoke and to whom they taught morality.

"How do I belong to the Jewish people? In what way am I a part of that community whose faults I too carry upon my shoulders? And whose wanderings I share?"

From time to time a poor man from out of town showed up at the study house who was different from the run-of-the-mill beggars who came to ask for alms or for a place to sleep and then went on their way. These paupers belonged to other worlds and knew how to tell tales of other lands. They arrived, ate a meal, and received a few groschen from the shammes, who collected money for them during the service, after which they disappeared.

Sometimes I thought, "These folk are traveling the path I will one day take." When I was a child, I had thought that the point at which the sky touched the summer meadows was the edge of the world. I used to look toward that horizon with yearning. Now I understood that this was all childish fantasy. The world was much bigger than that. Here was Yitskhok, who had been to London. But he did me no favors by telling me stories about that city. It was he who was responsible for my discontent with each fleeting day and my anxiety about the days to come.

I began to think, "Orle is not the best place for me. Why? Because it's too small." Even though I would always figure out my place in the synagogue, I was drawn to a larger city where there are bigger secrets. Yitskhok himself had confided to me that he would eventually leave Orle. That life at home had become too constrained.

Still, I passed that winter in Orle. After visiting home for Pesach, I went right back. It was still too soon for me to take leave of Yitskhok. In him I had found a well from which I drank wisdom and knowledge. And in the books he had managed to get hold of I found a distant world that was becoming more and more familiar.

Summer, from my very earliest years, had always lifted me onto its wings and carried me lightly over the earth. And so it was that the second term I spent in Orle came toward me with a shining, melodious countenance. With the arrival of summer unknown songs began to gush forth from me. The winter nights laden with anxieties that had so tormented me and had occasionally turned me into a young Job disappeared. I sang aloud poems by Heine that had been translated into Hebrew. Poems that for me were transformed into the Song of Songs.

It was then that I wrote my first letter to my uncle Avrom Tumener's youngest daughter, the dark-eyed Sheyne. Into it I wove half of the Song of Songs. I received a reply from her that contained even more beautiful thoughts and was written in a much finer hand than my own.

Yitskhok, during the course of that summer, was not such an assiduous scholar. The summer had made him seem younger as well. His stature matched his face better. You could almost take him for fifteen instead of twenty.

He and I strolled together on those late afternoons in the lovely fields behind the town and sang songs with words and songs without words. A fountain of song streamed from us, and the rye and the wheat fields heard us sing.

A Block of Wood for a Pillow

When I first showed up in Brisk to study with a teacher there—and also to learn how to chew glass—it never occurred to me to think that within five years I would be back again in Brisk as a student, a skilled scholar, but with quite a store of hidden heretical thoughts in my head.

Orle had turned out to be small for me. I was considering a bigger city where I could be nearer to those who were imbibing knowledge from the new well. Yitskhok had inspired me to leave Orle. I never thought of joining a yeshiva. I wanted to study on my own.

So I determined to go to Brisk. It was a big city, and yet it was not far from home. My oldest sister, Frishke, lived in Brisk, and I spent a few days with her so that I could take a little time to investigate the various study houses that were closest to the Great Synagogue. I visited the synagogues when prayers were being recited so that I could examine the householders who frequented them. In Brisk, the yeshiva student was known as the poor-student. So I looked over the various poor-students who studied in the distinguished synagogues.

I also visited the famous rabbi's house. Reb Yosef Ber was no longer alive. His son, Reb Chaim Soloveitchik, or Reb Chaim Volozhiner, as he was called, was the rabbi. His stature filled the great rabbinical house. His large head and huge dark eyes saw everything. He was often seen deeply engrossed in thought, arm in arm with his advisor, Reb Simcha Zelig, a well-known fanatic with a small black beard and blazing eyes. They walked together circling the room, arguing with each other, and in that way they managed the affairs of the city. In the rabbi's house, one might also see Reb Yosef Ber's daughter, who resembled her brother to some degree and who, playing the role of a rabbi's wife, discussed community matters with respectable householders. She could quote fragments of the Gemara, hammering her points with a downward thrust of her thumb, and she fit right in with the crowd of idlers that swarmed about the rabbi's house.

I was not drawn there. Nor was I drawn to the respectable study houses that surrounded the Great Synagogue. I looked in on a study session conducted by Reb Chaim for his brightest students as they went over a page of Gemara. I was not pleased by what I saw. I was a scholar, but I was not a pious idler or a fanatic. In the study houses that ringed the old synagogue I seemed to see nothing but pure idlers.

So I sought and found a study house on a broad, sandy street at a considerable distance from the respectable part of town, far from the main synagogue. There the congregants were artisans and wagon drivers. It was the Lisker synagogue, whose only source of pride was its couple of scholars and a few pious devotees. It was a new, not entirely completed brick building. It was being rebuilt after the famous fire in Brisk had burned down the former Lisker synagogue. Here the women's section was on the ground level, separated from the men's only by a grate. The women's section was also where they stored wood. A few cords of birch and pine continually gave off a pleasing smell.

Todres the shammes, a tall, erect, tidy fellow with a small brown beard and pleasant smile, made me welcome. He found me seven eating days. Mostly they were in the homes of poor people. There were three or four young scholars from elsewhere in the study house. They were good students who had secretly looked into Haskalah books. They knew private libraries where one could find books in Hebrew and in Yiddish. There were places in the study house where such "impure" books could lie hidden all day, waiting for the silence of night when they would be taken out so that one could secretly sip teaspoonfuls of the new learning.

There was plenty of room beside the two large stoves for the three young scholars who slept there. A tabletop had been set across the backs of the pews for me, forming a double-decker sleeping bunk. I chose a block of birch taken from the women's section of the synagogue for my pillow. That sort of bed made for comfortable sleeping, and the smell of the white birchbark at my cheek was delicious to my nostrils. During the week it was rare for a congregant to come in to do any studying early in the morning. It was a work-exhausted congregation that came to recite prayers in the Lisker synagogue. It was only on Fridays that, beginning at three o'clock in the morning, the reciters of Psalms, the scholars of the Mishna, and the various sermonizers kept the synagogue awake. It was then that we students had to get up and join the congregation.

In the middle of the week the synagogue was usually quiet by nine o'clock at night. Then, with quaking hearts, we drew out our hidden secular books. As we opened one of those books, our eyes were dazzled by the letters. For a little while we strained our ears, listening to every slight sound in the synagogue to hear whether there might not be hidden some secret watcher who would discover and then tell the whole world what the poor students were doing at night in the study house. I had a particularly good knowledge of Hebrew grammar. Secretly, quietly, I sat and composed Hebrew poems—always with trembling heart. Always we had the feeling we were living in a circle surrounded by a dark wall of mist. Though we were not locked in, though we could come and go whenever we pleased, so long as we were inside the synagogue we were still in that enchanted ring.

The thing that I wanted to do, that glowed strongly before me, I had to do secretly, even in a synagogue where simple folk said their prayers.

From the sidelines some foolish glances were cast at the few young scholars in the Lisker synagogue. There was a blond young man, a religious fanatic and a fool, who spied on us. He would occasionally "raid" us at night, when he would come to see what we were up to. He was in the habit of coming up to a scholar and caressing his cheek to see whether, perhaps, the youth was, God forbid, shaving. Though there was nothing yet on my face that could be shaved, he was suspicious just the same that I had some sort of trick by means of which I kept my beard from growing.

At night I read Hebrew and Yiddish. In that period Y. L. Peretz published the journal *Holiday Pages*, in which he printed things of his own under various names: Y. L. Peretz, Y. L. P., Lamp Polisher, and so on. It was easy to read all kinds of meanings into his work, which was full of flowery language. I felt the same way when I read Mendele Moykher-Sforim's *The Mare*. Wherever I looked in those books I found the People of Israel looking back at me, always animated by the spirit of the Tanakh and the Aggadah. They confirmed me in the belief that the voice I heard coming from between the lines of text was the voice of the People of Israel who were in exile and who wept and begged to be freed.

I shed many tears reading *The Dark Young Man* by Yankev Dinezon; I could also discern the face of the People of Israel in that book. Though I read more Yiddish than I did Hebrew, just the same I preferred to write in Hebrew. My handwriting, speckled with vowel signs, looked more respectable. I sent my verses to the only judge I knew: to Yitskhok, in Orle. His letters in reply encouraged me.

I found no traces now of my childhood residence in Brisk. It is no great distance from the age of eleven to sixteen. Five years. But in that brief five-year period I had several times outgrown my clothes and my boots had grown tight. I saw Brisk now through quite different eyes. My walks to the Mukhavets, the huge river, roused different feelings in me than before. Sitting on a bank of the river on summer afternoons as an eleven-year-old barefoot boy, my thoughts were carried away toward home. In my thoughts then I built a mill on every riverbank. I saw myself as a powerful miller who could carry on his shoulders heavy sacks of grain from a wagon to the mill and from the mill to the attic and the hoppers.

Now it was just before Pesach and winter was over. The ice on the river began to melt and crack and the floes heaved up and down in the water, rising only to sink back again with a splash, heading into the stream that flowed with newly liberated energy toward the nearby Bug River. Now as I watched I had no memory of my home, of Lippe's mill standing beside the huge river. This spring-liberated river seized my spirit; together with the ice floes, it carried my very essence in the direction of an unknown world.

The time had come when I began to look beyond my home and the mill. A huge, hairy, bony hand emerging as if from a cloud had torn up my roots, which had been sunk so deeply in the dark, moist soil around the pond where my family drew its livelihood. My home was being emptied of its inhabitants. The older children had already left. Kalmen had married and opened a little shop in town. Bebl had married and now also lived in the shtetl. Her husband was a dyer who dyed wool and thread for the peasants of the region. Moyshe went off to work as a painter for the railroad. At home there were only my father, my mother, and little eight-year-old Soreh. My father had to hire an outside laborer to help him with his work.

Just the same I went home at Pesach time, but only for the holiday. This time I brought a bundle of secrets with me—secrets meant to remain hidden, though it was conceivable that I might confide in my mother. I had found other roads and paths leading me to a different life, to a world she had once herself imagined. As I traveled toward home it was with the intention of returning to Brisk that summer. And I traveled as an adult.

But home is home. No matter the distance I had traveled, no matter how good other people had been to me, none of that had succeeded in creating a new home for me.

Home is home. Particularly when my father and mother came out to greet me and when I was met by the springtime countryside and by my own river, whose odor I knew so well; when I was met by the sound of the water rushing under the two mill wheels and the lively *clip-clop, rattle-rattle* of the paddles; when I was greeted by the warm smell of freshly ground kernels of wheat. Then "elsewhere" disappeared.

The warmth of childhood embraced my entire being, as if I had just then been newly born. I was glad to be home once more.

The Call of the Outside World

When after Pesach I returned to Brisk for my second term, I took springtime with me in my coattails. But then I experienced a new anxiety. Though Brisk itself seemed brighter and purer, and the weather drew me out of doors, and though the great river attracted me, the melody of the Gemara did not ring true. A yearning gnawed at me.

One spring afternoon, when the sun poured through the southern windows of the Lisker synagogue, I was at my reading stand with the Talmud tractate Nedarim open before me when all of a sudden I couldn't believe my eyes—there was my friend Yitskhok, standing in the open doorway. I ran to greet him. When we embraced we actually trembled. We tried to restrain our tears. I looked into his face—his wide forehead, his pure blue eyes. Yes, it was my friend. I did not ask "How come you're in Brisk?" He would have to tell me of his own accord. I noticed that though he was five years older than me, I was the bigger one. He treated me now as if I were the older one.

We sat down, both of us serious and gravely preoccupied. He told me his mother had died. And that he had decided to leave his birthplace, where his every move was watched. That he was going out into the world to discover some purpose in life. He planned to study Talmud and the commentaries with even greater diligence.

He would try to be ordained as a rabbi.

"One can be a rabbi," he said earnestly, "and be an enlightened rabbi. One can study with intensity and still have time to look into secular books. We'll do it together."

For a while I sat, confused. He had made it clear that I was no longer a child. He had done it without using words. In a time of despair, with no other recourse, he had come to me, who was much younger than he.

Well, then, I had to show him that if not the older, I was the stronger of us two. I made a decision: "One thing is certain, he will not have to eat days. If he can't speak for himself, then I'll speak for him. I'll find a synagogue that will provide money for his support."

That very afternoon I went to one of the wealthier synagogues not far from the Great Synagogue. I managed to convince the shammes that one could not permit the son of the Rabbi of Orle to eat days nor could he be expected to sleep on a synagogue bench. I managed to arrange everything for my friend on that same day. The synagogue promised him a ruble a week, and they also found him a place to sleep. Because it had been hard for me to think of my delicate, frail friend crossing the thresholds of strangers to eat days, I was happy now to know he would be sleeping in a bed. When he was provided for I went back to my own synagogue. It was already late, but that night I could hardly sleep a wink.

The coming of my friend had not brought me peace. He had, rather, put a new burden on my young shoulders—the responsibility for looking after him. He seemed to me to be an older, smarter, and more scholarly brother who looked up to me because I was the one who had the natural energy, who, when he was stumbling, could reach out a stronger hand to him than his own.

But the winds that had broken a window in my own life would not let me rest. And my friend who had come to Brisk with the exclusive intention of immersing himself in the sea of Talmud—he arrived like a restless spring wind from elsewhere. But he had not gauged for himself the distance that lay between him and the old synagogue.

Perhaps the two worlds, secular and religious, had made peace within him. Perhaps he, who was the son of a rabbi, could imagine himself as a rabbi, answering questions on ritual matters, presiding over rabbinical trials, becoming the spiritual leader of a city or a shtetl. Perhaps he could come to terms with such a life and could disregard the contradictions that had been roused in me, a miller's son, who until that moment was still rooted in the good earth, who could still feel the spring wind moistening my face just as it moistened the budding springtime branches.

Ah, no. In my blood, such contradictions could not live in peace. Had I not secretly written verses like those written by the poets of my time? It was Yehudah Leib Gordon whose poems had exalted my mind. His mockery of pious idlers; his fierce attacks against Jewish traditions. The spears he had flung against the fanaticism of my world—these had made a permanent impression on me. And this was why, even in my thoughts, I could not see myself in the guise of a rabbi who answered ritual questions and who abided by all the traditional rules.

Yitskhok had, as usual, spent the whole day studying in his study house. At night he came to join me. Sometimes I went to meet him. Together we walked the quiet streets of Brisk, often arriving at the yard of the Great Synagogue and going to the banks of the Mukhavets River, where we talked endlessly about our future.

It was something to wonder at. It was he, the older one, who had thrust secular and Hebrew books at me, who had helped me by giving me my first lessons in grammar, and who had roused in me the desire to write poems. It was he who had predicted that in time I would become a poet, he whose own first attempts at poetry were in Yiddish. It was he who, in Brisk, had somehow dug up Yiddish books and brought them for me to read. And it was he who loved the work of Yitskhok Leybush Peretz and who taught me the hidden meanings in his writing.

"Peretz lives in Warsaw. If I could go to Warsaw and see him face to face I'd let him see what I've written so he could print it in *Holiday Pages*."

My friend quite unexpectedly opened an entire bundle of Yiddish works heavily influenced by Peretz.

About that time a famous orator came to Brisk who spoke of Mother Zion and how she yearned for her children and for their return home. He spoke to a packed crowd in the Great Synagogue, and his fiery words inflamed the congregation. He sent my young imagination off in a disturbing direction. Later I lay on my bench thinking of a way to get to the Land of Israel. That night I wrote a poem in honor of Mother Israel.

And yet it was my friend once again who suddenly and unexpectedly steered me onto another path.

One evening at the end of summer my friend came to the synagogue from which, as was our custom, we went out for a walk. He was radiant as he described his plans. What he now thought was this: since no purpose could be accomplished if one's soul was filled with contradictions, then it was wrong to be a rabbi without faith. That being so, we would have to change our present course of life.

"I've heard," he continued, "that there are students in Grodno who take no payment for preparing young people to be admitted to gymnasia or to the universities. After the holidays you and I are going to Grodno."

I grew dizzy. It was as if the ground had suddenly fallen away from under me and I was standing on the edge of an abyss. It was all too sudden. My mind was usually unhurried, calm. And now he had projected a life for me of quite a different order. We would go to Grodno? And tear up, once and for all, the bonds by which I was still tightly bound? How in the world could I do that? I trembled as if from cold. I had trouble finding my way back to the synagogue where I was supposed to sleep. True, in my own study house there was another young man who by day studied assiduously and at night was secretly teaching himself secular subjects. Before me now lay the option to choose one of the two. Only one of the two.

My first thought was that I should go my own way. Grodno? Where was Grodno? Who did I know in Grodno? And what if I went to a gymnasium? To what end? To acquire a skill? Why couldn't I do what my father and brothers had done? Did I intend to study more deeply? To study for the sake of knowledge, for the sake of wisdom? A new sea opened before me. Where were its shores?

Where did it begin and where did it end?

Day after day passed. The Gemara lay open on the lectern. I looked again at the text I'd been studying, and my mind refused to take it in. The case seemed unfamiliar to me, as if I had forgotten everything that, until now, I had so diligently learned.

I was glad that summer was ending. I felt ill at ease in the study house. I began to regret the years that had passed, and I . . . Was I really one of those about whom Perets Smolenskin had written at the beginning of his book *The Wanderer in the Paths of Life*? Was I one of those wanderers on the paths of life? Young as I was, had I been wandering around for so long?

Yitskhok and I agreed we had to leave Brisk. I would go home for the holidays, where I would think the situation over on my own. He would go back to Orle, where he had an older sister. After the holidays he would join me and, if necessary, give my family some explanation—or perhaps not—of why we were going so far away, to Grodno, the provincial capital.

No. Better not to explain.

It was agreed: Yitskhok would come to us. It would do him good to see Lippe's mill, my home. Perhaps it would please him; it might be that he would decide to stay there in the mill with me. We could study and be good millers at the same time.

It was decided we would each go away for a while and think about it on our own. Life stretched two hands out to me, and it was hard to choose the hand which was to lead me.

Beggars, Idlers, Preachers, and Orators

When I was young I did not understand where they came from so unexpectedly, nor did I understand where they disappeared to, those poverty-stricken travelers who wandered through my life: those beggars, idlers, preachers, and orators.

What would life in the small towns have been like in those days without those amazing folk who came among us with their hands outstretched, palms up, demanding what was due them, an amount that varied with their impudence or their own sense of self-worth?

As a boy when I slept in the study house in Meleytshitsh, such a stranger, when he came and slept near me, would rob me of my sleep. Sometimes I was afraid to shut my eyes—who could say what the peculiar man might do? Even later, when I was a bit older and had enough courage to talk with one of those poor fellows who wound up in the shtetl's synagogue, looking everyone and everything over with an all-knowing glance, I had trouble understanding what sorts of people they were.

Among them were ragged beggars with a sack hanging from a shoulder. Those sacks reeked of sourdough bread and the sweat of filthy foot bindings. They were shaggy men who had feathers in their hair. They were unwashed and shifty-eyed, and their smiles lurked somewhere inside a tangle of beard and mustaches.

Such a fellow would arrive with an outstretched hand and go

from house to house begging for coins or bread, eating along the way whatever food he was given. He continued his begging among the men in the synagogue, where there was always room for people like him. And there was warmth—though not necessarily near the stove, even in winter. His body was insulated from the cold by rags wound around tatters, one piece of torn clothing over another. Dressed like that he would collapse onto whatever spot happened to be free. And when toward midnight the synagogue had emptied out, he would light a candle by whose glow he would count what he had begged during the day. Then he would take an inventory of the things in his sack. Finally, when that was done, he would, by the light of the same candle, begin a search for lice in his bosom.

Such a fellow wandered on foot. I was of the opinion that when he spent the night in the synagogue he tainted the place with his presence. He left a shadow over the spot in which he and his sack had rested. Even days after he was gone, the place where he had slept would give off whiffs of his stench.

On the other hand, there were times when a poor man came to the synagogue who brought with him a sense of piety and shyness. He was a needy man, and yet he was not a beggar. Yes, he was dependent on the generosity of others and had been for some ten or fifteen years. But he was neatly dressed; his beard was combed. He would not look you directly in the eye, and his glance, out of shame, was directed to the ground. He would pray for a long time and look into a book. He waited for the shammes to ask him, "Pardon me, is there anything you need?"

"A small contribution. I'm the survivor of a fire. I've an older daughter who needs a dowry." After which the shammes would collect some money for him from among the congregants. Sometimes two householders went around gathering donations for him, or else people would go out into the community to collect money, going from door to door. The man himself, in the meanwhile, went about looking secretive, speaking little, looking into a book now and then, saying only a few words while his eyes were fixed on his text.

These were visitors I felt compelled to follow with my eyes; I wished I could guess when they would arrive and leave. I felt drawn to engage such men in conversation, to hear the voice of someone of whom I was somewhat suspicious. Sometimes it seemed to me that such a fellow was not really poor. That he had a home somewhere, and a wife and children. In his own town, and in his own home, he was undoubtedly talkative and quite capable of laughing out loud. And that his wandering was a way of testing the world, to discover whether there were still generous hearts to be found among Jews. I fancied that he had very little pleasure from the money he collected and that most of the time he gave it away to needy folk.

Sometimes the person who walked into the shtetl was half beggar and half idler. He too carried a sack and a pack and gave off the smell of sourdough bread, but he came to town as if he were his own man—begging nothing, just demanding. He might deliver a sermon to the congregation.

He would arrive in the evening and spend the night in the synagogue. In the morning, during the morning service, the shammes would bang the top of the Torah table and announce, "The congregation is urged to come to the early evening service because just afterward a preacher will be speaking."

In the course of the day the preacher would have invited himself into several prosperous homes, where he was well fed. Nor would he have turned down invitations to eat in the homes of the poor. He was a garrulous type, exchanging small talk with the resident scholar, however young he might be. He talked of shtetls where the people were generous and of shtetls where the householders were stingy, where it was a waste to visit.

Between the afternoon and evening prayers, such a preacher would stand on the reading platform and lecture the congregants who sat, chins in hand, listening to the drizzle of his speech but becoming neither better nor more pious. His listeners might drop a coin without much feeling into the plate the shammes passed around. These were run-of-the-mill, everyday preachers who, even if they stayed in town over Shabbos, did not add much to the holy day. They simply added to the general sleepiness of a congregation that had been stupefied by the heaviness of their Shabbos cholent.

Sometimes a fiery preacher came to town. Dark or rosy complexioned, blond-haired or gray, with blazing eyes and an envious glance. His mission was not to collect money but to punish his sinful hearers. He did not beg. He had come, he said, to wake those who were dozing away their lives in exile.

When he spoke to the congregation, he did not speak as if they were his contemporaries. He seemed to have come out of a distant past and to be indifferent to time and place. People, time, and place—all of that served only as allegory, as an occasion for drawing a moral.

"Why are you asleep, my Jews, when the sea sends its waves over your heads? Why are you asleep, my Jews, when sin has brought the very foundations of the earth to rack and ruin? Why do you snore, my Jews, when the Daughter of Israel laments her miserable fate?" No one slept as this preacher gave his sermon. Curses frequently sparked forth from the preacher's lips. And he stood there snapping a figurative whip, lashing at the necks of his "snorers" and "sinners."

For a fellow like that, a couple of householders would canvass the town, collecting money. For a fellow like that people gave in a heartbeat. "Ah, so this is for the preacher who spoke yesterday. I've heard that each word he spoke was a pure pearl. They say it was utterly amazing."

"Ah, so it's for him. My husband has already given something, no doubt. But be good enough to take a few groschen from me as well."

More rarely there would be a different sort of visitor, a pilgrim who wandered the world expiating some sin whose nature he would not divulge. One of those who did penance for the dispersion of the Jews and wandered farther and farther away from his own shtetl and home.

"Where are you from?"

"From far away. No one here will have heard the name of my town." Or: "To tell you the truth, I've actually forgotten the name of the place. The whole world has become one town, so what difference does it make what its name is?"

One such fellow passed through Brisk and found his way to the Lisker synagogue, where he stayed for several days. The melody with which he recited Gemara was so strange it seemed hardly to be Jewish. He was a young man who habitually tugged at his small, dark-brown beard, which had given it a patchy look. And the way he held on to his peyos you could not tell whether they were short or long.

On one of those late study nights, toward dawn when one's mind wandered from the Gemara to an appreciation of the summer morning, that pilgrim, who had also been awake all night, came quietly over and confided in me, "I've been to Paris. A sinful people live there. A sinful folk. The populace is steeped in whoredom. I've been to Jerusalem. The city is a dilapidated wasteland. You can hear the howling of jackals. And the sound of the Daughter of Zion weeping. I've also been to Berlin. The Germans are very wise and hate Jews. You really want to become a rabbi? You'd do better not to. There's no point in it. The Torah is like a frayed garment that is no longer respected."

When he departed the next day he had left me with a hidden secret. An undisclosed secret. Paris . . . Jerusalem . . . Whoredom and the weeping of the Daughter of Zion.

I wondered, who was this man? How did he know, though I had been studying so diligently, that I wasn't really intending to become a rabbi?

It seemed to me that this stranger, who was perhaps three times my age, nevertheless had some connection to me. I felt a kinship with him. I knew that as I got older I might end up looking like him. That like him I would wander the world, bearing my secret with me. When that man left I felt melancholy and older.

Oh, how many times have I lived on my own, not at all connected to my childhood years! What has youth actually had to do with me? Did my young age keep me separate from the older men in the synagogue? Those out-of-town visitors, those passersby, who awoke in me the feeling that my destiny was linked to theirs. I too went as they did from city to city; I went begging from house to house . . . seven houses a week to which my not-at-all bold steps led me.

At such moments my mind sought to recall Lippe's mill, where for now I was not regarded as a stranger nor as a beggar. Where, though I was a grown lad, I could still run and leap like a boy or climb a tall tree from which I could survey the world below.

But the coming and going of these visitors increasingly carried my home farther and farther away from Lippe's mill. These strangers and visitors finally showed me that the world is large. In my thoughts I followed them on their way to strange and unknown worlds.

✍ Gone Is the Joy from My Home

At summer's end I left Brisk to go home for a visit. It was an oppressive time around Lippe's mill. The usual fatigue of the month of Elul was on the willows by the millpond. It touched the water rustling under the mill wheels and the bare, withered meadows that extended to the western horizon. It affected the barnyard fowl, the old roosters, and the young ones testing their voices.

My home . . .

Had my home aged along with my parents, along with the children who had already left for the shtetl?

Yes, the years had affected Lippe's mill. It had shrunk. And whenever I looked toward it from a distance and saw the house or the mill on its pilings over the water, I felt an ache in my heart.

Why did I now have so little to say to my family? And why did my father look at me with regret? Was it that he had an inkling that his gifted Peretz, who was intended to be a rabbi, had come home too soon because he had strayed from the righteous path?

My mother was . . . a mother. She would in any case have preferred for her children to cling to her. It's indeed a welcome occasion when a child comes home—never mind from where. And particularly if that child is the one who can resolve her doubts and who was following a path into the distance where her own mind frequently strayed.

She asked me, "How do people live in such a big city as Brisk? Is anyone really able to look after someone there? What do you think, my child? Wouldn't I like to have a look at how people live in the world!"

For her it seemed that a child away from home, apart from the fact that he was studying Gemara, would also get to know the world at large.

In the synagogue, no matter how loudly I chanted passages from the Talmud, the people of the shtetl regarded me with a suspicion that passed from the eastern wall to the benches around the stove and from there all the way to the marketplace. "Lippe's Peretz is looking into impure books."

The trees on both sides of the road; the pond shadowed from beyond its edges; the ducks thrusting the water behind them with their red, webbed feet; the broad leaves of the water lilies—all of these spoke to me, demanding a justification for my absences from home summer after summer. Now I understood what it meant not to have joined the trees at the beginning of springtime when, swollen with inner life, they burst into thick leaves and buds. I could see now that I had pulled my roots up from their native soil with my own hands. That I had cut the holy bond I possessed with the moist and verdant earth, with which I had been so intimate as a child.

There was a time when every blade of grass, every seedling that emerged around our mill and in the nearby meadows in spring and the beginning of summer, had been dear to me. Everything was essential; everything made the summer lovely. Everything that sprang from the earth told me to take a full measure of delight. And I had drunk delight as avidly as I drank the water from our river. I accepted as needful the swarms of flies that filled our little house with their humming all summer long. A fly had no evil intent even when it fell into our food. Flies did no harm even when they gathered around the rim of my plate when I ate my meal of farfel and potatoes. I put up patiently with the mosquitos that took what they needed from my body. When we slept outside and woke in the morning all bitten and bloodied—why, that was part of the healthful experience and the sweet dreams that came with sleeping outdoors. Ah, but that was long ago. Long ago.

Now at the end of summer, having come as a secret secularist whose eyes were on distant horizons, whose heart was aching, whose mind was already diverted from its course, I walked the familiar paths like a stranger. Those paths that began on both sides of the dam and led from the mill to town, paths that had, day in and day out, been refreshed by my family's footsteps. Now it was on those very paths that I lost my footing. I had become too delicate to walk on muddy ground in my bare feet. I would now not tolerate dust or a bit of dried mud. Being stung by nettles while reaching for a late raspberry growing at the base of a tree no longer excited me.

Just the same, for now that discontent was only my own. It was my secret. During the two weeks before Rosh Hashanah I helped around the house and the mill the way I used to do when all the children still lived at home. My brother Moyshe was off at work as a painter for the railway in the vicinity of Bialystok. My father now had a Gentile boy to help him with the work. The paddles clapped inside the mill as always, but the cheerfulness of the past was no longer there.

The sound of the water rushing under the mill wheels sometimes accused me, "Look what's become of you. You've gone off to wither away, to wrinkle your cheeks and wear out your eyes over useless books."

It was the beginning of the month of Elul. The Days of Awe depressed my father. He complained often that his children had left home. He spoke often about my brother Moyshe and wondered whether he would come home for the holidays. How good it would be if his surviving children came home for the holidays.

Little eight-year-old Soreh was following in Bebl's footsteps. Sometimes she seemed a flower among flowers, sometimes like a bird among trees, lively, getting into everything. Hers was the only natural, vibrant energy around the house.

The shtetl folk came more frequently to Lippe's mill than they did before. Young people from town whom I did not know well, and sometimes respectable householders in whom I had little interest, came for the clear water under the wheels.

They came to Lippe's stream but not to Lippe the miller. The

229

young girls who used to come when Bebl was a girl, who used to sing and dance and stroll about the meadows, had with the passing years turned stolid and set in their ways, just as my dancing and singing sister Bebl had. Beset by all sorts of cares, she now lived in town and was the mother of two children.

My older brother, Binyomin Khayem, and my brother Kalmen both lived in town. They had become suddenly pious, long-bearded, worried Jews, as if they had not grown up in Lippe's mill. As if it were not they who had drunk the water from our river, who had mischievously climbed trees, or walked along the dam striking the branches as they passed to wake them from their contemplation.

Urtshe, who lived in the village of Probi and who used to make his way "across the bogs" from his village every summer, now had gray hair in the broad, blond beard that hid his face. He still made his way every Monday from his village to the Kleshtshel market. He would arrive barefoot, carrying his boots over a shoulder. Then he washed his muddy feet in the water behind the mill, after which he put his boots on and came into the house to wish us a good day.

Now, leading up to the Days of Awe, a strange thing happened to Urtshe. It was just before Rosh Hashanah, at Lippe's mill. Something uncanny, contrived by Satan himself. What a tale!

Here's what happened. My aunt Rivke, my uncle Avrom Moyshe, the miller's wife, and another woman came to visit us. Though it was the end of summer it was a hot afternoon. The two women decided to go bathing behind the mill where the water was cool and pure. Evidently they were tempted to go into the deeper water, where they were swept into the whirlpool near where the mill wheels turn and where, within seconds, they risked drowning without anyone taking notice.

Just then Urtshe arrived from his village. He had come "over the bogs" barefoot, and his legs were muddied to the hip. Meaning to wash off the mud so he could put his boots on before he came into the house to wish us his usual good day and to talk with us about the coming Days of Awe, he went behind the mill. And there he saw the two women in the throes of drowning. Two naked women. Naked as the day they were born.

The sight made him dizzy. Just think of it! Naked women. It was not to be endured. But prohibitions be damned when a life must be saved. Especially Jewish lives. Even though it was before the Days of Awe. Perhaps *because* it was before the Days of Awe.

Of course Urtshe rescued the two women. He pulled them from the water, laid them down on the grass, and called the people from the house. The women were not in danger. He had snatched them away from the grasp of the Angel of Death.

But Urtshe! Urtshe sat in our house looking like a felled tree. Pale as the wall, he sat barefoot, his trouser legs rolled up above the knee. With my father's approval he undertook to perform a penance: he would fast every Monday and Thursday for a month. That vow made, his heart was eased a bit. He put his boots on and went off while my worried father watched him from a window.

This somehow brought Yehudah Leib Gordon to my mind . . . Yehudah Leib Gordon and his satiric poems. My mother could not see in what way Urtshe had sinned, though indeed she did not see how being naked was revolting. My mother, who had in secret chosen to bathe in our river instead of in the dirty mikveh in town. I was tempted to tell her about Yehudah Leib Gordon and about how he scoffed at Jewish superstition; how he lamented the fate of Jewish women. I thought of telling her but I did not, unwilling to reveal my secret thoughts to my family.

On this visit home I discovered how deeply my father loved his children. My brother Moyshe sent word that he would come home for Rosh Hashanah. He would arrive on the Friday before the holiday and would be on the evening train that went from Bialystok to Brisk.

So we all went out to the railroad tracks that passed near the mill to wait for the train bearing Moyshe, who would undoubtedly be outside on the rear platform, from which he would see us as the train went on to the station a few versts away. We were all there waiting beside the tracks.

The train came and went, and Moyshe was not there.

"Evidently they're not going to give him time off to go home for the holidays. That's how one becomes a slave," my mother said sadly.

My father said nothing. He stood leaning against an alder tree, his head bowed. Tears rolled down his cheeks. My brother Moyshe did not come home for Rosh Hashanah. He sent word that he would come at Sukkos time. So we greeted Rosh Hashanah sadly. Even though Peretz was home from Brisk, my father and mother both knew his place was no longer with them. They tried to imagine just what that distant world was like to which, after the holidays, their child would return.

Their sadness pressed upon me, the same sadness that lay heavily around Lippe's mill at the end of summer.

We Go in Search of Students

The rainy autumn came all too soon, drenching the dams around Lippe's mill. You had to stamp your feet hard to get the mud off your boots before crossing the threshold and entering the house. It was just after Sukkos that the sky descended, hanging gray clouds across the district.

It was on such a rainy Shabbos afternoon after the holidays that Yitskhok came to visit us. He had come to help his younger friend Peretz leave with a lighter heart for distant places—in this case, all the way to Grodno, the district capital, which to us seemed somewhere at the very edge of the world.

The family regarded Yitskhok with wonder. Such a small fellow. With such a high forehead. Such a deep voice. When he spoke he had an air of rabbinical authority—so learned, so refined. Hearing him they half understood and were half perplexed by him. But they were pleased by his friendship with me, though both my parents were puzzled by the trip we planned to Grodno. "Is there no way to study in a synagogue nearer to home?" my father asked, shrugging his shoulders.

"It's so far you won't be able to come home for the holidays," my mother said, grieved.

They studied my friend. Clearly a rabbi's son. What a curious fellow. My mother, knowing that he was an orphan, tried in the few

233

days he spent in her house to feed him up so he would get stronger or, since he was so small, to make him grow a bit. She noticed his helplessness and was sorry that scholars had to be weaklings.

I showed Yitskhok around, explaining to him the way a mill turned grain into flour. He regarded the muscular members of the family with respect. As he walked among the leafless alder trees with their dark trunks, he looked even smaller and more delicate than usual. He had difficulty understanding my family's isolation from the rest of the world. Visitors were rare in our house. We had little to say about anyone else, and we turned silent easily.

The two of us agreed not to tell my family what our real purpose was in going to Grodno. We decided that we would say that one studied with more enthusiasm away from home: the farther away you were, the farther and deeper were you able to swim in the sea of Talmud. Perhaps from Grodno we would go on to the yeshiva at Volozhin. Perhaps even to Vilna. The names of those big, distant cities elicited surprise and consternation in the faces of my parents and siblings. Neither my friend nor I were entirely clear about why we had settled on Grodno. Perhaps it was only because of the rumor that in Grodno university students came to the synagogues to teach yeshiva boys secular subjects, the seven liberal arts.

The house turned even gloomier when the overcast, wet Shabbos was over and I began to tighten the leather bindings of my homemade suitcase. That Shabbos Bebl, who with her husband now lived in town, visited us. My brother Binyomin Khayem and Kalmen with his wife also came from town. My brother Moyshe who all summer long had been painting signal posts for the railway had come to spend the winter at home. All of us felt an indefinable anxiety. Only my brother Moyshe agreed that it was a smart thing to leave home. He had gotten a taste of faraway places and was envious of my coming journey.

I had made it clear that it was impossible for me to study somewhere closer, so there was nothing for the family to do but stand around shaking their heads as they tried to imagine the distant places where their own blood, their own child, was about to be cast away. On that fall night after Shabbos was over we sat around until late, talking much and not talking at all. Or sharing long, inconclusive silences.

My father grubbed about and found a few rubles for me; my brother Moyshe added some that he had saved from his work last summer. No one had calculated just how much my trip would cost or what my expenses would be. Neither my friend Yitskhok nor I had any idea what our travel expenses would be.

At the beginning of the week, at midday, my family watched, teary-eyed, as the train carried us away. There were mute glances, mute blessings, joy, grief, and fear on the faces of our well-wishers.

That was how my friend and I left for Grodno. From our train windows we saw little enough of the scenery through which we passed. I hardly noticed the autumn landscape as it waited for the coming of winter.

The day passed and then a long night, during which we lay on the hard benches of the compartment. The wheels rattled under the cars but offered no consoling word to raise our spirits. The world seemed a greater riddle the farther away from home we went. The nearer we came to Grodno the more anxious I was that I might not have made the right decision.

When we arrived in Grodno in the morning, we were met with a big-city racket. On the faces of Jews and non-Jews alike we saw expressions of indifference. Just the same there was someone who, anxious to earn a little something, approached us and offered to take us to a very inexpensive hotel. My friend and I put our money together and then divided it in two. I kept one half and he kept the other. He was better at numbers than me, after all; he was older and had even taken some trips.

To get to our hotel we had to pass through a muddy courtyard where there were harnessed and unharnessed wagons. When we got into our dark, narrow room each of us had the same look of anxiety. Yitskhok and I gazed at each other mutely and I searched his face for an answer to the question, "What's to become of us now?" Here we were in Grodno, in a narrow room, where some Jewish woman, a stranger, had just brought us two glasses of tea and some black bread for which she demanded a couple of groschen.

Our task was to search among the study houses for yeshiva students and, using great caution, ascertain whether it was true that in Grodno secular students came secretly to the yeshivas to teach the scholars and prepare them for entry to the gymnasia.

It was nearly noon when we found our first synagogue. There were no congregants in it. There was a single yeshiva boy who sat beside the stove reciting Russian rules of grammar aloud. When he caught sight of us he hurriedly closed his book and hid it under his seat. Then he looked with wonder at these two strangers, who looked back at him just as amazed.

Yitskhok and I both felt ashamed, as if it were we who had been caught at forbidden studies. Yitskhok, being more courageous than I was, went up to the yeshiva boy and asked him about Grodno, yeshiva boys, and students. He did not tell him about our purpose in coming to Grodno. He said that we were simply traveling through the city on our way to Vilna and that we had made a stop here. Perhaps it would prove the right place.

"And what do you do here?"

The yeshiva boy smiled broadly and a bit foolishly, then brought his grammar book out of its hiding place and showed it to us. "I certainly can't show this to any of the congregants. If you like, I'll recite a Russian poem for you."

Unasked, he began to jabber a Russian poem at us. But it sounded ridiculous coming from his mouth and made us laugh. It was not long before my mood darkened again. I noticed a similar sadness on Yitskhok's face.

We learned from this yeshiva boy that Grodno was not really the place where we could draw up full pails from the well of Haskalah. "Ah, if I could only get to Vilna. That's the place to be. Vilna is where the true students are, the ones who come at night to teach the yeshiva boys all sorts of wisdom. I envy you, going to Vilna."

We spent a sleepless first night in the hotel. We both felt as if we had been plucked out of our familiar world and had been flung far away into this strange one. Never mind that we were still among Jews, among study houses. What was the point of going secretly into a forbidden garden to gather forbidden fruit, the way the yeshiva boy we met that day was doing? If we were going to do everything in secret, if we were to hide our hunger for secular learning, we might as well have stayed in Brisk, where at least we had received food and lodging.

We counted what money we had left. We calculated that we could pay for our hotel until Shabbos was over. After that we would have to go begging. In the meantime we searched out a few more synagogues, investigated, "took the pulse" of the shammes, and it looked as though eating days were hard to come by. Danger was staring us right in the face. We both felt completely adrift.

It was Yitskhok who began to poke fun at the sort of scholarship we encountered in the synagogue in Grodno. And it was he who started to turn back. He pointed out that what we had learned up to this point need not be considered wasted. We had acquired considerable skill in Hebrew. And the Talmud itself required the deepest kind of scholarship. "To be a profound student of the Talmud can also mean that you are a learned man. And there's enlightenment in Talmud study too. Let's not spill out what we've already drawn from the well. We must get out of Grodno," he proclaimed heatedly.

I agreed. I too was afraid to stay in Grodno. I was not eager to go begging from house to house or to put up with further insults.

We learned that there was a little town called Kuznitse one train station away from Grodno in the direction of Bialystok. It was said to be a fine little town. We decided to use what little money we had left to go to Kuznitse for Shabbos.

And that's what we did. We got to Kuznitse on a Friday afternoon. Carrying our two wooden suitcases, we came to a Jewish inn. After we had taken the time to shake the travel dust from our clothes, we went to the one and only synagogue in town.

The shammes was setting candles in the candelabrum. The two of us took Gemaras from the shelves and went to the eastern wall. There we filled the empty synagogue with our Gemara song from tractate Nedarim.

The shammes came cautiously toward us, greeted us with a "Sholem aleichem," and asked, "Where are you from, and what's the purpose of your journey?" He also asked whether we wanted him to find us someplace to stay for Shabbos.

It seemed like we had been saved from drowning. I felt such gratitude for the unknown shammes, who had greeted us so cordially and who asked if we needed a place to stay for the night, I nearly cried.

❧ A Home Is Found

There should have been a bitter irony in the situation: to have traveled to Grodno so that we might meet students who would take us into their care and prepare us for entry into a gymnasium—and what was the result? More sedulous study, more singing over the Gemara, and more eating days.

It was as if we had fallen from heaven to earth. But it was to a gentle, friendly earth, which is what the town of Kuznitse turned out to be. With a certain inward embarrassment, both of us settled diligently to our Gemara study. My friend seemed to have shrunk into himself; his delicate body had been exhausted by our journey to Grodno. The failure of our mission had sapped his strength. At twenty-two, he needed a practical purpose. He regarded me, the youth of seventeen, as the stronger of us. As for me . . . there were undiscovered poems stirring in me, and I had no notion of how to extract them from my throbbing blood.

The shtetl welcomed us warmly. We were diligent students, and the synagogue goers regarded us with respect. In the midst of our studies there would come a sudden silence, and wordlessly we would wonder, "Where is this all leading?"

Kuznitse welcomed us. It provided us with good eating days. I was used to it, but eating days made my friend gag. I wanted to make things easier for him but had no idea how. He was, after all, older than I was and more experienced. And yet I felt responsible for him. He was the weaker one, smaller and paler with glittering blue eyes and a high, pale forehead.

It became a bit too much for me when all at once he got sick, laid low by a bad case of typhus. The whole shtetl worried and wanted him to get well. I was seventeen, but the few weeks of his illness matured me quickly. My friend's anxiety became my own. His years had their influence on me. Meanwhile, I was alone.

I became aware that in Kuznitse there were young men and women who had formed study groups. In some of the homes where I had my eating days there were grown children. At my Friday house there were a couple of pleasing, dark-eyed young women who studied secular books and Hebrew. This meant that on Fridays after I had eaten I lingered a little longer in that house. In order to show off their learning the young women brought out their Hebrew textbooks and recited aloud their Hebrew and Russian rules of grammar. A little later they brought out a textbook to test just how much Hebrew the visiting young man understood.

Suddenly, the eighteen- or nineteen-year-old daughter said, "Maybe you could teach me Hebrew, and I'll teach you Russian." The unexpected offer gladdened my heart. I felt the blood rush to my face as she spoke.

Their mother complained that the girls weren't letting the yeshiva student enjoy his food but were bothering him with their study questions.

"The study of Torah is no small thing," she said. "Torah on its own is plenty. You can't expect him to demonstrate a command of Torah and other kinds of knowledge."

The elder daughter argued that to study Torah one didn't have to be a good-for-nothing, one of those students maintained by the community. She spoke Hebrew to me. It troubled her that I had to leave to go back to the study house. She wanted to study Gemara with me.

It would seem, then, that some of what I had hoped to find in the big city of Grodno was available to me right here in Kuznitse.

On my Wednesday, in the home of a very pious couple who

owned a dry goods store, there was a young daughter who was a teacher of Russian. She too said a few words to me during one of the meals. She was blonde with intelligent blue eyes and a studious look on her narrow face. She too wanted to test the understanding I had gleaned at the study house. But in the process I forgot to eat and was carried away into another world.

There was a truly learned young man in the home of the cantor and shohet. He was a teacher of both Russian and Hebrew and owned books in a variety of languages. He too would chat with me on occasion and invited me to visit him. He was writing books in several languages, and if I liked he would make time to teach me Russian. Nobody in Kuznitse would find that strange, particularly since everyone knew that I was an assiduous student in the study house.

I slept beside the stove in a small room in the home of Avrom the tailor. He and his wife, both of them still young, had a couple of small children. It was a home that had a full measure of tranquility. It was good to live under the same roof with such kind and gentle working people. It was in Avrom the tailor's small house that I found true comfort. There was no limit to their generosity. Which brings me to a riddle.

Every couple of weeks I would find a couple of silver coins in the pocket of my winter coat that hung on a peg beside the synagogue door. A secret gift. For a while my suspicion was that this was the work of Avrom the tailor, who wanted to give me the benefit of his labor.

The first time I found a thirty-kopeck coin in the pocket of my overcoat I thought perhaps some member of the congregation had put the money in the pocket by mistake, thinking this was his coat. So I held on to the money for a while and did not spend it.

But when finding such coins became a bimonthly routine—thirty, forty kopecks in the pocket of my coat—I was overwhelmed by a warm feeling for some anonymous person.

Meanwhile my friend's health improved. He was no longer in danger. But the illness had left him considerably weakened. His blue eyes shone even more brightly. The acquaintances I had made while he was ill now stood him in good stead. He began by revising our plans. We would stay here in Kuznitse and turn it into our Grodno or Vilna. Here at our leisure we would go on with our parallel studies of the Gemara and could put our studies in order.

"It would be a mistake," my friend argued, "to have devoted so much time to religious studies without acquiring our rabbinical diplomas. Even if I don't want to be a rabbi, I ought to be ordained, and ordained by famous rabbis at that."

Evidently my friend had, during the course of his illness, decided to focus all his energies on the study of the Talmud and its commentators. He drew me along with him. That winter both of us studied our religious texts with great diligence, with time left to look into secular books as well. But while I was beginning to regard Kuznitse as my home and sensed that in the shtetl I would find what I was looking for, my friend's gaze was on the far horizon. He was waiting for a miracle of some sort that would transport him to some shore where he would find the tranquility that at his age he felt was due him.

The fact of the matter is, that's what happened. A marriage broker came to town and snatched my friend up. The marriage broker proposed a match for him with a bright young woman from Suchowola, in the Grodno administrative district. And that's what he did. He got married and left me there in Kuznitse, alone.

It was then that I felt myself to be fully an adult. I had learned a lot from my older friend. Now I saw my life in quite another light. When he left, everything around me seemed suddenly to have grown silent. Because we had studied together, I had become accustomed to the sound of his voice, and I didn't think mine would have the same resonance if I sang alone. When he left I lost some of my enthusiasm for study.

There followed a time when I tried to take stock of myself. It was clear to me that my friend had uprooted me from two distinctly different worlds: the world I knew at home around Lippe's mill and the world of the venerable study house. He had opened a door and revealed a free world to me, though I did not yet know for certain the true nature of it.

My home, Lippe's mill, was already far from me both geographically and conceptually. I didn't go home at Pesach but stayed in Kuznitse, where I began to seek new meaning in my life, which until then had been concealed from me.

I loved to wander at dusk in the outskirts of the shtetl near the railroad tracks, where I would beat my own path. I became aware of the blush that rose to my cheeks when young women, the daughters of the mothers who fed me, engaged me in conversations that reminded me I was now a man.

I was seventeen years old, not yet fully grown. So it took me by surprise to feel the beating of my heart when we gazed upon each other in astonishment. Life taught me that a Torah scholar is also a man; when a scholar is young, his youth is directed to the outside world by the murmur of his own blood.

I was aware that I had a small fame as a singer of Gemara melodies. As one of the young women in whose home I ate said, "When the windows of the study house are open, your voice can be heard three streets away." How could I make light of such a gift?

It was easy to find secular books in Kuznitse. Nobody seemed to mind. The good, simple folk in whose home I slept were pleased to see that their young Torah scholar, when he came home at night, found time to look into a Russian or a German book or to put pen and ink to blank paper.

On those first summer evenings when I wandered on the outskirts of town I felt a melancholy joy. I seemed to be walking with light steps between earth and sky, attuned to melodies that came from them both. It was the first summer that my life away from home, like a flower, opened its heart to the sunlight. For a while my life and my heart, undisturbed by contradictions, were at peace.

I Sing to the Daughter of Zion

The lovely summer through which I was living on the outskirts of Kuznitse stirred up memories of those lovely summers around Lippe's mill, my birthplace and home. There I had been surrounded by meadows. Here there were fields of wheat and rye. The railroad that cut through the area bound the two experiences together. The dreamy boy Peretz, who in previous summers used to run barefoot near the mill, was now, several years later, the dreamy youth who walked with measured steps out of the shtetl to witness the dusk, to accompany the evening sun as it set among wheat fields at the western edge of the horizon.

There were evenings and Shabbos afternoons when I was not alone. When, talking of high matters, I walked with the modern daughter of one of the pious families with whom I ate on Wednesdays. The subject was Dr. Herzl.

"Who is this man who has emerged from the thicket of the past to gladden the heart of the Daughter of Zion?"

"He'll gather the world's scattered Jews and lead them to the Land of Israel."

"He's convening a congress in Basel to which representatives from the four corners of the Jewish world will come and to whom he will hand over the keys to the Land of Israel."

It was like a fairy tale that everyone in the small shtetl embroidered and improved. They sang songs about the bent and veiled Daughter of Zion and of how she waited at the origin of all roads for the return of her children from the ends of the earth.

I knew the Tanakh nearly by heart. I knew the prophets. Their words of reprimand and of consolation to the Jewish people, their curses and blessings, lived in my mind. I knew three sections of the Gemara almost by heart, including the commentators and the narrative and allegorical passages. I knew as living events the legends that described the destruction of Jerusalem and the subsequent diaspora. I became aware that the very earth on which I walked, the wheat and rye fields where I was spending a pleasing summer, were foreign soil. That one had to plead for permission to walk in them. Above all else there was the Land of Israel, to which Herzl was summoning the People of Israel.

I felt songs rising in me in response to Herzl's call. Songs that came to me from a distant world, demanding that I put them on paper. Songs whose sounds I meant for the Daughter of Zion to hear along the road of all roads. The sounds would come to me from a nonexistent world and disappear into the distance. And, at dusk, on the outskirts of town, I wrote them down, humming a Gemara melody all the while.

The fathers of the shtetl knew me as the diligent student who, no matter at what early hour they arrived, was already there, filling the predawn synagogue with my song. And the daughters of the shtetl knew me as the yeshiva scholar who wrote poems in Hebrew, and even spoke Hebrew . . . For them he was, surprisingly, the one who pointed out to them all the lovely spots on the outskirts of town where the flowers grew, where the breeze rustled in the rye and wheat fields.

The Daughter of Zion carried me away from the world in which I lived. The Daughter of Zion pointed me toward the east with her finger, signaled and promised an eternal life to each one who would come to her and soothe her sorrow.

At harvest time, when men and women arrived singing to the wheat fields to cut the grain with their sickles, right at that time, instead of singing along with the reaper girl's White Russian song—

The sun circles the forest,
But does not enter it,
Just as my beloved circles my house
And does not come in

—I sang quite another "Harvest Time" song. In the song I sang, my heart lamented the devastation of my field: "I walk among reapers / who do not cut my field / who do not sing in my field."

What amazing days those were for this seventeen-year-old. The question whether to choose the synagogue or another life seemed not so urgent for a while. What wonderful evenings they were when, in the company of dreamy young Jewish women, I sang my Hebrew melodies into the dusk.

That was more than three decades ago, and now it seems to me that it all happened at some other time and in some other place altogether. As if I had died hundreds of years ago and then risen from the dead into a world where the sun no longer sets that close by, in which a young man and woman never again go on such intimate strolls, speaking through their blood and not their mouths, with their hearts and not their tongues.

I received letters from Yitskhok. He too had found what he was looking for: a home and a devoted companion. He sent me what he was writing. Yiddish essays! That seemed strange. Why not Hebrew, which he knew as well as I did?

I sent him my poems, and he praised them. I also had a letter from Sheyne, my uncle Avrom Tumener's daughter. It was a long letter with many dots between the sentences and disguised thoughts. She too knew of the Daughter of Zion; even she in her village had gotten wind of the coming redemption of the Jews from their exile. Her handwriting was even more refined and embellished. She wrote that she was now grown up and wanted to know whether I had also grown. She wondered whether I still meant to become a rabbi and asked whether there was any harm in the fact that her name, Sheyne, was the same as my mother's. "Ah," she wrote, "if I had wings I'd fly to you, if only for a moment, so we could look at each other, so we could see how each of us has grown over the last three years."

Gradually I was learning Russian. With the help of the cantor's son and the young woman in whose parents' pious home I ate on Wednesdays, I had already acquired enough Russian to speak and read books. I discovered the Russian poets. I could read and understand Pushkin and Lermontov, and I even tried my hand at writing Russian verse.

I discovered the poems of Ha-Metzayer Mané, pseudonym of Mordechai Zvi Mané. His poem "The Spring Sun Turns to the West," which is sung to a nostalgic melody, drove me from the synagogue and out into the fields.

But I can hardly say that it was poetry that took me away from the Gemara and brought me to the outskirts of Kuznitse until late into the night. No. It was the call of youth that would not let me rest. My long-dormant youth had begun to stir, like an infant bird that was beginning to peck at its shell, chipping a door through which it would pass into the twilit fields.

I thought occasionally of home. I conjured up images of my father and mother, of their quiet life in the presence of noisy waters beneath the mill wheels. Sometimes when I imagined my home from afar, it came to me in the form of a tearful mother pleading with me to come home. Telling me that in summer there was no place as beautiful as the world into which I was born. Asking, "Can your heart remain intact while being away from your parents and birthplace for a whole year?"

There were moments when I yearned to drink once again from my own river, when I was drawn to my original roots. In the end I felt like a wanderer who had found no earth in which to plant himself. The writing of my first poems, my first songs, had attached fledgling wings to my arms, and I desired only to fly upward; I wanted to detach my steps from the ground.

But whenever I was on the verge of going home to stay with my parents for a little while, I was overwhelmed by fear. There were new contradictions in my life. I had grown ripe and had fallen from the tree on which I had grown. Now that same ripeness had made Kuznitse seem like a shrunken place, too small to contain me. With the end of summer and the onset of fall it seemed that I heard the wailing of the harvested and withered fields as they pleaded with the autumn fogs to veil them. I felt within myself a similar yearning. And I waited for some sign that would cause me to leave Kuznitse before winter.

It came.

It came again from my friend Yitskhok. He was married, and all was well with him. But he felt himself "only halfway through my journey," and so, with the consent of his young, loyal wife, he was going to go to Vilna for the winter to study. Did I want to go with him? Together into the wide world, to the great city of Vilna.

At once the claims of Lippe's mill and of Kuznitse vanished like a fog. Vilna! My friend Yitskhok was presenting it to me. Awed, I took up Yitskhok's call. Vilna! The Jerusalem of Lithuania! How lovely was the road that led to it.

⟨⟨ To Vilna!

When the call from Yitskhok came to go to Vilna, I was nearly eighteen years old. I was well versed in the Talmud and its commentaries. I was ready to be ordained. Although I could read Hebrew and Russian, I was still in the forest of Talmud, with my mind off in the distant past. Still, I sensed that I was on the verge of leaving the world of the synagogue and that soon I would step out into an open and bright world.

"Perhaps a little too open and too bright?" Yes, open and broad as the broad, open sea that calls out to one lost in contemplation at its shores to stride into its depths.

The new cord that my feverish hands grabbed on to emerged from my essence and disappeared into the unfettered distance. I was writing Hebrew poems about the world and the Jewish people, poems in which I expressed my feelings about spring, about my love for the earth when it comes to life. I was reading secular books uncritically, published books that commanded my respect. I read both Yehudah Leib Gordon's blasphemies and Mikhah Yosef Lebensohn's lyric poetry. They were both as holy to me as the holy books from which I was beginning to turn away. I had assembled quite a bit of secular knowledge without noticing from whence it came. At the same time I was drawn to Russian literature and read Tolstoy, Turgenev, Nekrasov, Pushkin, and Lermontov. The world that I discerned there seemed closer to me than the one I found in Perets Smolenskin's work. At times I saw my own earth in those Gentile books: my mill, the meadows, and the surrounding trees that often awakened in me such longing and melancholy.

I thought often of the mill and of my bent father, walking in heavy boots from the mill to the shtetl, sowing his cares along the way into town. I thought of my mother, of her narrow face and shoulders, aged and shriveled before her time, also hurrying into town for something. She was full of disappointment because her still-young children were gone, leaving her alone among the aging trees around the mill.

Nevertheless, just as I could no longer wholeheartedly return to the sea of Talmud and its commentaries, I could no longer take root in Lippe's mill beside the shimmering pond. A voice was calling me farther and farther away from both the synagogue and the mill, and my heart wanted to follow this distant, familiar yet unfamiliar voice.

It was familiar because this voice was again coming from my friend Yitskhok, who had, by getting married, left me alone in Kuznitse. And now he was calling me to go off to Vilna with him, where a loyal guide was certainly waiting to lead us out onto the path of righteousness.

My friend Yitskhok, the rabbi's son, had found his match in Suchowola, in the Grodno administrative district, in the form of a woman of valor. After the wedding she encouraged him to go to Vilna to study secular subjects and to find his purpose in life. Now this friend was calling me to meet him on this path. We would go together to Vilna. There, combining our strength, everything would be easier. In a short time we would reach the sixth, the seventh, the eighth class in a gymnasium. After that, the university. And after that...

Late that autumn I set out to meet Yitskhok on the way to Vilna. The same day we got there we found a little room in a dirty little street in an even dirtier house. It was a tiny room with two dirty, hard beds—all for three rubles a month. Yitskhok paid the rent, and I felt a pang watching him. He was so small. Already he was yearning to return to Suchowola to his young wife, who was to him a lover, mother, friend, and supporter. Here, in the confines of this filthy little room in Vilna, it must have seemed to him that he had left a world full of good things and was now paying for the privilege of being shut up in prison.

We bought all sorts of Russian books: grammars, arithmetics, histories, geographies. But the new learning did not enter our heads easily. I often glimpsed tears in Yitskhok's eyes. There was a discernible distance now between us. Not so much the difference in age—rather it was that he was no longer alone. As for me, I felt as if I were a bird that had escaped one cage without having yet found another.

Our first few days in Vilna were exciting. It was, from our point of view, a big city in which Torah and Haskalah surged together like adjoining rivers. A city where modesty and degradation, piety and heresy, were to be found in the narrow alleys scattered around the courtyard of the Great Synagogue.

I had a great desire to look into the small Vilna synagogues and glimpse those studying there, to see my own likeness in them. And it was quite bizarre to me to find the entire courtyard filthy with the poverty that was spread out over the slippery cobbles. There were market vendors calling out their wares. Women cursing as they sold beans, bagels, rotten apples, fish, cookies, and animal hides. There were beggars who clutched at the coattails of passers-by. Little stalls like infected wounds on an unclean body. And above it all the sounds of scholars chanting in the study houses along the narrow alleys and around the stench-ridden courtyards surrounding the Great Synagogue.

This was Vilna, the Jerusalem of Lithuania?

If I talked with any of those students who seemed to be permanently affixed to their benches, I very soon discovered that they, like myself, had doubts about what they were doing, that the insolent "Why?" and "For what?" were always upon their lips. "Why let those years of youth be lost in desolation and pain?" Coming face to face with those studying in the small synagogues, I did not question my decision to take such a bold step away from the well that had until then filled my heart with such a delicious ache, that had filled my mind with burning dreams.

And yet, despite the fact that Vilna, from the very first moment I entered it, revealed its extreme poverty to me and exposed the dreadful mundanity in which its throngs of people were caught up, I continued to feel that in some corner of the city there existed the secret door that, when I came upon it, would open onto the new life for which my thoughts were reaching.

I felt, too, when I visited the Strashun Library, which was on the second floor of a building adjacent to the old Great Synagogue of Vilna, that the young men silently reading the secular books there were very much like myself. And the books on the shelves behind them looked out at me earnestly. Earnest—but not alien.

Meanwhile, what of my dear friend? Homesickness gnawed at him. Vilna had leached his strength. It was here that he first understood just how far from his grasp his new goal lay. It was because he was alone, because he was soon to be a father. At home, in Suchowola, his young wife was expecting a baby, and though she had encouraged him to go to Vilna, still she longed for him. His life force was draining away and his weak, delicate body was beginning to give in. At the same time, our poverty-stricken diet of bread and tea was putting a terrible strain on his body. He became ill, unable to withstand the difficult beginning to which he had led me, the younger one.

It was soon clear that he would have to leave Vilna. As for myself, without a groschen to my name, it was clear that if I didn't soon find a refuge with the coming of winter I would end up sleeping outdoors. I couldn't send for help from home. My parents couldn't help their castaway son from afar. My home only had loyal arms if a child came back to its embrace. My home could nourish someone who hungered, cuddle someone who was lonely, shelter him and find him a place to lay his head. But my home was no longer a home for someone who had been swept away by a storm.

That's how I sometimes felt in Vilna, as if I were carried there by a tempest and deposited into its narrow, poverty-stricken, beggar-infested streets. To become a beggar seemed like a horrible fate.

And so, though our rent had been paid for the month, I went

looking for a place to sleep in a synagogue. A synagogue that would not require that I be a pious Torah scholar. As for food, I would worry about that later.

I found what I was looking for on Nowy Świat Street. It was a cold basement synagogue in which porters and draymen prayed. The shammes, a blond, young ex-soldier, understood me quite well. Not only was he going to let me sleep in the synagogue, but he promised to find me twenty kopecks a week. It seemed a great stroke of luck at the time.

But my friend had fallen ill and was bedridden. The only thing that revived him was the hope that he would soon go to his devoted wife in his new, warm home.

Winter came, and I brought what little bedding I had into the cold synagogue on Nowy Świat. One freezing morning before dawn my friend Yitskhok was to leave Vilna to go back to Suchowola. I came out to accompany him. I had stayed up the whole night, helping him pack his case. And just before dawn, with his case on my shoulder, we silently walked through the streets of Vilna to the train station.

He was off to Suchowola to start his life as a Hebrew teacher there, leaving me to return, troubled, to my cold basement synagogue on Nowy Świat Street.

⤜ Hunger, Need, and Cold

Although my refuge was in a half-dark little synagogue on Nowy Świat, I had free access to the world of Vilna. The few Gemaras on the shelves of the poor synagogue humbly asked to be looked into from time to time, but my heart was no longer in the task.

Winter came, and I was insufficiently dressed. The twenty kopecks a week that the good-hearted shammes got me from somewhere were just enough for black bread, tea without sugar, and a white paper collar that I changed once every two weeks.

I slept in my clothes on a hard bench in the synagogue with an old prayer shawl at my head and, for a blanket, my overcoat and a few old curtains from the Torah ark.

The synagogue was so poor it was heated to a bare minimum only once every morning, so it was always freezing at night with a cellar-like cold that crept right into my bones. The congregants, draymen who popped into the synagogue in the morning, kept their heavy sheepskin coats on as they hastily prayed.

Hunger, poverty, and cold; hunger, poverty, and song.

Perhaps I should not even mention the hunger. Because if you have a piece of black bread and tea twice a day you don't actually starve. But you're still in need. The body demands something more. Sheer youth kept my spirits up. And song. And a new, soon-to-be-traced path to follow.

I was a bird suddenly freed from a dark forest flying over a bright, open field. Still, I knew it was winter, and cold. I knew that hunger rumbled in my stomach.

I was not alone in the cold synagogue. There were three other young men who, like myself, had left their former lives and were not yet well started on their new ones. The kind shammes was tolerant of us all and let us cluster around the cold stove, warming it with our thin bodies just as we warmed the hard benches.

There was among us a former child prodigy who had once been a diligent student in Volozhin. He was a round-faced, blond young man with a perpetual smile on his face—a short, broad-shouldered fellow who smiled warmly at me when we first met. His name was Eltshik, and he knew Vilna well. He was always on the move. No place in town was unknown to him. He used to go to the library at the Daughters of Zion and bring back all sorts of Hebrew books. He did not suffer from hunger because he used to eat at the cheap kitchen on Nowygrod Street, where the beggars went to eat their fill.

Eltshik knew there were writers in Vilna who contributed articles to the newspapers *Ha-Melits* and *Ha-Tsefirah*. And he was acquainted with old Kalmen Shulman, who by then was going blind.

When Eltshik read some of my most recent poems he became enthusiastic. He was exalted by them. It was almost as if the Divine Presence glowed in his face. He was determined to take on the world for my sake. He complained that I did not eat enough. "You can't survive on black bread and tea." And he offered to take me with him to the cheap kitchen, where he would get my bread and plate of food for me so I wouldn't have to stand in line with the beggars.

He also offered to introduce me to his friends, the contributors to *Ha-Melits* and *Ha-Tsefirah*, so I could read my poems to them.

One day he forced me to go with him to the cheap kitchen, but I was repulsed by the smell and by the sight of the beggars hastily slurping down their food.

I remembered what he had said about the writers he knew— that he usually encountered them in the Daughters of Zion library, that he shook hands with them and called them by their first names. That he even knew where they lived. "Gontshar," he said, "writes for *Ha-Tsefirah*. He's a hunchback. He looks just like Moses Mendelssohn. You can usually find him in a small synagogue in the courtyard. And the writer Markulis, who writes for *Ha-Melits*, his real name is Gorelik. He's house-sitting for a family that has gone abroad for the winter."

So, with beating heart, I went with Eltshik one morning to meet Gontshar, the hunchback who looks like Mendelssohn and who writes for *Ha-Tsefirah*. Eltshik kept encouraging me every step of the way. "You'll see. He'll be glad to see us. He'll read your poems, and he'll like them."

"There he is," Eltshik said, pointing to a diminutive, hunch-backed young man wrapped in heavy tefillin seated at the eastern wall of his synagogue. It was the time of the second morning service, and there were some twenty or thirty congregants. "That's Gontshar. We'll wait here until he sees us. You'll see; he'll recognize me and come down to us."

Indeed, that's what happened. Gontshar, an intelligent-looking man with an ironic smile, came down to us at the door and greeted Eltshik like an old acquaintance. Then he greeted me and asked who I was. "He's a young poet who writes in Hebrew," Eltshik said, introducing me with pride. "He sleeps in the small synagogue on Nowy Świat. He wants to read his poems to you."

I blushed fiercely. At the same time it seemed only natural to me that a writer for *Ha-Tsefirah* should be in a small synagogue wearing heavy tefillin. Perhaps he was even in the same quandary I was in.

"Come to my place tonight and bring your poems," Gontshar said, smiling. So he had an apartment somewhere, yet he still went to the synagogue to pray. I liked him.

Eltshik regarded the exchange as a great victory. He said, "Gontshar is a great writer. It'll be good for you if your poems please him. Tomorrow we'll go to Markulis's—Gorelik's, that is."

The next day, a frosty morning, Eltshik, enthusiastic as ever, took me with him to Rudnitsky Street to meet Gorelik, or Markulis. As we climbed the stairs to the second floor of the brick building, we heard the sound of a Gemara melody, but it was actually someone enthusiastically and loudly reciting a Hebrew poem. We paused on the steps and listened with bated breath. It was Bialik's poem "To the Legend" ecstatically read. We heard steps going back and forth inside and the reciting, again and again, with even more rapture.

Eltshik knocked on the door, and it was opened by a tall, pale young man with sunken cheeks and intense, blazing eyes. His large, unheated room was so cold that when the young man spoke, vapor rose from his mouth. His ecstatic singing drove off the cold. He invited us in with open arms.

When Eltshik introduced me as a young Hebrew poet, Gorelik said at once, "Take out all your poems and read them. I'll listen."

My teeth were chattering both from excitement and from the cold. I read him my poems.

"You're growing into a real Hebrew poet," he said, slapping my shoulder. "Where do you live? Oh yes, in the small Nowy Świat synagogue. Good. I'll come see you there."

Warmed up by his words, Eltshik and I went through the streets of Vilna, dancing and singing.

"We've still got to go see Kalmen Shulman. He's old now, but I want you to meet him," Eltshik said.

That meeting was not fated to be. Shulman died that winter. But Eltshik's efforts on my behalf were not wasted. He opened the door to the free world even wider for me. He helped me to lay the foundations of my life.

Eltshik found copies of the Warsaw weeklies *Ha-Dor* (in Hebrew) and *Der Yud* (in Yiddish) and brought them to the synagogue. It was in *Der Yud* that I first encountered works by Sholem Asch and Avrom Reyzen. Eltshik tried to persuade me to send my poems to *Ha-Dor*, whose editor was David Frishman. "You'll see," he said. "He'll accept your poems."

How fortunate one is to encounter an Eltshik in the course of one's life. To feel the glow of his generosity. Meanwhile, hungry and ill-clad as I was, I walked about singing.

Eltshik was so proud of me. But that winter I also gave him something to worry about. My strength began to fail me. I had dizzy spells and was unsteady on my feet. Eltshik said, "Listen to me. Come with me to the cheap kitchen. You'll get stronger if you eat a good meal once a day." I agreed and went with him a few times. But the food did not agree with me. I was too emaciated.

When spring came around I was overwhelmed to the point of tears with longing. I wanted to walk out of town so I could meet the oncoming spring and exalt my soul with its beauty. But by then I was really very weak. Eltshik took me to the hospital for the poor, where I was given a note to see a doctor.

A very young doctor, with little or no experience, examined my emaciated body. He listened to my lungs and my heart with his stethoscope. Then he asked me what I was doing in Vilna. He listened and smiled the way a father might smile at some clever thing his little boy was saying. Then he asked, "Do you have a home somewhere?"

"Yes. My home is in Grodno province. It's a watermill near the town of Kleshtshel."

"Your parents are living?"

"Yes."

"Have they enough to eat?"

"Yes. Millers don't lack for food."

"Do they have a cow?"

"Yes."

"Does she give milk in summer?"

"I suppose she does."

"Then forgive me, young man, but I must tell you. Go home at once, immediately. Go home to your parents at the mill, where you can get plenty to eat and drink. Otherwise, if you stay here, living in the synagogue, starving and writing poems, you will soon die."

"Soon die . . ." That was it. I felt a cold sweat breaking out on my body. I walked out into the clear day on unsteady legs and with tears streaming from my eyes.

I went to the outskirts of town to see how the outdoors was greeting spring. I regarded the trees drawing their sustenance from the moist soil. I pulled up a few green blades of grass. Tears still streamed from my eyes. "Die very soon . . ."

I did not want to die.

I confided my situation to Eltshik, who talked with the kind shammes. The shammes gathered some money together for my travel expenses. Then, weak, drained, pale, and carrying a bottle of medicine and a bundle of poems in my breast pocket, I went home to my parents, carrying my broken body homeward to the green meadows that surrounded Lippe's mill.

✍ I Go Home III

I left Vilna toward evening three weeks after Pesach. Because I did not want to frighten my family, I did not let them know I was coming. On the train to Kleshtshel I lay awake all night on a hard bench of the third-class car.

Ever since the young doctor in Vilna told me, "Young man, if you don't go home to your parents, you'll die," those fiery words stood out in my mind. More than anything, my awakened youth was craving life. My return home in the springtime was sad. I had never in my young life experienced such acute sorrow.

Kleshtshel, when I drove through it on the wagon that took me from the station to the mill, looked strange to me. My brothers, Binyomin Khayem and Kalmen, now lived here in the shtetl, as did my sister Bebl. I made a brief stop at each of their doors and then hurried on home, feeling like someone who, having left in his youth, returns in old age from a distant land to his birthplace. Though I was eighteen years old, I did not feel young as I drove through the Gentile streets.

Still, as the wagon passed the last barn, coming out of town to the fences and dams and starting down the road between the rows of alders and willows, I breathed in the fragrance of the spring blossoms and felt like a small child when he catches sight of his mother. The warm air struck my face. The meadows surrounding the mill were decked out in their spring finery. The row of willows beside the pond across from the house seemed somehow heavier than I remembered, bent lower over the water. Fish leaped toward the sun. The green grass of the surrounding meadows glowed in the early morning light. The mill wheels were turning, *clap-clap, clap-clap.*

Someone in the family looked out the window and saw me coming. Everyone ran out to greet me. "What's the matter? What brings you here?" my worried mother asked as she kissed me.

My father was astounded. "What . . . how come . . . You didn't come for Pesach, but why now, of all things?"

My ten-year-old sister Soreh, now the only child in the house, looked on, amazed.

A pale German boy, nearly my age and covered with flour, came out to meet me. "He's our new miller," my mother said. "There's no one else around to help your father."

We went into the house—the same house, and yet different. My home had become smaller since I left to explore the world. After living in a big city like Vilna, the house looked both smaller and emptier. All of the children but Soreh had left. Though I had been gone only a year and a half, my father and mother had aged. I, who had lived through a whole lifetime in the interval, understood that more than clock time had passed. It seemed to me that I alone had already lived out my life. The fact that the doctor from Vilna had called me "young man" proved nothing. He had, after all, ordered me to go home or I'd die.

My mother tried anxiously to find out what was wrong with me, but all I said was that I had simply been overworked in my studies. I had overestimated my strength and needed to rest. I wasn't eating enough in Vilna, and besides, I did not want to eat days there anymore.

I may say, in passing, that I felt glad to be home. I had been longing for it. As for the bottle of medicine given to me by the doctor, if I felt like it I'd take it; if not, I would also be fine.

Home is home. The child within me, which had been hidden somewhere, appeared as soon as my mother started to feed me, palpated every part of my body, and kissed my cheeks over and over.

Home is home. After several days my strength began to return. There was new color in my pale, drawn cheeks, and I understood why the clever young doctor had ordered me to go home upon examining my emaciated body.

During those first days, the familiar region took me to its bosom again. I walked barefoot in the meadows as I had done when I was a boy. Feeling the rawness of the earth on my feet, I felt that I belonged there. I had been wrong to go away. I had been wrong to turn myself into a bench sitter. To live like a beggar by knocking at other people's doors.

At times it seemed that the trees frowned angrily at me, as if they were asking why I had left them for so many years. Even the willows overlooking the pond looked at me askance. During that time back home, I was drawn to measure the meadows with barefoot strides. The mill had become a bit unrecognizable.

My father wanted desperately to know what I had been doing in Vilna. And why I had stopped eating days. He wondered when I would be ordained as a rabbi. He had been told in town that I was studying something else in Vilna, and now he wanted to know what that was.

My mother also noticed a change in me, but she was pleased by it. Now she could talk to me about the sorts of things one could only learn in a big city like Vilna. Over the years she too had lost some of her piety and some of her faith in the World to Come. She wondered what was being said in Vilna about that next world.

Home. Well, home is home. For a while I could feel my roots again in the moist earth around the mill. But I was soon affected by an autumnal feeling. The house itself seemed to have grown bent, and now that the children were gone it felt empty, like a nest whose birds have flown away at the end of summer.

I wanted to know why there was a barren spot in the grass on the other side of the bridge this year. Why the spot was the size of a person. My mother said sadly, "A peasant who used to come to the mill drowned near there last summer. He was taken out of the water, but it was too late. He was dead. The authorities let him lie beside the bridge for a full ten days. In time he began to rot, so the grass seemed as if it had burned, and this year there's no grass growing on that spot. A black spot the size of the drowned man. It's a fearful place at night."

"I'm afraid to go there," said Soreleh.

The young German who helped my father around the mill was pale and thin like me. Sometimes he spat blood. I knew him. His father, who was dead, was a German who had wandered through our region as a magician. His father would come back to us from time to time. He was good with his hands and knew how to fix the mill. One time he brought his only son with him, a small, pale boy. Now his only son was a miller with my father and sometimes he spat blood.

He felt like a brother to me. We became friends. Because the boy was ill, he felt drawn to me. Both of us had the desire to live. I helped him with his duties around the mill. Sometimes we went for walks in the meadows and bogs to look for currants. Roaming over the meadows, we looked like twins.

I grew stronger as the summer arrived, but the young German did not. His daily failing health saddened me greatly. My mother cared for him as if he were her own child.

"Wait," he encouraged me. "Wait till the raspberries ripen. Raspberries give you strength. We'll gather them and eat them. And get stronger." And so he waited for the raspberries to come. We looked for them everywhere and ate them wherever we found them. In one sense he was right. Later in the summer I felt much better. As my body paid its debt to the many uneaten meals and sleepless nights in Vilna, my youthful energy returned. Meanwhile the meadows were being mowed and the air was fragrant with hay.

One hot summer's evening, when the hay was being gathered, I was getting home from the shtetl. My mother put food before me and watched me with joyful sorrow as I ate. Suddenly my sister Soreleh ran in crying, "A peasant is drowning in the river!"

I flung my food aside and ran out to the stream behind the mill. Peasants were running in from the fields, all of them pointing toward the water, but it seemed not to occur to any of them to go into the water and save the drowning man.

I noticed that bubbles were rising in the water at a spot near the mill wheels. Throwing off my clothes, I jumped into the stream and swam toward the bubbles. Then I dived. A moment later I surfaced with a half dead young peasant—a giant of a man, three times my size—in my arms.

I managed to bring him out of the water, where the other peasants took him from me and laid him out on the grass. They pressed the water out of him, and lo and behold, to everyone's joy, he came to life.

A huge one-eyed peasant appeared. Falling on his knees before my mother he cried, "Forgive me, dear. Forgive me. I insulted you today. You are a holy person, and because I insulted you God punished me. Forgive me." Still on his knees he kissed my mother's hands.

"I forgive you," my mother said, crying tears of joy. "Now get up."

The resuscitated peasant also stretched out his arms with all his strength and asked my mother to forgive him.

The one-eyed peasant then announced to everyone that he had insulted the miller's wife that morning when he had asked her for the landlord's key to the bridge—the key the landlord had given the miller to look after because the landlord charged twenty kopecks per pood of hay that was transported over the bridge. And when the peasant had asked the miller's wife for the key and she had refused to give it to him, he had threatened to beat her and called her ugly names. And that's why God had punished him.

Then, weeping, he embraced and kissed me, saying, "You saved my only son. You who are so pale and thin, and he's so big. And yet you saved him. I will be beholden to you forever."

So even in my own home I achieved the status of an adult, and I felt a resurgence of the strength that had dissipated while living away.

That summer, when I considered what I had lived through in the last five years—eating days, the diligent study of Mishna, Gemara and the commentaries, Midrash and so many other rabbinical books—when I tried to put it all together and see how it could fit in around Lippe's mill, I couldn't find any place for it. I saw for myself how all the knowledge I had acquired in the confines of the study houses had nothing to do with my birthplace.

I sat under an old willow tree beside the pond and, my voice trembling, read my poems, my longings, and my uncertain gropings aloud to the trees that faced me. I felt as if my surroundings understood me, that everything inclined itself toward me to hear what I had to say.

At such a time and in such a mood, my home dominated me. The city of Vilna disappeared into a white fog. In such a mood none of the cities or shtetls in which I had lived immersed in Torah and worship had any importance. Powerful moments of my childhood years came back to me.

It was then that the summer spoke to me, saying, "Your home saved your life. Where else should you be directing your steps this time?"

Lippe's Mill and the Jerusalem of Lithuania

I went to work in the mill. I did it to help out the young, sickly German, whose dry cough reverberated everywhere. I was unhappy that, even as my health returned, the life force was seeping out of his emaciated body. His pallor made me very unhappy. I saw in him an aspect of my own dried-out figure of half a year ago in the synagogue on Nowy Świat. At summer's end he got a lot worse; his lungs labored to take in air without success. Finally he asked to be taken to a hospital. When he left the mill my mother, shedding tears, went with him as if he were her own child. But the life-hungry look in the young miller's eyes continued to haunt the mill with an acute sadness.

The second hay gathering had been removed from the surrounding meadows; a cold dew settled more and more frequently upon the trees and grass, turning them yellow.

Again, without warning, I felt ill at ease. It was the return of an old feeling that had come upon me years ago, and it had resulted then in my leaving home. Now what I got from being at home was a perpetually autumnal feeling. I had been sent back by my doctor in Vilna to where in familial surroundings I could recover my health. But now that I was well nature demanded her due. Once again, as on earlier visits, when I resisted re-immersing myself in the current of my life's search, my imagination seethed with plans that would keep me at home. I fantasized that I would become rich enough to buy the mill from the wicked landlord. That I would become the miller and would look after my parents in their old age. I never spoke about these fantasies with any of my brothers and sisters. What were they after all but the dreams of a twig by the side of aging trees?

As the summer progressed I anticipated the coming of fall. The sun declining over the woods to the west of the mill left long shadows on my parents' faces. The willows across from the house had aged, and the millpond, with islets and reeds encroaching along its edges, had grown narrower.

In the course of that summer I noticed that my mother went more and more frequently into town to visit her children who were married and lived there. Moyshe, as always in the summer, kept his distance from home. Ten-year-old Soreleh found her way into the shtetl by herself, and as I did at her age ran errands there for our mother when she needed salt or pepper.

As for myself, I kept my distance from the shtetl, though there were now several young men who, like myself, had gone off to other shtetls to study, to eat days, and to pore over volumes of Torah as well as snatches of secular learning. They were youths like me who came to visit home. Some of them were my former classmates from heder. I formed a friendship with one of them, Sanneh, a charming boy of about my own age. He was the son of Leyzer the windmiller. Sanneh came often to my home, and we would go out into the meadows, where I secretly read him my poems.

In the course of that summer I continued to turn my feelings into poems that never saw the light of day. Poems that spun a filamentary link between my life at home and my life in Vilna. Poems that waited to be read by those who would understand them.

My father often talked with me about the great rabbis in Vilna, and he wondered when I would myself become a rabbi. He imagined Vilna as a city full of great rabbis, of study houses packed from the eastern walls to the doors with people studying Torah and where the melodies of Torah study resounded everywhere. And in the midst of all that holy busyness, there was his son Peretz. "Why haven't you been ordained? Is it that they don't ordain eighteen-year-olds?"

That summer, without intending it, I often made my father unhappy. He would take a holiday prayer book down from a shelf and, putting on his spectacles, leaf through it till he found the Yom Kippur liturgy. Then, pointing to a passage, he would ask me to look, saying, "Do you see anything here?"

I would look into the book, translate the few lines he pointed to, and say, "No, I don't see anything special."

"What do you mean?" my father said. "Today, in the synagogue, they pointed to that specific passage as predicting the coming of the End of Days. The coming of the Messiah, who is expected soon."

But no matter how often I read the passage, I could find no such interpretation.

My mother watched us. She did not quite understand what was taking place, but seeing how I was making my father unhappy, she tried to help me out by saying, "Maybe the great scholars in Kleshtshel don't see anything there either." My father closed the prayer book, put it back on the shelf, and walked out of the house.

My mother, seeing her opportunity, took me aside to reassure me that she did not care whether I became a rabbi or not. She seemed to have grasped, and did not mind, that in Vilna I was acquiring secular learning as well as Torah. She was fully aware that in Kleshtshel people lived their lives in intellectual darkness and was pleased that at least one of her children would emerge from it.

She had her own vision of Vilna. I had spoken with her about Vilna many times. Unlike my father, she did not see it as a city of scholars fixed to their benches in small synagogues. For her it was a place where young women were not forced to marry at an early age, where they too could expect to amount to something, where they could hold their heads high.

"Do you think, my child, that I don't understand how people live in Vilna? I wish that I could afford to send you there with your expenses paid so that your health wouldn't suffer. My heart aches when I think what it must have been like for you."

Another time she said, "I know, my son, that there's nothing here for you. I know that the work of the mill would get done without you. If you stayed here at the mill you wouldn't have the chance to amount to anything."

At the end of summer the peasant with the blind eye whose son I had pulled out of the water a few months ago showed up, bringing a new oaken barrel he had made himself. It was a present for my mother.

"See?" he said, with tears in his only good eye. "See, I haven't forgotten what your son did for me. Or how I insulted you. I'm only sorry I have no cucumbers in my garden. Later I'll be sure to bring you some cabbage, which does seem to have grown successfully."

The tall, one-eyed peasant's face was suffused with blood, and sweat broke out on his forehead. He held the fragrant barrel in his arms as one might hold a shivering child and told my mother that he would have been as bereft as a stone if I hadn't rescued his only son, his support in his old age.

He hugged me, kissed my cheeks, and said, "I think it's wrong for people to hate Jews. Very wrong, I say. Here, for example, you went and rescued a Gentile. What does it prove, what? It proves that all people are brothers." Turning to my mother, he asked, "Why is he so skinny? Let me have him for a few weeks, and I'll fatten him up."

My mother said that she too wished that I were not so skinny, but there was nothing she could do about it. That I only came home for an occasional visit and that I would be leaving soon.

The peasant said, "Maybe God sent him home so he could rescue my son." And he stood silently looking at me and down at the ground.

Summer was over. The more the days dipped toward the winter side of the sky the sadder I became. My heart was heavy, and my thoughts turned more and more frequently to Vilna. There were moments when I was beset by fear as I imagined Lippe's mill in the winter frozen solid with ice and saw myself bundled and wrapped up going out to the waterwheels with an ax to chop away the ice.

Vilna was calling. Vilna was warning me not to stay home for the winter, saying, "Get away from there. You'll die if you stay in

Lippe's mill. Home can mother you, but it can also destroy you. Get away while you can!"

I poured my distress into my poems and hoped that finally I would hear a true voice from Vilna that would call me by my name. That a friendly hand would take hold of me and lead me away from Lippe's mill, where again my life force was beginning to drain away.

In the interval between Yom Kippur and Sukkos, the call from Vilna finally came. It freed me from the bitter despair that had assailed me as I stood next to my father in the synagogue on Rosh Hashanah and Yom Kippur.

In the small synagogue on Nowy Świat Street where I had been living there was a congregant, a respected Jew, a former landowner who had moved to Vilna for the sake of his children who were studying in a gymnasium. We had talked several times last winter. Apparently, he had his eye on me. It was now he who sent me word through a young man from the synagogue that if I would return to Vilna for the winter, he would hire me to teach his younger children Hebrew. He promised, moreover, to pay me fairly for the work.

It was a timely call to which I responded at once. This summer my home had put its sickly son back on its feet and sent him off with tears in his eyes, back to far-off Vilna for the winter.

✐ On My Own Two Feet

As I lay on the hard bench of the third-class carriage in the train, I heard again the anxious conversations I had participated in that summer. "The mill isn't what it once was, my son," my mother had said, her lips trembling. "Your father is all by himself, and it's getting harder and harder for him to do the work. It's not too bad in summer, but when the winter comes . . . it's frightening to consider living here in the middle of nowhere. That's when thieves come. They wait for the water to freeze, then they climb into the mill at night and steal sacks of grain."

My father too spoke of how hard it was to be alone. The landlord pressed him for the rent money. It was hard to scrape together the hundred and twenty rubles for the year's rent. It was frightening to be alone.

Though he was already seventy, my father had not aged much. He was like an oak tree, broad, hard, deliberate. But he suffered from the departure of his older children. My little sister Soreleh, who was a sprightly ten-year-old, could not by herself fill the house or the outdoors with vitality in the way that ten years ago the children had made the house seem full.

My return to Vilna was sad, even though I was traveling with the knowledge that there were pupils there waiting for me to teach them Hebrew and that I wouldn't have to seek out a refuge in some synagogue.

It was a sunny fall morning when I climbed down from the train carriage in Vilna and went to a cheap basement inn not far from the station, where I would stay for a little while. I ordered tea, and while I waited I took out a bottle of raspberry syrup my mother had made that summer. There was always an abundance of raspberries in the woods near the mill, and it was the berries I had picked that my mother had turned into syrup. It was one of those bottles of syrup, made and corked by her own hands, that I started to open. She had packed it among my things with a cloth carefully tied around it in case it leaked.

But evidently the rattling of the train during the night had shaken the bottle, and gases had formed in it. Now, as I untied the string, the cork popped out with a bang, spewing raspberry juice to the ceiling, which then dripped onto my face. The smell of raspberries, the smell of my lost home, filled my room at the inn. It brought tears to my eyes that were long overdue. My mother's pallid face appeared in my imagination, and without her saying a thing I read in her eyes: "A bad sign, my son. A bad sign."

That same day I returned to my former refuge, the small synagogue on Nowy Świat where I had written Hebrew poetry and worn my health down. The shammes told me that my would-be employer was expecting me. I went at once to the rich man's house and met with him and the two gymnasium students whom I would be tutoring. I learned that I would be expected to teach them two hours each day, five days a week, and that I would earn six rubles a month.

Six rubles! What could be better? I would be immediately independent. Not only that but my two pupils had an older brother and an older sister who were students in the university in St. Petersburg, who kindly offered to teach me Russian as well as the other subjects I would need to know if I meant to take gymnasium or university exams.

After that meeting I went off into the side streets of Vilna to look for a place of my own to live in. I found what I needed in the home of a young couple, herring vendors. They set up a bed for me in their kitchen and showed me a couple of rooms that they were prepared to set aside. The rent would be two rubles a month, which would include a free glass of tea each morning.

I couldn't do better. Rent at two rubles would leave me with four rubles a month to spend. Almost nineteen years old, I would finally be able to stand on my own two feet. I wouldn't have to plead or beg or be dependent on anyone else. Nor would I have to go hungry. Now, on my return to Vilna, I felt that I was fully grown up at last.

The autumn passed and winter came. My pupils were pleased with me, and their older brother and sister, my teachers, were also pleased with me. The previous years I had spent studying away from home were like being buried deep in a dark cellar. Now the Vilna through which I strode, with its network of streets and alleys running uphill and down, with its filthy courtyards and its overflowing gutters, seemed to have been reborn. I explored the city and its outskirts, where pine forests stood guarding the town. I could feel my slight body growing taller; my clothes were getting tight and short. All the while poems flowed easily from my pen.

I visited the small Vilna synagogues quite often and talked with the young scholars who were there for study and worship. Occasionally I was moved by the way they sang a Gemara tune. Sometimes I was prompted to open a Gemara and to utter my heartfelt song to the vaulted roof overhead.

But I recognized, both in their eyes and in their songs, that these young scholars in the small synagogues were possessed by the same longings and the same sorrows that had once crushed my spirit. When I spoke with them I found that some of them were fanatics while others were skeptics. I proposed to them that we form a group to be called "Torah from Zion." We would gather a few times a week in a synagogue, where we would all study a page of Gemara but in a more enlightened, progressive manner. The main thing was to study Hebrew and grammar.

The idea pleased them. Several dozen youths, bigger and older than I was, joined the group. They came on time, and we talked about the larger world as well as about the Land of Israel and the Daughter of Zion. We spoke of the Jews' return to the Land of Israel. Though we ostensibly met to study Gemara, we pored fervently over Hebrew, grammar, and secular books as well.

I explored all around the little synagogues, looking into the deep, damp courtyards and peering into tiny cellar windows as I got to know Vilna's poverty. With one excuse or another I was admitted to those cellars, where I spent an hour or two with "the dwellers in darkness," as I called them in my as-yet-unpublished poems. I met people of my age or older who had abandoned religious studies and, captivated by the new learning, were trying out their talent for writing poetry. They were enthusiastic about Bialik's work and could recite his poems by heart.

I tried my hand at describing Vilna's poverty in Yiddish, a language that was at once easy and hard for me to write in. Without quite knowing why, I ended by writing stories in Yiddish and poems in Hebrew. It may be because the Daughter of Zion required that one sing to her in the Holy Tongue. In the years I had spent studying in synagogues, on those late Thursday nights, I had often addressed her in Hebrew, and she too had spoken in the language of the prophets and the great legends.

The life that vibrated around me and of which I was a part did not make heavy demands. Since I had lived in poverty I had grown used to finding my own fresh air to breathe. Having huddled alone and in corners for so long, now that I was able to stand on my own two feet I devoted myself to the process of my development. While I felt compassion for those who were withering away in the dark cellars, I was not yet ready to protest against those who lived in the upper stories. More than anything, I put my hope in the redemptive spirit of Zionism, which would gather up everyone from the Jewish streets and alleys and lead them, to the music of pipes and cymbals, to the Land of Israel.

I acquired two more pupils so that, for three rubles a month, I could rent a room of my own. It was a second-story room on a cleaner side street. A room that looked out on trees. And here I readied myself to entertain those of my newfound friends who might be willing to hear this young poet recite his unpublished poems.

Still young myself, I was amazed by the new world of youth pulsating in Vilna. A world of young people who, like me, were moving toward new horizons. Young people who were not dismayed by cold or hunger and who could content themselves with a piece of black bread and a sweetened glass of tea.

Then there was the pine forest on the outskirts of the city and the castle mount and the road along the Viliya River. Ah, what a summer I had in store for me after that first winter in Vilna on my own two feet.

In the spring, when I watched the broken ice floating downstream on the newly awakened Viliya, my river from home appeared before my eyes, agitated, awakening from its frozen slumber. The image of my father came to mind as he stood on the bridge at the open mill sluices, with my mother and sister at his side, hacking at the ice with a heavy iron crowbar and sending it downstream with the current. "Is it true?" I asked myself. "Am I uprooted from my home forever?"

I fantasized again my old fantasies: I would get older; I would buy the mill from Shrinski, the landlord; I would become the miller and would have my parents at my side. The mill would be my home, and the waters of the millstream would taste forever sweet on my tongue.

I outgrew my clothes before the year was out. The description on my passport that said I was of short stature and had a "longish nose" would have to be rewritten.

It was true. Vilna had received me as a child and had commanded me to grow. I had obeyed and grown.

✐ "Longings"

My return to Vilna had been quiet, and quietly now I roamed its streets. Sometimes the city frightened me; at other times, it demanded that I love it.

Vilna had many secrets and many corners that were now known to me. The threshold of the old synagogue felt ever farther away. Now when I passed a study house and heard Gemara melodies, they seemed to come from a distant world veiled in mystery. Still, it must have been some loyalty to that past life that prompted me to form study groups of young scholars with whom I occasionally turned a page of Gemara, studied Hebrew and grammar, and whom I helped along on their quest whenever I could.

In time the secular city, far removed from synagogues and holiness, revealed itself to me. I was captivated by the noisy flow of life buzzing through the streets and alleys. I still clandestinely wrote poems and short stories. And my eyes began searching beyond the synagogue and longed to find a new, vital essence.

Meanwhile I had sent a Hebrew poem and a short story to a publishing house in Warsaw. The poem was distilled from my own longings; the story in Yiddish described the life of those who spent their days and nights in the dark cellars of Vilna. My request was that the poem be published in the Hebrew weekly *Ha-Dor* and that the story appear in the Yiddish periodical *Der Yud*. I was sure that neither the poem nor the story would be accepted, but my heart beat more quickly whenever I imagined that some editor in Warsaw was looking at my work.

The city stirred my blood. I was moved by the pine- and fir-covered banks of the blue-green Viliya River that flowed to Kovno and that, at Slabodke, fell into the Niemen River. And standing beside the Viliya I thought a bit sadly about the great yeshiva in Slabodke and its students studying parables on morality. My path may have once been leading me there, but I had turned aside only yesterday, cutting myself loose from what had been my direction since childhood. What a sudden leap, from my synagogue days to the streets of Vilna. From the timeless antiquity of the religion to which I had been bound, body and soul, to the gray, workaday life of the city. I now roamed the streets of Vilna quietly.

There were times when I felt as if the very ground under my feet was falling away from me and that I would be left suspended in midair. Though I wanted to condemn the religious knowledge I had gathered through so many days and waking nights, I found myself unable to do so. The new learning I drank so thirstily had not yet provided me with an adequate foundation. My slim notebook of Hebrew poems and the few Yiddish stories I had written were bits of honey I had gathered in this new beehive. The stored honey of the soul, strange honey that elicited sweet pain from hidden sources. Bizarre honey that intoxicates youth and obscures both the past and the days to come.

I often walked the streets at the time of day when the students, boys and girls, were coming out of the gymnasia together. They were a different generation from the one I had known. Seeing them I tried, without success, to glimpse the spirit that had bound me to the synagogue. I also tried to recognize in them my current aspirations, also without success.

I was walking downhill on Nowygrod Street, contemplating the poverty of Vilna, which lay covered in dust. That poverty was wordlessly calling to me. The more I walked on toward the poverty of Vilna the more familiar its face looked to me.

Can I really say that I left the life of the synagogue as an adult and that my steps, though soft, were confident? Certainly not. Just as my voice resounded loudly reciting Gemara in the study house and freely streamed out of the open summertime windows, now it was the opposite. Since I had shut the volumes of the Talmud my voice was getting quieter and quieter. My free-thinking speech was also soft spoken. My unfettered movements were quiet movements.

Vilna had motherly glances for me as well as the harsh glances of the miserly. I knew that beyond Vilna there was no other recourse for me. In Vilna I was to be reborn on the other side of the old synagogue. This was now where my new ups and downs would be. I loved earning my own living. I kept watch over my pupils and made sure that my modest salary was justly earned. I was carrying the responsibility of a teacher. After all, I was already twenty years old, even though I didn't know how to put those twenty years in any kind of order. My experiences from home were now the most useful ones for living my life. Out of all the achievements I had attained at the study house through constant diligence, I was only able to make use of the knowledge that I had secretly learned in those hours I had stolen from my own night's sleep.

It was my first beautiful summer in Vilna, even though it was soon to be two years since I had first arrived there. Once I even went off childishly to the Viliya, to try to drink a mouthful of its water, tilting my face toward its blue-green stream . . .

Then one day I went into the Strashun Library and started leafing through the new issue of the weekly *Ha-Dor* that had just come from Warsaw. Suddenly my eye fell upon a narrow, longish Hebrew poem entitled "Longings." The poem was signed "Peretz Hirshbein."

I flushed. I felt a throbbing in my temples. My knees trembled, and I really felt as if I were about to keel over. I rushed right out of the library to the booksellers on German Street, where I bought the same issue of *Ha-Dor*. I had no hope that in this issue I had just bought I would find the same poem with the same poet's name printed beneath it. I turned and turned the pages, my hands trembling.

"Longings." The same narrow, longish poem, with the same signature.

I folded the issue in half lengthwise, put it in my breast pocket, and went off, wandering the streets of Vilna. The issue of *Ha-Dor* was burning a hole in my pocket. I came to the Summer Garden, then hurried to Castle Mountain, where at the very top I took out the *Ha-Dor* and turned to the poem: "Longings." Yes, the poem was still there. No one would take it away or erase it.

I tried to consider rationally what had happened, but it was beyond my understanding. There were tears in my eyes. All the piety that all my life I had been taught to have for the printed word, all the reverence I had for the writers whose names I had read beneath their works, kept me now from grasping that it was my name on the page, printed in black on white. My name, my poem, written in the small synagogue on Nowy Świat Street at a time when I was cold and hungry.

I hurried toward that synagogue thinking that I might find friends there who were in need. Who knows? I might find Eltshik, and I could show him the poem. I might even read it to him right there between the walls of that basement synagogue, where I had anxiously read over my poem "Longings" so many times.

Instead I found myself in my small room with the door closed. There I sat in a dreamy stupor in which I did not know whether to sing or to cry.

A wave of feeling overwhelmed me, and I felt a huge sense of responsibility. For whom? For what? For my own words. For the new course of my life.

When, later, I met my friends, it was not with a feeling of pride but of shame, and my cheeks burned when they treated me with reverence or disbelief. "Did you actually write this poem?"

"Yes. A year and a half ago, when I was sick. When I lived in the Nowy Świat synagogue," I said, guiltily.

I could not sleep for the first few nights after I found that my poem had been published in *Ha-Dor*. After days and nights of deliberation, when my mood had cooled off, I was overcome by weariness, as if after a sudden and grave illness. For several days I avoided meeting any of my close friends. I even neglected my pupils for a couple of days. I wanted to come to an understanding of what had happened by myself.

Some inner voice kept asking, "So what if you've published a poem? Does that make you a real poet? Is that all?"

A feeling of insignificance came and cooled my enthusiasm. I was flung back into a world of new pursuit. That inner voice counseled me, "Don't send your poems out for a while. Wait. Don't deceive yourself. Now that your name is no longer your own, don't let it be bandied about so lightly."

Yes, it seemed to me that such fame as I now had came too easily.

Out of My Childhood Shoes

It would be a mistake to think that my years of diligence over the Talmud and its commentaries were years thrown to the winds. I was neither a cement pit that lost not a drop of its contents nor a mushroom growth that absorbed everything. Such talent as I had was more like that of the winnower who can sort the grain from the chaff.

I was comfortable very early with some of life's contradictions. Quite early on I made peace with natural phenomena. I sought no boundaries for God and His great wonders. So, though superficially it was a bold leap, it was not really difficult for me to cross the bridge from religious to secular studies, from my past to my future. Out of what I had studied so diligently, I picked and chose what was useful to me. The new seed fell, as it were, on a well-plowed field. Secular studies came easily to me.

Since my first poem printed in *Ha-Dor* was in Hebrew, it linked me for the foreseeable future quite specifically with my knowledge of Hebrew and the sources from which I had absorbed that knowledge. It was now time to deepen my understanding of things. It was time to draw closer that which I had been estranged from and a time to push the familiar away. It was a time of weighing and measuring what I had already achieved and experienced. I was already well read in Haskalah books; I'd read plenty of poetry and prose by refined poets and ordinary bards alike, who submitted their works to every type of contemporary anthology. Though Perets Smolenskin had absolutely no influence on me, I read everything I could get my hands on by Yehudah Leib Gordon—and he didn't add much to my own view of Jewish life, which was festering in darkness. I couldn't stand the poems of Adam ha-Kohen Lebensohn. On the other hand, I knew almost by heart the poems of his son Mikhah Yosef, who died young.

My memory had free will. It assisted me in forgetting what my nature could not endure and in remembering with no effort whatever suited my mood at the time.

The verses of poets who had made a name for themselves while still young resonated for me, like Bialik, Tchernichowsky, and those who followed in their footsteps; as for the older poets, it had become difficult for me even to open one of their books.

A work that created a tangible bridge for me between my past and future and over the abyss that had for a short time gaped wide beneath me was Graetz's *History of the Jews*, which I read with great thirst. It reconnected me to the ur-sources where I had glimpsed signs of Judaism in its purest form. Jewish survival in the diaspora among hostile nations, the calm and confident way in which Graetz depicted the Jewish past—as I enthusiastically read *History of the Jews* it seemed as if Graetz had removed a veil for me from time and from the Jewish people in the diaspora. The fresh breezes on the Jewish street cleared away that haze yet more from my consciousness.

Sometimes I was saddened by my readings in the classical Russian authors, who with no special effort seemed to be so far superior to anything I had read in contemporary Hebrew literature or in what was then a still poverty-stricken Yiddish literature. I knew perhaps half of Lermontov and Pushkin by heart. It was easy for me to memorize the longer poems of those poets. In Tolstoy and Turgenev, both of whom I read thirstily, I encountered God's world, how great it was in its four seasons, and I saw how I was a mere speck of dust in the great world of these non-Jewish writers. At times it made me feel discouraged.

Even though I followed a specific program in my studies, keeping in mind when exams were, when gymnasium was ending, and the possibility of entering the gates of the university, literature nevertheless got the upper hand. Moreover, while history, geography, and other subjects were easy for me, I had no fondness for mathematics at all. Arithmetic crowded my mind and was, with regard to all other subjects, like a parched desert around the edges of an oasis.

I read Shakespeare and the first part of Goethe's *Faust* in Russian translation. Then, out of nostalgia for those days in the study house in Orle when my friend had sung me Hebrew translations of Heine's poems to a Gemara melody, I began searching for the primary source. I bought a German-Russian dictionary and a copy of Heine's *Book of Songs* and sought out those poems that four years ago I had already known by heart only in Hebrew.

The issue of *Ha-Dor* in which my first poem was published was torn in half lengthwise too soon. The poem "Longings" by Peretz Hirshbein was also torn lengthwise. At that time my spirit was carried away to distant worlds, and more than once I looked over with disgust at that worn-out copy of *Ha-Dor* lying on my writing table among all sorts of thick books, huge books of poets who had been long dead and books of poets whose footsteps I could still hear wandering among the living.

The summer was over, winter had come, and without my fully realizing it the publication of my long, narrow poem several months earlier in *Ha-Dor* had produced a circle of good friends around me—students and part-time students who were already demanding something from me. They looked nostalgically at the young, pale poet who had only published a single poem. That made the young, pale poet feel his smallness, his insignificance.

Nevertheless, a gang of young men and women persuaded me to teach them Jewish history. Consequently, when winter came, I felt for the first time upon my youthful back the rod of the oppressor, because even to do something as innocent as teaching Jewish history to a small group of ten or twenty young people, we had to find a hiding place where the police wouldn't catch us. And we did find such a hidden spot in a basement apartment on Zaretcha Street. Every Friday evening, with hearts beating wildly, we went down to Zaretcha, down into that basement where young enthusiastic faces looked out at the young poet who had already published a poem.

How different it was going down to that hidden cellar on Zaretcha where young men and women were awaiting my arrival—compared to my meetings with the "Torah from Zion" society in a small Vilna synagogue, with the students who had chosen me as their temporary teacher! That was also something out of the past. I had come there as one of their own, paged through the Talmud, taught Hebrew grammar. And now I was meeting with strangers who were becoming my friends.

These strangers were looking to me as a source of knowledge; they wanted to drink their fill from me. And I—my heart was trembling so much. I felt I was too young and poor to fill their cups. And further, after sneaking back in the dark from the secret meeting to my individual room, I sat there staring into the distance, where I saw my double, which had been dissociated from me and gone off far away and was waiting for a rapprochement: for recognition and reintegration.

I had come home drained and weary from the clandestine cellar where a dozen people with a thirst for knowledge had depleted me with their curiosity. It took me a long time to fall asleep. It seemed as if I would have no more knowledge to share with my new students at the next meeting. And nevertheless, in the span of a week, the sources had replenished themselves, and my eagerness to give and to be emptied was refreshed, and with a renewed throb in my heart I set out once again in the dark down to Zaretcha to that basement apartment with blackout curtains in the windows. And again I met with those strangers who were becoming ever more familiar and close to me.

Later, one evening when my students had already gotten whatever they could from their teacher, out of the quiet they launched into a long song about labor and hardship. When they came into the dimly lit basement apartment on Friday nights, they came in as workers, bringing with them the aroma of tobacco, the smell of the factory where one of the girls worked making cigarettes; the carpenter bringing with him the fragrance of pine wood; the harness maker the stench of the pelts; and the tailor the odor of fabric, ticking, and cheap cotton cloth.

They spoke softly of conspiracy and of those narrow alleys they came out to at a determined hour of the evening. Looking intently into each other's eyes they tossed smoldering words back and forth to each other: words of liberation.

I started to suspect that the Vilna police were watching me, following me wherever I went. They were keeping an eye on me as I left the library with books under my arm. It was clear to me why my heart was beating harder and why a chill went up my spine as I walked past the main police station on German Street.

The people in whose building I lived in my tiny room on the second floor had a beautiful daughter who kept to herself in her room on the other side of the stairwell. She was famous in Vilna for her beauty—dark eyes, black hair, and passionate features. One winter's day she knocked at my door. Though I had caught glimpses of her through a window, I saw her now directly for the first time. She was not taller than me, but she seemed more mature. Her presence filled my room. She sat for a while on the edge of my bed, studying me. Then she went over to my table, where she looked through the Russian books piled there. Then, looking candidly into my eyes, she said, "I've been told you're a poet. Is it true?"

I didn't know what to say. I felt myself blushing with embarrassment. I could tell from her face as she took my hand that she was trying to determine from the lines and marks on it what my talents were. For a while she stood examining my fingers, seeming to count them so as to verify that I had the correct number. Then she laughed secretively. "Yes," she said, "I can tell that you're a poet. Be a poet like Pushkin and I'll love you."

"I'll never be a poet like Pushkin," I replied, a bit more boldly. She laughed a deep, resonant laugh, then, giving me her hand as she was taking leave, she said again, "Be a poet like Pushkin and I'll love you."

That same winter I had unexpected evidence that I was a grown-up. My family wrote to tell me that the authorities wanted to "take a look at me" because I was due to report that fall to the draft board in Bielsk.

Though I had been born in Kleshtshel, I was registered as a resident of Bielsk, so I would have to report to the draft board in Bielsk. They wrote to say that since my brother Moyshe, who had reported to his draft board in Brisk, had been released early, they wanted me to remove my name from the rolls in Bielsk and reregister in Visoke-Litovsk, where my father was a registered resident, so I could report to the draft board in Brisk.

Examining myself in my mirror, I felt a pang of grief. Was I really an adult? There were times when I still felt myself a child. A child of mother Vilna, the Jerusalem of Lithuania.

When spring came I turned my thoughts toward home. I was destined once again to feel that I was going home to my mother and father.

⚞ My Last Time at Lippe's Mill

I came home a few weeks before Pesach. The region was thawing; the water in the dams was rising. Trees were bursting into life. The soaked ground around my home enticed me to repeat a springtime frolic from my past when, against my mother's will, I ran barefoot over the soft earth.

The great city of Vilna, along with its cobbled streets and wood-planked sidewalks, had been whispering something into this nature boy's ear. Vilna was telling him a big-city secret through the sound of the water running from the tap in his own room.

I changed my clean city clothes for the dusty garb of a miller and became helpful around the mill. My brother Moyshe, who was already engaged to a girl from the shtetl, worked as head miller during the noisy time before Pesach. My father, despite his age, continued to work hard. He carried heavy loads and stayed awake in the evenings, when the younger folk were falling on their faces.

Although everyone was busy with the pre-Pesach abundance, with the lines of peasants waiting their turn to have their wheat ground or with sifting Pesach wheat, a gloom nevertheless hung over our home. Everyone was preoccupied.

My mother said, "I'm afraid we are going to have to leave the mill. The landlord has warned us that starting around Shavuos, if we don't pay him a hundred and fifty rubles rent a year instead of the hundred and twenty we're paying now, he'll rent the place to someone else . . . to Jews, evidently, who have offered to pay that much."

That's what my mother told us.

It was utterly impossible. There was no way they could work hard enough to earn one hundred and fifty rubles for the year, even if they made some extra money renting out the horse and wagon. So now they had to think of leaving the mill in which I had been born and where they had lived for the last twenty-one years. How far would they have to go? Maybe to the shtetl? For Lippe the miller and the rest of his family, the shtetl was quite a distance. They had moved here from a village, country folk for generations. Now, at their age, they were supposed to pick up and move into town? It looked as if my parents had concluded, "It's no use. We've lived out our lives."

My parents regarded the days to come with trepidation. With an air of anxiety, both of them, my father as well as my mother, studied their guest who had come back home to have his name removed from the Bielsk census only to register with the census in Visoke-Litovsk so that he could stand before the draft board in Brisk. Yes, they were worried: "What if they take him? What if they turn him into a soldier?"

Just before Pesach my father got a taste of childlike joy when the shammes promised to call his Peretz, as befitted a guest in the shtetl, to read the maftir in the synagogue on the first day of Pesach. My father was sure that the shtetl folk would finally look upon his Peretz as he deserved, something he had been secretly hoping for all those years his son was away. "At last," he said, blushing bright red, "you'll get to read maftir. You'll show them who you are." I did indeed show them who his son was, but it did not happen quite the way he expected.

In the synagogue, on the first day of the holiday, when it was time to take out the Torah, the shammes auctioned off the aliyahs, the privilege of reading a Torah section, as was customary. Normally when there was a guest in the synagogue, the aliyah to which the guest would be called was not sold. So this time they certainly didn't need to sell the maftir.

Then imagine my father's and my brother Moyshe's astonishment as they stood together and heard the shammes, who had already sold all the aliyahs, calling out, "One gildeyn for maftir!" My brother Moyshe paled. Looking toward the lectern he announced, "Two gildeyn."

"Two gildeyn," echoed the shammes. But one of the people sitting near the eastern wall then bid three gildeyn. Moyshe signaled four gildeyn, and from the eastern wall there came the challenge: "Five gildeyn . . ." And then: "Six gildeyn and twenty groschen!" Nearly a whole ruble. It was unbelievable. Somebody meant to tear the maftir away from the miller's family by force.

But Moyshe wouldn't back down. He stood there, flushed, doing battle with the whole congregation. With all of the wealthy men who sat near the eastern wall. The eastern wall bid more; Moyshe bid even higher. He meant to triumph even if he had to pay a fortune for the maftir—and finally he had his way.

The shammes looked toward Moyshe, who indicated me, his younger brother. Then, for the first time in the Kleshtshel synagogue, the shammes called out, "Young Peretz, Lippe the miller's son—maftir."

Well, now I needed to show that Peretz, Lippe the miller's son, was worthy of the maftir. I recited as clearly, resoundingly, and as grammatically as I could, enunciating correctly. Then I sang the haftorah blessings in the Vilna manner. All in all it was obvious that Lippe the miller had triumphed.

When the service was over, men from the eastern wall came up to greet me and to exchange a few words with my father. My mother also was given her due by the women, who could see that she, the miller's wife, had a right to be proud of her youngest son.

When we got home, we talked about what had happened in the synagogue. Everyone, including Moyshe, who had spent a fortune for his victory, felt how unjust it had been. Everyone in the family felt they had been seriously dishonored. They had deceived my father in the same way that a peasant is deceived in the market. Maybe it hadn't even occurred to the men at the eastern wall to bid on the maftir. They simply did not want to allow my father the pleasure.

In the intermediary days of Pesach, I was to go to Bielsk to meet with the authorities and later to Visoke. When I was done that day, since I knew no one in Bielsk, I went straight back home. Another day I went to spend the night with my uncle Avrom Tumener. He had been put out of his rented estate and now lived in Visoke.

His children too had grown up. His youngest daughter, Sheyne, who was more or less my age, was the girl whose handwriting was more beautiful than mine and with whom I had corresponded. She had written me several love letters containing lofty thoughts separated by many dots.

My uncle Avrom and my aunt Soreh treated me as an honored guest, but for Sheyne, who had grown into a pretty and clever young woman, my visit was a dream come true. Her parents, aware of her feelings, contrived to leave us frequently alone, or encouraged us to take spring walks on the outskirts of town, where there was a windmill on a hill.

We went out at dusk and found our way to the illuminated windmill. In the still evening, the mill loomed with its wings reaching toward the sunset. We stood there wordless because, though the sun was setting, we felt within ourselves a rising dawn. So many years had gone by. We were finally really looking at each other: I saw her black hair, her dark eyes; she saw me, blond-haired with blue eyes. How could feelings such as we were having come to two young people who were the children of sisters? It seemed to us that, having lived in separate worlds, a miraculous hand had brought us together.

"Do you know, Peretz, I never stopped thinking of you. There were always boys hanging around, but I never saw any of them."

"But what will happen to us if I'm drafted?"

"So what? I'll wait for you. Is waiting four years such a big deal?" And a bit later, "You're well-educated. I've also studied. Together with you I'll learn even more. All our years, I will keep learning."

Here's what we decided: If I went before the draft board and they didn't draft me, I'd take her with me to Vilna. Of course that would only happen with the approval of her parents.

She sighed, "Oy, the minute the time comes that you're finally free . . . And what about the fact that my name is Sheyne and my aunt's—your mother's—is Sheyne?"

But who cared what our mothers' names were now when an utterly nameless life suddenly shuddered and was born at the edge of the western sky where the sun had just set?

Back at her house after such a long and late stroll, it was understood that the children had found their happiness. Of course her parents and the older children were able to read it in our faces.

Before the final days of Pesach I took the train home—drunk, but not from wine—so I could spend those final days of the holiday with my parents.

But what sadness had taken hold of my home on that last day of Pesach! My parents and the elder children had gotten it while praying in the shtetl synagogue. They didn't say a word of it to me. I saw my mother in silent tears. My sister Bebl came to us during the day—and it was the same with her.

As we ate, people's faces were disturbed; the holiday was spoiled. Did it have to do with my imminent departure? Was it about the possibility that at any moment they might have to move away from the mill?

That same last day of Pesach we all went to Uncle Avrom Moyshe's windmill. And as soon as we walked into the house, still at the door, Aunt Rivke burst into tears. And everyone all at once started crying.

"What's the matter?"

"Avrom Tumener's daughter Sheyne was poisoned . . . She didn't survive."

Everyone looked at me. They were trying to see what was going on in my face. I asked, "How did that happen? What happened?"

"It was an accident. Yesterday morning as she was getting ready to go to the synagogue to pray Aunt Soreh prepared a plate of matzoh meal and mixed it with poison for the mice. She had forgotten to tell the children to be careful with it. So the girls made latkes from that matzoh meal. The younger one, Sheyne, was the first to eat it, and the tragedy happened. All day yesterday she was on her deathbed. Doomed . . . Such a tragedy, such a tragedy!"

"How did you find out about it?"

"Yesterday a sick patient was taken to the doctor in Visoke. They came back today and were telling everyone how all of Visoke was devastated because of the tragedy."

Grief, endless grief, took hold of my life. Grief from the inside, grief from the outside. The spring outside was grieving. I practically couldn't see anything through the window. The pond looked glazed over, with the heavy, aged willows sinking into it.

"I'm leaving for Vilna tonight. There's a train at midnight for Bialystok that I'll be taking . . ."

No one in the family was offended that I was leaving in such a hurry, even though I had intended to stay at home for a couple of weeks. Stuck in a profound silence, I could barely wait for it to be time to go to the train. Since I had almost no baggage it was decided that Moyshe and I would walk along the tracks to the station.

The night was dark. I took a wordless leave of my grief-stricken parents. We walked along the muddy dam in silence. At the edge of the pond I slipped and fell off the dam into the water. I jumped out of the cold pond, and Moyshe, feeling in the darkness how wet I was and afraid that I would get sick, wanted me to go back home. I didn't answer and kept on walking, soaking wet and filthy, until we arrived at the station.

There was still a good long hour to wait for the train. An hour of intense darkness. When the train came Moyshe hugged me silently, then helped me into the railroad car in which a single candle burned. Once the train was in motion, I sank down beside the hot cast-iron stove to dry my soaking wet clothes. All night long I sat there drying them while the tears coursed down my cheeks.

That was the last time I was a guest in Lippe's mill, my home. Half a year later, at the end of the summer, when I came to Kleshtshel to report to the draft board, the mill was no longer ours. My parents and Soreleh, my youngest sister, had found a small house almost outside of town, on the road that led to the train station.

The cramped house smelled of damp. Through the small windows one could see the sandy road that led to the train and a sparse strip of land where geese and scrawny horses cropped the grass.

My father, like an uprooted oak, and my mother, like an uprooted birch, started wilting before their time. Their voices were even more hushed than usual.

One day at the end of summer, the three of us, my mother and father with me between them, went off to see what was once Lippe's mill. We walked slowly along the path our family's footsteps had made over the years. We cast affectionate glances at the trees on both sides but could find nothing to say. The trees too were silent as they felt our pain. We never reached the mill. Our steps were not up to the task.

And that was how on that day, though I walked between both my parents, I took leave of my childhood years for good.

END

Carmel, New York
1931–1932

Peretz Hirshbein (1880–1948) was a Yiddish playwright, novelist, journalist, travel writer, and theater director whose work was pivotal to the development of Yiddish theater in the early twentieth century. Born in 1880 to a family of flour millers outside of Kleshtshel (Kleszczele), a town then part of the Russian Empire and now in northeast Poland, Hirshbein was a rabbinic prodigy, and it was thought he would enter the rabbinate; instead he discovered secular literature and became a writer, first in Hebrew and later in Yiddish. The rustic setting of his youth provided the backdrop for much of his writing, including his two-part memoir and a series of naturalistic plays he wrote in the 1910s that are considered masterpieces of the genre. One of them—*Grine felder* (*Green Fields*, 1918)—was turned into a movie in 1937, becoming one of the best-loved Yiddish films. After visiting New York around 1912, Hirshbein spent much of the next twenty years traveling the world together with his wife, Esther Shumiatcher-Hirshbein, whom he married in 1918. In the mid-1930s, the couple settled in Los Angeles, where Hirshbein died of Lou Gehrig's disease in 1948.

Leonard Wolf (1923–2019) was a poet, author, teacher, and translator. Born in Vulcan, Romania, Wolf immigrated to the United States in 1930 with his family. He began writing poetry in his teens while attending public school in Cleveland, Ohio, and served in the U.S. Army during World War II. After the war he moved to Carmel, California, where he became part of the "Berkeley Renaissance" along with poets like Lawrence Ferlinghetti and Allen Ginsburg, and later earned his PhD in English and creative writing from the University of Iowa. Wolf taught English literature at several colleges and universities and authored twenty-seven books, including his own novels and poetry collections. He became particularly renowned as a translator of Yiddish literature and published a Yiddish version of *Winnie the Pooh*.

About White Goat Press

White Goat Press, the Yiddish Book Center's imprint, is committed to bringing newly translated work to the widest readership possible. We publish work in all genres—novels, short stories, drama, poetry, memoirs, essays, reportage, children's literature, plays, and popular fiction, including romance and detective stories.

whitegoatpress.org
The Yiddish Book Center's imprint